JOHN THE LOYAL

JOHN THE LOYAL

STUDIES IN THE MINISTRY OF THE BAPTIST

BY

A. T. ROBERTSON, M.A., D.D.

BAKER BOOK HOUSE
Grand Rapids, Michigan

Paperback edition issued 1977
by Baker Book House

ISBN: 0-8010-7644-7

PHOTOLITHOPRINTED BY CUSHING - MALLOY, INC.
ANN ARBOR, MICHIGAN, UNITED STATES OF AMERICA
1977

TO

THE HONORED MEMORY OF

WILLIAM HETH WHITSITT

SEEKER AFTER TRUTH

PREFACE

The literature on the ministry of the Baptist is not large, as the Bibliography at the close of this volume shows. Our most ambitious treatise is still that of Reynolds, "John the Baptist," which was the Congregational Union Lecture for 1874. He lamented then the paucity of books on this great theme. To be sure, all the great lives of Jesus give considerable attention to the work of the Forerunner of the Messiah, and the recent Bible dictionaries have able articles about him. It is proper that John should be overshadowed by Jesus. It was what he himself wished and what he foresaw. But, just as Paul is a beacon-light in the Apostolic Age, so the Baptist stands on the other side (and partly parallel with the life) of Jesus. One furnishes the true prospective view, the other the just retrospective interpretation. Jesus towers in the middle, far above both of them, but both John and Paul must receive adequate treatment. Paul has fared better than John, partly because of the wealth of original material from him and about him, partly also because of the fuller light that blazed around him. John was like the morning star in the early dawn, a very bright and shining one indeed. John wrote nothing himself, though probably "Logia of John" were preserved in Aramaic which were used in the fragments of his preaching preserved in Matthew and Luke.

I have written the present book because of the fascination which John has for me. I have attempted a positive interpretation of the life and work of the Baptist for the general reader, in the light of the new knowledge of his time. This is an age in which everything is challenged, even the very existence of Jesus. But merely technical points are put in the foot-notes so as not to disturb the reader who does not care for them. Other questions of a more erudite nature are also reserved for the notes. The book is not meant as an apologetic, and I do not feel called upon to justify every statement in the Gospels for the benefit of the modern disbeliever. I have treated such questions as occasion arose, not from a sense of compulsion. It is John himself that I wish to bring before the reader, if I may, with something of his powerful personality. Vitality throbs in his words to-day as when he first spoke them to the multitudes. I have called him "John the Loyal" from no sensational motive, but as an aid to just understanding of the man. The term "the Baptist," so indissolubly and justly linked with his name, has one peril. It puts accent on the new ordinance which attracted so much attention then. But John was not a ceremonialist. The spiritual element was the main thing in his nature. He "followed the gleam" and was loyal to his vision. That is the dominant note in his life.

The material for a study of John is not very extensive (the gospel fragments, a little in Acts, a paragraph in Josephus), but it is remarkably rich in suggestion. His figure stands out with marvellous clearness when the various items are brought together and rightly interpreted. He was one of the great spirits of human history, and deserves our best efforts to understand him. He is still the Voice crying in the Wilderness, and the people are ever eager to hear his words.

A. T. Robertson

Louisville, Ky.
February 1, 1911

I am indebted for the excellent indices to three of my students, Rev. Powhatan James, W. J. Nelson, and J. B. Weatherspoon.

A. T. R.

TABLE OF CONTENTS

JOHN THE LOYAL

CHAPTER I

EQUIPMENT

"For he shall be great in the sight of the Lord, and he shall drink no wine nor strong drink; and he shall be filled with the Holy Ghost, even from his mother's womb" (Luke 1 : 15).

1. *The Hand of God.*—This is the point with which to begin the study of John's life, as it is indeed with that of all men in one sense. The presence of God in history is the great lesson that the serious student of history learns. Nothing but God's hand in the history of the race can explain the great movements upward and onward. But the narrative[1] which tells us all that we know of the birth of John draws a far more intimate picture of this child's relation to God or, rather, of God's interest in him. "The hand of the Lord was with him"[2] as a child. One loves to think that heaven is near the life of every child.

[1] Holtzmann ("The Life of Jesus," p. 108) bluntly says: "The story of John's birth (Luke 1: 5–25, 57–80) is a legend of late Christian times, which John 1: 31–34 contradicts." For the life of me I fail to see what there is in these verses in Luke which contradicts the statement in John that the Baptist had not known Jesus till the baptism of Christ. It is expressly stated in Luke that Mary left Elizabeth about the time of the birth of John. The acquaintance between Elizabeth and Mary (Luke 1: 36–56) does not prove acquaintance between John and Jesus (John 1: 31 ff.). As to the "legend" notion of Holtzmann, anything is "legend" with him that bears the mark of the supernatural.

[2] Luke 1: 66.

But we are at once ushered into an atmosphere of the most intimate communion with God. The curtain is lifted and the hand of God is seen reaching out before this child is born. Time was when the mere mention of the possibility of God's making his will known by angel or other miracle was the occasion of supercilious scorn in many educated circles. But we have lived to see the day when religious experience is considered a subject worthy of scientific investigation and belief.[1] Besides, when cold scientists like the late William James and Sir Oliver Lodge believe in the possibility (even actuality) of communication with the dead, one is surely not called upon to assume an apologetic air if he avows his belief in the power of God to manifest himself to men.[2]

2. *The Value of the Record.*—The testimony of Luke is sometimes discredited on the score that he alone records the account of the Baptist's nativity. But Luke is not now without able champions among modern scholars.[3] "That Luke is ever at variance with other historians has still to be proved; and the merit of greater accuracy may still be with him, even if such variance exists."[4] It is worth noting also that the story of the Baptist's miraculous birth comes immediately after the classic introduction[5] in which he

[1] Cf. William James, "Varieties of Religious Experience."

[2] This argument does not, of course, prove that God sent his angel Gabriel to Zacharias. It leaves the question to be examined on its merits.

[3] Cf. Ramsay, "Was Christ Born at Bethlehem?", "Luke the Physician," "St. Paul the Traveller"; Chase, "The Credibility of Acts"; and even Harnack (on most points), "Luke the Physician," "The Acts of the Apostles."

[4] Plummer, "Commentary on Luke," p. 6.

[5] 1: 1–4.

has stated his painstaking thoroughness in the examination and use of his sources of information. It is beyond controversy, therefore, that Luke had what he considered reliable testimony for what he here relates in so vivid and captivating a manner. Whether it was an Aramaic document or whether he learned this beautiful bit of biography from Mary, the Mother of Jesus (or from one of her circle), during his two years' sojourn with Paul at Cæsarea,[1] may never be known. But the whole tone of Luke's narrative lifts it far above the late apocryphal stories which have come down to us.[2] "In any case, we have here the earliest documentary evidence respecting the origins of Christianity which has come down to us—evidence which may justly be called contemporary.[3] It may be added that the drift of modern criticism has been distinctly toward a comparatively early date for the Gospel of Luke (from A. D. 58–80), so that the old notion of a late invention of the miraculous birth of John as being necessary for one who was to be the Forerunner of the Messiah falls to the ground.[4] Besides, the whole spirit of the narrative here is pre-Christian, an impossibility for a late inventor. Then again, the very language of this narrative (like that of ch. 2) is quite Hebraistic (Aramaic), while Luke's

[1] Acts 23–26.

[2] "To appreciate the historical sobriety and manifestly primary character of this early Jewish-Christian source, we have only to compare the first chapter of Luke with the relative sections of the 'Protevangelium Jacobi,' and especially with those chapters (22–24) which Harnack calls the *Apocryphum Zachariæ*." Lambert, in "Hastings's D. C. G."

[3] Plummer, "Commentary on Luke," p. 7.

[4] Marcion does omit this section from his mutilated edition of Luke, but he did so upon doctrinal, not upon critical, grounds. Cf. Plummer, "Luke," p. 6.

introduction is the most classic bit of construction (literary form) in the New Testament. Luke is here "a faithful collector of evangelic *memorabilia*" which he "allows to speak for itself."[1] His keen sense of historical values is probably the very reason for the preservation of this most important detail which escaped the notice of Mark and Matthew.

But the narrative is attacked on its inherent character, irrespective of its early date or documentary nature. "Some have found in this a fabulous element, modelled upon the history of such men of God of Old Testament times as Isaac, Samson, and Samuel."[2] This objection assumes that these Old Testament stories are without value because of the birth of children under unusual conditions.[3] It is true that there is the point of similarity in the birth of a son to aged parents, but, unless God is to be ruled out of human life, the narrative is not to be discounted on that score. Indeed, Luke seems here to be reporting events out of harmony with popular expectation which is naïvely introduced in a way that guarantees the historical character of the narrative. The people were amazed at Elizabeth for naming the child John, and the traditions in the Hill Country confirm his account.[4]

Criticism has its place in the study of the ministry of the Baptist. The fragmentary accounts must be

[1] Bruce, "Expositor's Greek Text," *in loco*.
[2] Weiss, "The Life of Christ," vol. I, p. 234.
[3] "This calamity [barrenness] is grievous to all Orientals, and specially grievous to Jews, each of whom is ambitious of being among the progenitors of the Messiah" (Plummer, p. 10).
[4] Weiss, "Life of Christ," vol. I, p. 235.

combined, sifted and co-ordinated.[1] "By the ordinary, uncritical reading of the New Testament Scriptures, one gets a very imperfect and one-sided view of John the Baptist." [2] It may be retorted that the uncritical have no monopoly in the matter of one-sided views of the Baptist, for assuredly the critics do not agree in their interpretation of him. But Mr. Bradley lays the blame for this state of affairs on the New Testament writers, to whom John "is a person of secondary importance." "Under the circumstances the strange thing is that they should have preserved at all some of the facts which they furnish regarding John." His point is that the gospels exalt Jesus at the expense of John, that John was not the Forerunner of Jesus as "the gospel writers grew more and more to view him." Incidentally, this criticism of Bradley answers those who claim that Luke has overpraised the Baptist in the birth narrative, but unfortunately Mr. Bradley has to pursue processes entirely too subjective to be convincing. The narrative of Luke "is full of poetry, no doubt, but it is the kind of poetry which bursts like a flower from the living stem of actual truth." [3] In a word, then, it may be said at once that minute study of the New Testament

[1] It is true that in a general way the material from the Synoptic Gospels goes together (Matt. 3 : 1–12; 4 : 12; 9 : 14; 11 : 2–19; 14 : 3–12; 17 : 12 f.; 21 : 23–27, 32; Mark 1 : 2–8, 14; 2 : 18; 6 : 17–29; 9 : 13; 11 : 27–33; Luke 1 : 5–25, 36–45, 57–80; 3 : 1–20; 5 : 33; 7 : 18–35; 9 : 9; 11 : 1; 16 : 16; 20 : 1–8), while that of the Acts (1 : 5, 22; 10 : 37; 11 : 16; 13 : 24 f.; 18 : 25; 19 : 3 ff.), of John (1 : 6–8, 15, 19–40; 3 : 22–36; 4 : 1; 5 : 33–36; 10 : 40–42) and of Josephus ("Ant.," xviii, 5, 2) is distinct. But the various threads can be picked up and pieced into a whole.

[2] W. P. Bradley, "John the Baptist as Forerunner," *The Biblical World*, May, 1910, p. 327.

[3] Lambert, "Hastings's D. C. G."

picture of John gives the result of a coherent whole, a primitive figure, whose rugged outlines left so deep a mark upon his time that even the greatest Figure of all time has not effaced that impress, even when he crept close beside the Son of God and stood in his light.

3. *The Home to Which He Was to Come.*—It is a great thing for any home when a child enters it. He comes as a prince, a fresh gift from God. No child had come to the home of Zacharias and Elizabeth. They had borne their burden with silent sorrow, but with chastened spirits. They were far advanced in their days, as Luke expresses it in the Old Testament phrase.[1] Step by step they had together gone, though the patter of no child's feet was heard by their side. Hand in hand also[2] they had journeyed[3] (were still journeying) "in all the commandments and ordinances of the Lord." They had kept in the path all the way, God's path, and so were righteous[4] in the sight of God.[5] They had walked uprightly with God, and were blameless[6] in the sight of men. They had grown rich in grace, and ripe in piety for the journey's end. Of all the homes in the Hill Country there seemed not one where a child would have fared better or been more welcome. It was a priestly family on both sides. Elizabeth was a daughter (descendant) of Aaron, and Zacharias was still officiat-

[1] ἀμφότεροι προβεβηκότες ἐν ταῖς ἡμέραις αὐτῶν ἦσαν (1 : 7). Cf. Gen. 24 : 1; Josh. 13 : 1. The periphrastic past perfect looks back over the long years before this time.

[2] ἀμφότεροι (1 : 6).

[3] πορευόμενοι.

[4] δίκαιοι (from δίκη, δείκνυμι, show the way).

[5] ἐναντίον θεοῦ.

[6] ἄμεμπτοι. It can be referred to God's point of view also, but it is a stronger word than δίκαιοι, which was used of God's view.

ing as priest, as he had the right to do.[1] There had been twenty-four classes of priests since the days of David, and the course of Abia was the eighth.[2] Zacharias and Elizabeth are both in Jerusalem, for it was the turn of Zacharias to serve his week in the temple worship. But it was a great day in the life of Zacharias, for it had come to him to offer incense on one of these days.[3] There were possibly twenty thousand priests, and no priest was allowed to burn incense in the Holy Place but once in his lifetime. This honor many priests never received at all, but now it had come to Zacharias in his old age. The officiating priest was allowed to have two helpers, but they retired and left him alone in the Holy Place.[4] Luke gives another touch to the picture. The people kept praying[5] outside in the temple courts.[6] Luke is fond of noting prayer. Inside the Holy Place was Zacharias, fulfilling the duties of his great hour, knowing full well that it was a great hour, but little understanding what God had in store for him. It is usually at just such a time and in such a spirit that God opens his treasures to us. The hour of climax is in the path of duty.

4. *The Child's Character Foretold.*—Zacharias was alone in the Holy Place. One moment he saw nothing unusual. The next there stood[7] an angel of the Lord. He was face to face with the angel. Luke

[1] Levites were superannuated at sixty, but not priests. Cf. Plummer, *in loco.*

[2] I Chron. 24 : 10.

[3] ἔλαχε τοῦ θυμιᾶσαι. The lot was cast both morning and evening.

[4] Plummer, *in loco.*

[5] ἦν προσευχόμενον.

[6] τὸ ἱερόν, but not ὁ ναός.

[7] ἐστώς (standing).

says that the angel "appeared" to him.[1] It is the word that Paul uses of the appearance of Jesus to him on the way to Damascus as well as to the other disciples before.[2] It is worth little to explain the vision away as a mere subjective impression due to overwrought nerves. Curiously enough Zacharias, as we know, refused to accept the message of the angel, and so can hardly be accused of having imagined the vision. The theory of a mere optical illusion is equally fanciful. The unseen world hovers nearer to all of us than we usually understand.[3] If one admits the possibility of the miraculous and the normal credibility of Luke, there is little ground for refusing credence here, unless one considers the birth of the Forerunner an event unworthy of such a special manifestation of divine power. One need not discuss the psychological possibilities of the case[4] save to agree with Plummer[5] that "the unique circumstances contributed to make him conscious of that unseen world which is around all of us." Zacharias was instantly thrown into violent agitation[6] at the sight of the angel at the right hand of the altar ("the place of honor" [7]) facing him. "Fear fell upon him" like a bolt of lightning. He was too much afraid to speak. The angel broke the silence. "Quit being afraid,[8] Zacharias," he said. That was reassuring and Zach-

[1] ὤφθη. Cf. Luke 22 : 43. Punctiliar action. It all happened in a moment.

[2] I Cor. 15 : 6 ff.

[3] Cf. II Kings 6 : 17.

[4] Cf. Lange, "Life of Christ," I, p. 264.

[5] *In loco.*

[6] ἐταράχθη. Effective aorist.

[7] Plummer, *in loco.*

[8] μὴ φοβοῦ. Μή with the pres. imper. usually means to stop what one is doing.

arias would listen. The prayer[1] of Zacharias has been heard.[2] He had apparently been praying for offspring[3] in this great hour of opportunity, his one great hour. Plummer[4] doubts whether Zacharias would make his private wishes the subject of prayer at such a time, and whether he would have prayed for a son at his age, or would have doubted the angel after having prayed for a son. But one can cite the case of the disciples who disbelieved the answer to their prayer about the release of Peter.[5] Besides, a prayer for a child is in harmony with the Old Testament atmosphere of this whole incident. At such a time one is likely to give vent to the deepest longing of his heart. Many a time he and Elizabeth had prayed for a child, and now he had once more uttered what might seem an impossible appeal even to God. Certainly the birth of this son had a direct bearing on the coming of the Kingdom for which the people constantly prayed. The angel proceeds. He even gives a name to the son, the name John or Johanan.[6] The name was new to the family of Zacharias, but most suitable to the circumstances. The first blessing will come to Zacharias (and Elizabeth). There will be to him "joy and exultation."[7] The second word means extreme joy. He will be glad to have a son, and gladder still to have such a son.[8] But he will bring

[1] δέησις, a special prayer for personal need (δέομαι) as opposed to προσευχή, general prayer.

[2] εἰσηκούσδη. A difficult aorist to translate. The action is punctiliar and is stated as past, but it is just past.

[3] So Bruce, *in loco*. [4] *In loco*. [5] Acts 12.

[6] Ἰωάνης. Cf. II Chron. 28 : 12, etc. It is an abbreviation of *Jehohanan*, Jehovah's gift.

[7] χαρά σοι καὶ ἀγαλλίασις. [8] Bruce, *in loco*.

joy[1] to many others also upon the occasion of [2] his birth. The angel is looking to the future work of the Forerunner. The love of the people for John will be one of the notable things in New Testament times.[3] He shall be great in the eye of the Lord. Great[4] is sometimes greater than the superlative (very great, for instance). In this context "great" includes also goodness, for it is in the eye of the Lord. The praise of Jesus will accord with this high standard.[5] The vow of a Nazirite will be his, and for his whole life, as was true of Samson and Samuel. This vow was usually for a short while.[6] All kinds of intoxicating drinks are to be avoided.[7] This ascetic life will harmonize with the wilderness, though Nazirites did not necessarily dwell apart. It is to be noted that Jesus was not a Nazirite, and Paul only on occasion. But the most significant thing about John is the promise that he will be filled with the Holy Spirit from his birth. It is a promise of the revival of prophecy. It had been some four hundred years since the voice of prophecy ceased with Malachi. And now a real prophet was to come again. Thus equipped he will turn[8] many of the sons of Israel to the Lord their God. It was a day of backsliding. This prophecy also came true. The quaintness and originality of the phraseology make it difficult to think that this is a mere composition of Luke put into the mouth of

[1] χαρήσονται. A durative second future passive. [2] ἐπί.

[3] "The Pharisees did not dare say that John was not a prophet (Matt. 21 : 26); and Herod, until driven to it, did not dare to put him to death (Mark 14 : 5)" (Plummer).

[4] μέγας in absolute sense.

[5] Luke 7 : 28. [6] Acts 18 : 18. [7] οἶνον καὶ σίκερα.

[8] ἐπιστρέψει durative future, repetition with πολλούς.

the angel. He shall go before the Lord [1] in his office as prophet. The word "him" could refer to the Messiah only by supposing something else said by the angel not here recorded. But, still, the idea doubtless is that God "comes to his people in the person of the Messiah" (Plummer). John's work will be "in the spirit and power of Elijah." He will not be Elijah himself, as some of the Jews expected and as John denied.[2] But he will be the real fulfilment of the return of Elijah as Jesus will himself show.[3] He will reproduce this great prophet's work, though he will work no miracles. It will be like the days of old. This second coming of Elijah will introduce the days of the Messiah. No wonder that he will turn the hearts of the fathers to their children when such a child as this has come. Parental affection had sadly languished and the child had lost its place with many.[4] The word "turn" [5] is conversion, the idea in John's word "repent." He will make ready a prepared people[6] for the Lord, yes, and for his Messiah. It was a wonderful picture. Every word was pregnant with meaning. And these words came pouring into the ears and heart of Zacharias. Could they be true? Were they not too marvellous to be true?

5. *The Scepticism of Zacharias.*—The demand upon Zacharias's faith was too great. He had not dared to

[1] ἐνώπιον αὐτοῦ. Cf. Isa. 40 : 1–11; Mal. 3 : 1–5.

[2] John 1 : 21.

[3] Matt. 17 : 12; Mark 9 : 12. The great prophets in the minds of the Jews were Elijah, Jeremiah, Daniel.

[4] Cf. Sirach xlviii; Isa. 63 : 16; Matt. 19 : 13.

[5] ἐπιστρέψαι. It was the common word with the prophets.

[6] λαὸν παρεσκευσαμένον.

ask for such a child, perhaps had not felt worthy of such a son. Indeed, if truth be told, he may not have really believed that he would be given a child at all in spite of his petition for one. It was a natural reaction, when the angel ceased his wondrous story, for Zacharias to ask: "Whereby shall I know this?"[1] He does not squarely deny the possibility of such an event, though he sees at once the obvious difficulty of such a hope in view of the old age of himself and Elizabeth. Perhaps the angel had overlooked this point. At any rate it will do no harm to ask for proof.[2] Zacharias could excuse himself by the example of Gideon and Hezekiah, who asked for signs,[3] and by that of Moses and Ahaz, who had signs without asking.[4] At such moments one's mind works rapidly, but not always correctly. One naturally recoils when his "day-dream is objectified."[5] The case of Martha at the grave of Lazarus is in point.[6] But, after all, however specious and excusable, it was doubt of the angel's word, of the message of God, and doubt in spite of the miraculous presence of the angel, itself proof enough if any was needed. The beautiful faith of Mary stands out in sharp contrast to the doubt of Zacharias.[7] The angel feels called upon to justify himself. He tells who he is.[8] We know the names of two angels in Scripture, Gabriel,[9]

[1] Luke 1 : 18.

[2] κατὰ τὶ γνώσομαι τοῦτο. His question asks for a sign by which to gauge (κατά) the promise.

[3] Judges 6 : 36–39; II Kings 20 : 8.

[4] Ex. 4 : 2–6; Isa. 7 : 11. Cf. Plummer, p. 16.

[5] Bruce, *in loco*.

[6] John 11 : 27, 39 f.

[7] Luke 1 : 38.

[8] "Gabriel answers his ἐγώ εἰμι with another" (Plummer).

[9] Dan. 8 : 16; 10 : 21.

"the Man of God," "the angel of mercy," and Michael [1] (who is like God?), "the angel of judgment," the opponent of Satan. Gabriel was apparently chief of the angels sent on errands concerning man's redemption.[2] He stands in the presence of God always ready.[3] It was a high place to fill. He had been sent[4] to speak to Zacharias, and it was good tidings[5] that he had brought. It was a sharp rejoinder. Zacharias had disbelieved an angel and a special messenger to him. The proof that Zacharias asked for will be given and in a form to leave no room for doubt on his part. It will come in his very person and will be in the nature of a punishment for this doubt. He had used his tongue to speak his doubt, and now his tongue will be silent[6] till the fulfilment of the prophecy. It is put positively and negatively[7] for emphasis. The angel does not leave Zacharias to interpret the reason for this kind of proof. His words will be fulfilled to the letter[8] in due time.[9] The dumbness began at once, and Zacharias was not allowed a reply. Meanwhile considerable time had been consumed. According to the Talmud the

[1] Dan. 10 : 13, 21; 12 : 1: Jude 9; Rev. 12 : 7. In the later Jewish books other names are given and different ideas of these two occur. Cf. Plummer.

[2] Cf. Heb. 1 : 14, *ἀποστελλόμενα.*

[3] *παρεστηκώς.* Note *παρά* by the side of.

[4] *ἀπεστάλην.* Sent from God himself. Cf. Heb. 1 : 14.

[5] *εὐαγγελίσασθαι.* The first use of "gospel" (*εὐαγγέλιον*) in connection with the mission of John or Jesus.

[6] *καὶ ἰδοὺ ἔσῃ σιωπῶν καὶ μὴ δονάμενος λαλῆσαι.* The *ἰδού* solemnly calls attention to his penalty. *Ἔσῃ σιωπῶν* is durative future made plain by the periphrastic form.

[7] Cf. Acts 13 : 11, *ἔσῃ τυφλὸς μὴ βλέπων.* Bruce, *in loco*, thinks the dumbness was "the almost natural effect of his state of mind—a kind of prolonged stupefaction."

[8] *οἵτινες*, not *οἵ.*

[9] *καιρόν*, not *χρόνος.*

priests were expected to return soon to prevent anxiety.[1] The fear of harm to Zacharias was natural in the Levitical religion, which viewed God as far from man.[2] The people were in a state of eager expectancy[3] and were already wondering[4] at the continued delay[5] of Zacharias in the temple. He finally came out, but he could not say a word, not even pronounce the benediction, as was the custom.[6] He probably made signs so that they preceived[7] that he had seen[8] a vision in the temple. It is not made clear how they knew so well that he had seen a vision. Besides his signs and the dumbness there was probably a look of rapture on his face. Zacharias was manifestly in a state of keen excitement, for he kept on making signs (nods)[9] and remained[10] dumb. After his week's service[11] was over, Zacharias went back to his home in the Hill Country of Judea.[12] He went a humbler, but a wiser man, full of thoughts of what he had heard and felt. We do not know the location of this home. Hebron has been claimed by some,[13] others urge Juttah (also a priestly town),[14] others still,

[1] Plummer.

[2] Bruce. Cf. Wünsche, "Beiträge," p. 413; Lev. 16 : 13.

[3] ἦν προσδοκῶν. A strong word (cf. Luke 3 : 15) and note periphrastic form.

[4] ἐθαύμαζον, descriptive imperfect (slightly inchoative).

[5] χρονίζειν, durative present. [6] Num. 6 : 24–26.

[7] ἐπέγνωσαν. Note ἐπι and see Acts 3 : 10; 4 : 13.

[8] ἑώρακεν, vivid historical present perfect retained in indirect discourse.

[9] ἦν διανεύων. Periphrastic imperfect again.

[10] διέμενεν. Both imperfect tense and διά accent the durative idea.

[11] λειτουργία (λέως equals λαός, ἔργον) was work for the people, public service. In Greece it was often public work rendered by a citizen at his own expense. In Egypt, as the papyri show (Deissmann, "Bible Studies," pp. 140 f.), it was used in a ceremonial sense of the work of the priests in the temples. Thus it came to the Septuagint and the New Testament.

[12] Luke 1 : 39. [13] Othon, "Lex. Rabbin.," 324.

[14] Josh. 15 : 55; 21: 16.

Ain Karin,[1] or, yet again, *Mar Zakaryā*.[2] We only know that at some town in the southern hills Zacharias had his home.[3]

6. *The Joy of Elizabeth.*—It was a great day for Elizabeth when she discovered that, old as she was, she was indeed to be a mother. Zacharias had, of course, written out for her the promise of the angel, though Luke does not say so. The motive of Elizabeth in so completely[4] hiding herself[5] is not told, nor can we clearly conjecture. It is possible that her statements were at first met with ridicule by her friends, or the solemn dignity of the event may have called for seclusion, or, indeed, it may have been just to avoid talk. But she had exultant joy. "Thus hath the Lord done[6] unto me in the days wherein he looked upon[7] me, to take away my reproach among men."[8] She can now lift up her head. And yet for a long time she hides her head. Her cup was so full that she must be alone with God. This attitude of exalted joy continues with Elizabeth. Much is written these days about the science of eugenics, but at least this is true. A child is entitled to a joyful welcome by both mother and father. Much in the

[1] Didon, "Life of Christ," Appendix D.

[2] Cheyne ("Encycl. Bibl.") mentions this as the traditional place of John's birth, but does not accept it.

[3] Smith ("In the Days of His Flesh," p. 25) agrees with Caspari that it was probably Khirbet-el-Jehud, near *Ain Karin*.

[4] περι. It is a voluntary silence with her, not enforced as with Zacharias.

[5] περιέκρυβεν ἑαυτήν. Reflexive expressed rather than the somewhat rare direct middle. It is not certain whether περιέκρυβεν is a late second aorist (constative) or a late imperfect (so durative).

[6] πεποίηκεν. Present perfect to accent permanence of the blessing.

[7] ἐπεῖδεν aorist (so punctiliar) sums up God's mercy.

[8] Luke 1 : 25.

child's life depends on the welcome in the home. It was to be this child's privilege to enter an atmosphere of deep religious fervor, of genuine spiritual life. That fact will have its influence on his life, for he will one day confront and condemn the mere formal religiosity of the time.

7. *Fellowship with Mary.*—The same angel who had brought the wonderful news to Zacharias revealed to Mary her exalted destiny. Mary asked for no sign, but one was granted her, a gracious one without a penalty.[1] The sign was what had already happened to her kinswoman,[2] Elizabeth. Mary was prompt to go and receive her proof from Elizabeth. It was a hallowed meeting between these two chosen women, the sacred privacy of which we must not roughly disturb. But Luke mentions several details. One is the fact that the babe responded to the salutation of Mary with a leap.[3] Another is the inspiration of Elizabeth. Mary apparently had told Elizabeth nothing of what Gabriel had told her. She interpreted[4] the babe's leaping to mean that the mother of the Messiah stood before her,[5] with all a mother's sympathy and the high ecstasy of the Holy Spirit's enlightenment. In reality, her outcry in so loud[6] a voice was a rhapsody of intense emotion. But it was a sober and clear insight, though on so high a plane.

[1] Plummer, *in loco.*

[2] *συγγενίς.* Not necessarily "cousin" nor proof that Mary belonged to the tribe of Levi rather than that of Judah. Levites could marry with other tribes.

[3] *ἐσκίρτησεν.* Cf. Gen. 25 : 22; Ps. 113 : 4, 6. Probably felt by Luke to be the first instinctive greeting of the coming Messiah by the Forerunner.

[4] Luke 1 : 43 f.

[5] Bruce, *in loco.*

[6] *ἀνεφώνησεν κραυγῇ μεγάλῃ.* Cf. Acts 26 : 24.

Elizabeth counted it a great honor to have received this visit from "the mother of my Lord." [1] This song of Elizabeth (with Hebrew parallelism) is the first of the New Testament hymns. It is also the first beatitude in the New Testament and a double one, though different Greek words[2] occur in verses 42 and 45, which are translated "blessed." The one accents the idea of credit as blessed, the other (cf. beatitudes of Jesus) the notion of inherent happiness. Both were true of Mary. Elizabeth now knows the story of Mary's happiness, whether by inspiration or from Mary. She felicitates Mary on her faith,[3] perhaps with memories of the doubt of Zacharias, and on the certainty of fulfilment[4] for her. The souls of the two saintly women are now strung to a high note of adoration and praise. Mary answers with her wonderful "Magnificat," [5] which it is not my province here to explain. On the return of Mary to Nazareth the three months soon sped by. The birth of a son to Elizabeth created a great stir among all the neighbors[6] and kinsfolk.[7] They acknowledged that God had "magnified" [8] Elizabeth (a "Magnificat" for her also). They kept a season of rejoicing with her,[9] the

[1] κυρίου here not in sense of courtesy, but in the Old Testament sense equals Lord Messiah (Ps. 110 : 1). She thus grasps the deity and humanity of Jesus. Cf. Christ's use of this Psalm in Matt. 22 : 42 ff. The phrase "Mother of God" is not in the New Testament. Cf. Plummer, *in loco*, *vs.* Didon, "Vie de Jésus," p. 111.

[2] εὐλογημένη (perfect passive participle) and μακαρία Cf. Deut. 28 : 4; Matt. 5 : 3 ff.

[3] ἡ πιστεύσασα. Attributive participle expressing antecedent action.

[4] τελείωσις.

[5] Μεγαλύνει. A few critics wrongly refer this song also to Elizabeth.

[6] περίοικοι equals dwellers around the house.

[7] συγγενεῖς, the usual word, not the late συγγενίδες.

[8] ἐμεγάλυνεν.

[9] συνέχαιρον. Imperfect (so durative).

first fulfilment of Gabriel's prophecy about John.[1] It was more than mere congratulation. It is with simple dignity and charm that Luke has thus portrayed the birth of the Baptist.

8. *The New Name in the Family.*—The Jewish law about circumcision[2] was ceremoniously observed.[3] The friends[4] who had come for the ceremony wished to name the child also as a part, in fact, of the ceremony.[5] To name him Zacharias was surely most appropriate and common.[6] So they began[7] calling the boy Zacharias, and thought that the ceremony was over. But there was a sudden interruption[8] on the part of Elizabeth. Zacharias had probably written on a tablet that the child's name was to be John. But the friends would not surrender their point without protest.[9] They even appealed earnestly by nods and signs[10] to Zacharias to get his wish in the hope that he would take their side in the matter against Elizabeth. It is curious the keen zest that people have in all that concerns a baby. It is possible that Zacharias was deaf as well as dumb, as is often the case,[11] or they may have wished to spare the feelings[12] of Elizabeth by so doing. At any rate, Zacharias understood the signs, if he had not already overheard the conversation, and asked for a tablet.[13] He asked, of course, by signs. He wrote: "John is

[1] Cf. Luke 1:14. [2] Cf. Ex. 4:25. [3] Luke 1:59.
[4] Note ἦλθαν plural. [5] Plummer, *in loco*.
[6] Josephus, "Ant.," xiv, 1, 3.
[7] ἐκάλουν. Inchoative-conative imperfect. Cf. Matt. 3:14.
[8] οὐχί, ἀλλά. [9] Luke 1:61.
[10] ἐνένευον. Iterative imperfect. Cf. ἦν διανεύων (1:22).
[11] κωφός (1:22) can mean this. [12] Meyer, *in loco*.
[13] πινακίδιον equals a little tablet covered with wax.

his name."[1] That settled it. But the friends wondered at this strange agreement between husband and wife on the new name. They took it as an omen of something, but did not know what. But a real marvel came now, for the mouth of Zacharias was instantly opened and he began[2] to speak. Now he blessed God. No more had he doubt. But it was too much for the crowd of neighbors, who were filled with fear, a touch of reality that bears on the genuineness of the story.[3] So Zacharias had felt when the angel appeared to him.[4] It was awe. But other tongues were loosed besides that of Zacharias.[5] The talk went on[6] throughout the length and breadth of the Hill Country. Others, the more thoughtful and spiritual, laid it all deep in their hearts with the query, "What then[7] will this child be?" No one could answer that question. With all the talk there was the hush of mystery and reverence. Luke adds his own interpretation,[8] which was in harmony with the deeper conviction of the people in the Hill Country. But he introduces it as an additional[9] point of view, more in accord with the real facts, for Luke had the benefit of the later developments. The expression, "the hand of the Lord," is indeed peculiar to Luke[10] in the New Testament, but it is common in the Old Testament.[11] No

[1] Thus the Greek order in Luke 1 : 63.
[2] ἐλάλει. Inchoative imperfect.
[3] Plummer, *in loco*. [4] Luke 1 : 12. [5] A zeugma in 1: 64.
[6] διελαλεῖτο. Imperfect (descriptive durative).
[7] ἄρα. In view of all that had happened.
[8] A habit of Luke it is to add such comments. Cf. 2 : 50; 3 : 15; 7 : 39, etc. [9] καὶ γάρ.
[10] Acts 4 : 28, 30; 11 : 21; 13 : 11.
[11] Cf. Ex. 7 : 4, 5; II Kings 3 : 15; Ezra 7 : 6, etc.

other explanation is possible to-day as one faces all the facts preserved concerning John the Baptist. The hand of the Lord was not merely upon[1] him, but with[2] him, with him all the way to the very end, with him from the very beginning, as Luke has now made clear. One does not depreciate human freedom in recognizing this to be true, nor is it unscientific. If men to-day take a hand in the breeding of finer kinds of animals, it is surely not impossible for (least of all, unworthy of) God to place his hand beside the life of the child who is to be the Herald of God's own Son. The highest blessing possible for any child is to receive in a real, if in a lesser, sense the blessing of God's hand in his life.

9. *The Insight of Zacharias.*—The prophecy[3] of Zacharias was probably spoken at the time that his tongue was loosed. The first word "Blessed" seems to take up the "blessing" of verse 64. Luke has finished his picture of the effect of that wonder, and now resumes the narrative of the song of Zacharias ("Benedictus"). The day of prophecy has come back and Zacharias, like Elizabeth and Mary, is filled with the Holy Spirit. He was probably not himself a very learned priest.[4] Moreover, the rabbi, not the priest, was now the leading figure in the public eye.[5] As a "common priest" from the hills he was not one from whom to expect a lofty or learned exposition of high

[1] ἐπί. [2] μετά. [3] ἐπροφήτευσεν.

[4] Edersheim ("Life and Times of Jesus the Messiah," vol. I, p. 141), says he would have been called an ἰδιώτης (cf. ἰδιῶται about Peter and John in Acts 4 : 13) priest, an *amha-retz*, a "rustic" priest, to be treated with benevolent contempt.

[5] Geike, "Life and Words of Christ," 1877, vol. I, p. 87.

themes, that is, not from the point of view of the learned priests and rabbis. Under Agrippa II "ladies bought the high-priesthood for their husbands for so much money,"[1] and the priests, as a whole, were a sort of national religious aristocracy. But God has often passed by the high and the mighty when he had a gift to bestow. He seeks out the choice spirits, those who have an ear open to his voice. They are often found in the Hill Country. It was necessary for God to reveal his purpose through prophecy in order "to revive, primarily in the small circles of the pious in Israel, the long-sunk Messianic hopes of the people."[2] The New Testament era has thus opened some time, probably, in the year 6 B. C., with no blare of trumpets, but with the definite outreach of God's hand. In the midst of the prevalent coldness and formalism, not to say corruption, there were found some who would, and did, respond to the moving of God's Spirit. Zacharias was not, probably, a great man in native gifts, though he was to have a really great son. The springs of greatness or genius are hidden to mortal eye, and do not follow laws of heredity that have been as yet traced. Nature practises leaps as well as sports. But Zacharias was just and pious and familiar with the Old Testament prophecies. "As the 'Magnificat' is modelled on the Psalms, so the 'Benedictus' is modelled on the prophecies, and it has been called 'the last prophecy of

[1] *Ibid.*, p. 89.

[2] Weiss, "The Life of Christ," vol. I, p. 140. "These prophecies in the circle of the pious, in the Hill Country of Judea, greet the first morning red of the new time of salvation, which is already dawning full of hope" (*ibid.*, pp. 245 f.).

the Old Dispensation, and the first in the New.' And while the tone of the 'Magnificat' is regal, that of the 'Benedictus' is sacerdotal. The one is as appropriate to the daughter of David as the other is to the son of Aaron."[1] That is clearly shown by parallel columns which reveal the kinship to the language of the Old Testament.[2] During the months of silent waiting one can well imagine that Zacharias had turned often to the rolls of Isaiah, Ezekiel, Jeremiah, Malachi, the Psalms, to see what, after all, the Old Testament did say concerning the Messiah and the Forerunner. The text of Westcott and Hort divides the song of Zacharias into five strophes (68 f., 70–72, 73–75, 76 f., 78 f.).[3] But there is a manifest cleavage of the poem at verse 76 which breaks[4] it into two parts. The first part (68–75) is an exclamation of praise to God for his goodness in the wonderful birth of the child. The second part (76–79) is an address to the child concerning his career in the kingdom. In the one he describes the work of the Messiah, in the other that of John.[5] "Zacharias sees in his son the earnest and guarantee of the deliverance of Israel."[6] The words are so rich in meaning that they command discussion. The three strophes of 70–75 set forth in exultant strain that the blessing of redemption through David has come true at last (68 f.), that God has remembered his holy covenant of old (70–72), that God has kept his oath with Abraham

[1] Plummer, p. 39.
[2] Cf. Plummer, p. 39.
[3] Plummer, pp. 39 f.
[4] καὶ σὺ δέ, παιδίον.
[5] Godet, "Commentary on Luke," p. 69.
[6] Plummer, p. 40.

(73–75). The second part has two strophes; one shows John as the Forerunner and the preacher of forgiveness (76 f.), the other explains that the new light will go even to those who sit in darkness and the shadow of death (78 f.). Most of the phraseology is found in the Septuagint, but it is not a mere chain of quotations. They are welded into a real unity of thought, and give a masterful and poetic interpretation of the dealings of God with Israel. The past finds its real justification in the present. It was for this that God was patient and never gave up this rebellious people. The promise is now reality. The birth of John is a guarantee of that of the Messiah.[1] God has visited,[2] God will visit.[3] It was surely time for God to come again after so many centuries of silence. Zacharias seems to have some conception of the incarnation,[4] though "redemption,"[5] in his mind, may have included political salvation[6] as well as the deeper and antecedent spiritual and moral elements of personal renewal.[7] The popular notion of the Messianic kingdom had sunk to the level of a mere political conquest and deliverance. The heel of Rome pressed hard upon the neck of the patriotic Jew. But that is a subordinate idea with Zacharias. The "Moses of salvation" who is to come through the house of David is the Messiah soon to be born

[1] In 70–75 the aorist indicative occurs; in 76–79 the future indicative.

[2] ἐπεσκέψατο. Punctiliar, but so recent that we have to say "has."

[3] ἐπισκέψεται (א BL). Future, but certain. The word is not unlike "visit," from *video*, and suggests "the familiarity of a friend and the tenderness of a physician" (Reynolds, "John the Baptist," p. 112).

[4] Godet, p. 69.

[5] λύτρωσιν from λύτρον (ransom) 1 : 68.

[6] σωτηρίαν ἐξ ἐχθρῶν ἡμῶν (1 : 71).

[7] 1 : 75, 77. Cf. Plummer.

of Mary. Abraham and the prophets are at last justified. Freedom from oppression will give the privilege of service to God in holiness and righteousness. With the eye of faith Zacharias now sees it all as a reality. He turns to the child. He will walk before Jehovah to make ready[1] his ways. He will bring knowledge of salvation which is found in forgiveness of sins.[2] John will lay chief stress on the spiritual elements. He concludes with a graphic picture of night in the desert as of a lost caravan. Jews[3] as well as Gentiles sit in darkness, and the shadow of death which has settled like a pall over all the world. But, because of God's mercy, "the dayspring[4] from on high" will shine like a bright star in the darkness "to guide our feet into the way of peace."[5] It is a noble utterance. With it the voice of Zacharias is heard no more, and he drops back into the routine of his simple life in the hills. But his heart is on the boy and he looks wistfully into his eyes and into the future. Was it, after all, only a mirage of the desert?

10. *The Hidden Years in the Hills.*—"And the child grew and waxed strong in spirit."[6] Luke with these words draws a veil over the life in the home of the young John. The child grew and grew, a joy to

[1] ἑτοιμάσαι. Cf. Luke 3 : 4. John will quote the same word.
[2] The first mention of "remission of sins" in the gospels (Plummer, p. 43).
[3] ἡμᾶς, ἡμῶν.
[4] ἀνατολή. Cf. Isa. 9 : 2 for the image.
[5] Luke 1 : 79. Peace was the word borne by the heavenly host on the birth of Jesus (Luke 2 : 14). Alas, how slow the world is to walk in this way!
[6] Luke 1 : 80. ηὔξανε. Imperfect (so durative descriptive). Likewise with ἐκραταιοῦτο.

his parents, whose strength inevitably was rapidly going with their advanced years. He kept on gaining strength with his years. It was strength of spirit, not merely that of body. Dr. John A. Broadus, as long ago as 1874, made a few brief notes toward a life of the Baptist. Alas! that the busy years found no place for the completion of that congenial task. I quote a few sentences at this point. "Not simply strong in body, in mind, in passions, but in will—and this not in self-will, but as a self-ruling will, strong in self-restraint and self-impulse. A fearless, resolute, determined, persevering, unconquerable character. But does it not also include what we call distinctively spiritual strength—strong faith in the unseen and eternal, strong desire and purpose to lead a holy and useful life?" It was then the normal life of a child in a small town in the hills; he will soon be much out-of-doors. One is at liberty to imagine the talk between Zacharias and Elizabeth as some new development in the boy gave fresh confirmation to the words of Gabriel or of Zacharias. It was just as God had said. We do not know how soon the old couple died, but it is hardly stretching the probabilities to suppose that they lived long enough to create in John, or rather cultivate what was inborn in him, a love for the Old Testament and its great stories of mighty men and its unfolding of a matchless future for Israel if Israel were only faithful unto God. Elizabeth could tell of Abraham almost in the very neighborhood of the cave of Machpelah.[1] And Zacharias could show

[1] Reynolds, "John the Baptist," p. 116.

many of the places where David used to hide from Saul in this den or in that. Not far away was Bethlehem where he had tended his father's sheep. Here was a comb of wild honey such as David had sought. There is nothing more fascinating than a boy's growing appreciation of his world as it unfolds around him. I quote a few sentences from Dr. Broadus's notes on John already mentioned: "He was a child of the mountains. Whenever education and religion take hold in a mountain region, the result is great strength of character. The only son of a priest was likely to be carefully educated, all the more when the child of such promises. He was doubtless taught to read and write, and from a child knew the Holy Scriptures. At twelve or thirteen he would begin to attend the feast of the Passover as a 'Son of the Law.' We cannot judge of his pursuits in early youth. The strict Jewish custom that every son must learn a trade would not apply to Levites, especially not to priests, as they all had a calling divinely appointed. One thing we know, he drank 'no wine nor strong drink.'" Did Zacharias and Elizabeth tell John what was in store for him? Or did they leave that to God? They most naturally told him. The talk about John would die down among the neighbors as he grew on like other boys. Now and then a reminiscent old woman would recall the early excitement and tell it as a wonderful incident. But the years went by. Will Zacharias and Elizabeth live to see the entrance of John upon his great work? They knew, of course, of the actual birth of Jesus at Bethlehem and of the death of Herod the Great. But it is growing late in the evening for them both. The light is dim. They draw the strong, noble boy closer to them. He has already become fond of the hills, and sometimes wanders far. They have left their mark upon John—a precious heritage of faith and spiritual fellowship. One day the boy saw the light die on the face of one or the other, and then of both. He was alone. Already the voice of God had been calling to him in a strange, mysterious way. Now he had no other voice to call. He will follow that. He knew now that the hand of God was with him. He will hold it fast. Had not Zacharias and Elizabeth told him to keep his heart open to the gate of heaven?

11. *The Voices in the Desert.*—"And was in the deserts till the day of his shewing unto Israel."[1] But when did he go to "the deserts"? It is hard to think that John would have left his aged parents while alive. It may be assumed that they are now dead. John was now probably grown (twenty or twenty-one, not yet thirty, the Jewish legal manhood). Josephus was sixteen when he went to the desert to study three years under Banus, the famous Essene.[2] The point is that it was no raw, callow youth who withdrew to the desert in a fret or for adventure.[3] John had doubtless come to full consciousness of himself, of his powers, of his mission. Besides, he knew his world, as is plain when he emerges from his

[1] Luke 1:80.
[2] Josephus, "Life," § 2.
[3] Josephus (*ibid.*) says that he went to the desert to learn the doctrines of the Essenes (he had dabbled in those of the Sadducees and the Pharisees) "that I might choose the best." He was a theological "taster."

voluntary retirement. He had "acquired personal independence. His wants were religiously limited, his tastes simple, and his dependence on his brother-men therefore reduced to a minimum."[1] Where did he go? The expression "the deserts"[2] means "the deserted regions." He did not have far to go to find the barren rocks and cliffs of Judah, and had probably made so many excursions into these regions that he felt at home here. Love of solitude had become a passion with him. "Meet foster-mother for one who is to be the censor of his time."[3] The general region called "desert" covered all the eastern portion of Judah and part of Benjamin. It was in reality about a third of Judah.[4] It was (and is) not an absolute desert, though badly cut up with wadys or canyons. The soil was largely washed away, but grass would grow where the soil still held, and shrubs and trees would be found here and there. It was a mountain highland that sloped down from a height of some three thousand feet at Hebron to the abyss of the Dead Sea, one thousand two hundred and ninety-two feet below the Mediterranean. It was a wild, grand, picturesque place. There were few inhabitants save in the towns at the head and lower end of the Dead Sea and on the higher plateau. There were sparse settlements here and there, some Therapeutæ, some Essenes. But all in all it was to most people of the time a forbidding region, full of hardship and even danger. Jerome found no farms here, but shep-

[1] Reynolds, "John the Baptist," p. 117.

[2] *ἐν ταῖς ἐρήμοις* (sc. *γαῖς* or *χώραις*).

[3] Bruce, "Luke," *in loco*.

[4] Keim, "Jesus of Nazara," vol. II, p. 219.

herds came with their flocks.[1] Here the vipers would be seen in clusters (broods) on the rocks. Not all of John's familiarity with nature was gained in this region. The winnowing fan, the axe at the root of the tree he was familiar with before he came to the desert. John had no settled abode in the desert. He moved from place to place "in the deserts."

Why did John go to the wilderness? Hermits went to the wilderness of Judea, as Josephus[2] tells us about Banus who "lived in the desert, and used no other clothing than grew upon trees, and had no other food than what grew of its own accord, and bathed himself in cold water frequently." Josephus "imitated him in those things" for three years. Keim[3] thinks that John also led a "hermit life." Certainly he lived a solitary life, but, when he comes forth at last, it is not as a hermit or man of the woods. He did indeed lead "a rural life away from the capital," [4] but it is by no means clear that he was an anchorite, though many of them came to these regions. It has, indeed, been urged that John went into the desert, like Josephus, to study the doctrine of the Essenes and that he became one. But there is no foundation for this idea. These cenobites had monasteries along the shores of the Dead Sea. They numbered some four thousand in all. The Essenes were an offshoot of Pharisaism with ascetic tendencies concerning animal food, marriage and animal sacrifices, but

[1] Keim, "Jesus of Nazara," vol. II, p. 219. Cf. Smith, "Historical Geography of Palestine." [2] "Life," § 2.

[3] "Jesus of Nazara," vol. II, p. 220.

[4] Smith, "In the Days of His Flesh," p. 25.

with an admixture of the philosophy of Parseeism and Pythagoreanism, including the worship of the sun.[1] But there is no real reason for thinking that John had any contact with them; certainly he did not accept their cardinal tenets about animal food (he ate locusts)[2] nor marriage, which he did not condemn, nor about sun-worship, which he did not practise. He did practise the ascetic life as was true of many others not Essenes, but he came forth and lived among men. "He preached the Kingdom of God; they preached isolation. They abandoned society; he strove to reform it." [3] It is true that he fasted frequently, as his disciples did later.[4] But that was a common thing with all Pharisees, who were surprised that Jesus and his disciples did not fast. John was not peculiar because of his stated fasting. Both John and Jesus abstained from oaths and honored poverty as the Essenes did.[5] "The Essenes had renounced every Messianic expectation; the soul of John's life and ministry was the expectation of the Messiah and the preparation for his work. The Essenes made matter the seat of sin; John, by his energetic calls to conversion, shows plainly that he found it in the will." [6] The Essenes were pessimists who gave up the world; John was a reformer who came to make it better. It is true that John's retirement to the desert was a protest against the prevailing luxury and corruption.[7]

[1] See Schuerer, "The Jewish People in the Times of Jesus Christ," second division, vol. II, pp. 189–218; Keim, "Jesus of Nazara," vol. I, pp. 365 ff.; Lightfoot on Colossians, pp. 158–179.

[2] Cheyne ("Encycl. Bibl.") takes locusts to mean carob-beans.

[3] Plummer, "Luke," p. 44.

[4] Matt. 9:14.

[5] Reynolds, "John the Baptist," p. 180.

[6] Godet, "Luke," p. 73.

[7] Lambert, "Hastings's D. C. G."

His predecessor Amos "had been a herdsman and a dresser of sycomores in that very region eight centuries before." [1] Like Amos, also, he would meditate upon this high calling better in this wild and desolate region. But John was no mere imitator of any one. He was *sui generis*, and all the more so because of his grapple with himself in the wilderness. He did not go apart, as the usual monastic does, to gain merit with God,[2] but to face his life problem and to adjust himself to it. His going was "an absolute break with the prevalent Pharisaic type of piety." [3] He went, not to stay, but to get ready to come back, to come back to save his people.[4] But John "learned his lesson at the feet of no human teacher." [5] Reynolds[6] has a fine word: "His education was the memory of his childhood and the knowledge of his commission, and was effected by the Spirit of the living God. His schoolmasters were the rocks of the desert of Judea, the solemn waters of the Dead Sea, the eternal Presence that fills the solitudes of nature, the sins, the shame, the vows, the hopes, the professions of his countrymen." [7]

He had withdrawn in no selfish spirit, certainly not to shirk his duty. Much of the hermit and monastic

[1] Smith, "In the Days of His Flesh," p. 26.
[2] Keim, "Jesus of Nazara," vol. II, p. 222.
[3] Lambert, "Hastings's D. C. G."
[4] Keim, "Jesus of Nazara," vol. II, p. 222.
[5] Nourse, "Standard Bible Dictionary." [6] "John the Baptist," p. 118.
[7] Cf. Wordsworth:

"He knew the rocks which angels haunt
On the mountains visitant;
He hath kenned them taking wing. . . .
His daily teachers had been woods and rills,
The silence that is in the starry sky,
The sleep that is among the lonely hills."

life of the ages has really been a species of selfishness, as citizens to-day withdraw from politics and leave the government of the cities to the "bosses" and corrupt professional politicians. The precise example of John in his wilderness life is not necessarily a model for us, certainly not for all. But it is beyond doubt that in our restless, feverish age men would be greatly helped by taking time for reflection and meditation. John gained much by his voluntary and temporary withdrawal to the desert. He gained robust health from simple, wholesome fare and life out in the open air. This sturdiness of body will stand him in good stead during the severe strain of open-air preaching to great crowds.[1] It is a curious notion held by some people that emaciation is a sign of piety.

It is without doubt true that John's imagination was cultivated by the wild grandeur all about him. The deep gorges, the high cliffs, the daring leap of a wild goat, the flight of an eagle, the flash of the lightning, the fury of the storm on the bare rocks—these would all have an exalting influence on his mind. He may have had rolls of the prophets with him, which he would read in these impressive surroundings. He often quotes the picturesque passages of the Old Testament.[2] Nature has also a distinct influence toward devotion when one yields himself to its noblest impressions. He would worship in the temple of nature, but not the sun, but Jehovah, the God of

[1] Farrar ("Life of Christ," vol. I, p. 107) considers John emaciated.

[2] Tasker, "Hastings's One Volume Dictionary." Thus (Luke 3 : 17 and Acts 9 : 9; Isa. 66 : 24; John 1 : 23 and Isa. 40 : 3; John 1 : 29 and Isa. 53 : 7).

Israel (the true Israel), and of nature. Jesus went often to the mountains to pray alone with the Father.

Was not the hand of the Lord still with him in the desert? Is it mere speculation to suppose that John "was led by the Spirit into the wilderness" as Jesus was in later years? Indeed, it is hardly probable that the devil left John alone during these years in retirement. Those who flee from society merely to escape temptation should remember that Jesus met the devil in the desert as well as on the pinnacle of the temple.

John had a new angle of vision in the wilderness. He could contemplate from a distance the moral and spiritual condition of his people. He could seek to discover the causes of the lapse in public life. He could search for a remedy. If he was to be a reformer he must be more than a denunciator of present conditions. It was not hard to criticise the Pharisees and Sadducees. Could he offer the people anything better?

12. *The Call to Cry.*—He knew, we may assume, his mission as he had been told it by his parents. He had communed with the master spirits of the olden days. But the prophetic fire had not yet blazed within him. He was willing to bide his time. One must not forget the self-restraint of John during these years. "The nature of John was full of impetuosity and fire. . . . If he had won peace in the long prayer and penitence of his life in the wilderness, it was not the spontaneous peace of a placid and holy soul. The victory he had won was still encumbered with

traces of the battle. . . . While he was musing the fire burned, and at the last he spake with his tongue. . . . In solitude he had learnt things unspeakable; there the unseen world had become to him a reality; there his spirit had caught a touch of phantasy and flame. . . . He had received a revelation not vouchsafed to ordinary men—attained, not in the schools of the Rabbis, but in the school of solitude, in the school of God." [1] Probably it was gradual, this conviction on John's part, that he must speak. The message was taking shape in his mind. Possibly reports came to him of unusual shortcomings on the part of the religious leaders in Jerusalem. "As he brooded on the signs of the times, the barren trees of the desert fit only for burning, and the vipers fleeing before the flaming scrub, became emblems of the nation's peril, and lent color to his warnings of impending wrath." [2] Yes, and the Spirit of God put a live coal upon his lip. The fire burned within his heart. He felt the woe of the true preacher upon him if he did not speak. But, after all, who was he, a man of the desert, a Nazirite, poor and unknown, who was he to lift up his voice against the great forces of Jewish life in Jerusalem? He doubtless had his moments of reaction, but the call came back, and louder. There was no peace. He had to speak even if no one heard. He dared not go to Jerusalem in his garb, nor would he be likely to gain a hearing there. He had his voice if he had no synagogue nor temple court. Indeed, he

[1] Farrar, "Life of Christ," vol. I, pp. 108 f.

[2] Tasker, "Hastings's One Volume Dictionary." Cf. Smith, "Historical Geography of Palestine," p. 495.

had no audience but the eagles, the goats, and the vipers. But he must speak. "The day of his shewing[1] unto Israel" had come. Plummer[2] suggests that John may have gone up to Jerusalem for the feasts. But the word "shewing" hardly means that, though it does imply a rather formal installation into office.[3] But it was in the wilderness that God met John (cf. Moses at the Burning Bush). In the wilderness John began to cry.[4] "The word of God came unto John the son of Zacharias in the wilderness."[5] He had long been listening for that word. Now it has come, and it finds him ready.

[1] ἀναδείξεως. Luke 1 : 80.
[2] "Luke," p. 44.
[3] Godet, "Luke," p. 73.
[4] Matt. 3 : 1.
[5] Luke 3 : 2.

CHAPTER II

CHALLENGE

"Repent ye, for the kingdom of heaven is at hand" (Matt. 3 : 2).

1. *The Time.*—Matthew[1] merely says "in those days," while Mark[2] succinctly and vividly describes the appearance of John as "the beginning of the gospel of Jesus Christ the Son of God." Matthew is not concerned with exact dates. Mark is justified by the word of Jesus[3] in making John the beginning of the New Dispensation. The actual outward beginning was when John lifted up his voice in the wilderness. "Until John," Jesus said. There was a grand, an awful silence in the preceding centuries till the new prophet spoke.[4] "It was the glory of the Baptist to have revived the function of the prophet."[5] Holtzmann[6] (Oscar) thinks that "scarcely any great intellectual movement that the world has known has had a simpler and less pretentious beginning than Christianity."

Luke is fully conscious that the new era opens with John. He has the historian's sense of the importance of the beginning of the new time. He seeks to relate

[1] 3 : 1. [2] 1 : 1. [3] Matt. 11 : 12 f.; Luke 16 : 16.
[4] Edersheim, "Life and Times of Jesus," vol. I, p. 255.
[5] "Ecce Homo," p. 2. Cf. Bengel, "Hic quasi scena N. T. panditur."
[6] "The Life of Jesus," p. 109.

it to the world by a sixfold date after the fashion of Thucydides with his sixfold date of the entry of the Thebans into Platæa.[1] This synchronistic date[2] includes the political and ecclesiastical rulers of Palestine. The political rulers are naturally the Emperor Tiberius Cæsar, who ruled over all; Pontius Pilate, the new governor of Judea under Tiberius; Herod (Antipas), the Tetrarch of Galilee (and Perea), whose subject Jesus was, and to whom he paid taxes; Philip, the Tetrarch of Iturea and Trachonitis, where Jesus found refuge (Cæsarea Philippi). The mention of Lysanias, the Tetrarch of Abilene, is not so natural. It is possible that Abilene had once belonged to Herod the Great, since Claudius gave it to Herod Agrippa I.[3] The word tetrarch[4] literally means ruler of a fourth part.[5] The four great divisions of Herod's kingdom would thus receive mention. Luke's accuracy has been challenged on the ground of this mention of Lysanias of Abilene, which is unsupported by any other evidence, though one by that name is known who lived six years before.[6] But Schuerer contends that Luke is thoroughly correct. Philip ruled from B. C. 4–A. D. 39, Herod Antipas from B. C. 4–A. D. 39, Pontius Pilate from A. D. 26–36.[7] The only exact note of time is in connection with Tiberius,

[1] Plummer, "Luke," p. 80.
[2] Holtzmann, "Life of Jesus," p. 109.
[3] Godet, "Luke," p. 108; Josephus, "Ant.," xix, 5, 1.
[4] *τετρααρχοῦντος* 3 : 1. Three times here.
[5] Cf. the four provinces of Thessaly in Eur. "Alc.," 1154. This is the only mention in the New Testament, but see Josephus, "War," iii, 10, 7. Cf. Plummer, p. 82.
[6] "The Jewish People," etc., div. I, vol. II, p. 338. Cf. Godet, "Luke," p. 107.
[7] Holtzmann ("Life of Jesus," p. 110) puts his date A. D. 27–37.

in the fifteenth year of whose reign John made his public appearance as a prophet. Now Tiberius was emperor from A. D. 14–37. So fourteen years plus fourteen would equal twenty-eight. Holtzmann[1] so takes it, and justifies Luke's date. But Jesus was probably put to death at the Passover of A. D. 29 or 30. He seems to have entered upon his ministry when thirty years old ("about thirty")[2] and was six months younger than John. This interval between the beginning of John's ministry and that of Jesus cannot, of course, be known with absolute certainty, but the period of six months seems probable. However, A. D. 28 appears to be too late for the beginning of John's work, since the ministry of Jesus was at least two and a half years long. It is known that in the provinces Tiberius was associated with Augustus in the rule for two years.[3] It is entirely possible, even probable, that Luke, writing about the provincial rule, and in the provinces himself, has this in mind. If so, A. D. 26 would be the latest date for John's ministry possible, and more probably A. D. 25, unless the mention of Pilate (A. D. 26) is conclusive for 26. We do not know the time of year when John began his ministry. It is hardly worth while to tarry over Luke's use of the untechnical "governor"[4] rather than the more exact "Procurator."[5] The ecclesiastical rulers mentioned are two, Annas and Caiaphas.[6]

[1] *Ibid.*

[2] Luke 3 : 23.

[3] Suet., "Tib.," xxi; "Vell. Paterc.," ii, 121. Cf. Godet, "Luke," p. 106; Plummer, p. 82.

[4] ἡγεμονεύοντος.

[5] D reads ἐπιτροπεύοντος.

[6] Note idiomatic use of ἐπί. The mention of ἀρχιερέως only once is "probably not accidental, and certainly not ironical" (Plummer).

The same expression occurs in Acts 4 : 6 ("Annas the high-priest and Caiaphas"). As a matter of fact, Annas was actual high-priest from A. D. 7–14, when he was deposed. His son-in-law, Caiaphas, was high-priest from A. D. 18–36. They either shared the office between them or Annas was considered high-priest *de jure* and Caiaphas *de facto*. This situation explains the connection of Annas with the trial of Jesus.[1]

Thus, then, Luke gives us an outlook upon the world of John's time. John, so far as we know, had no special dealings with Tiberius, who perhaps never heard of the new sensation on the Jordan. But he did have direct dealings with Herod Antipas. John was not the kind of preacher who made an absolute divorce between religion and politics. He tried to put religious principles into politicians. We have no evidence that Annas and Caiaphas ever saw John, but they took notice of John, as we shall see.[2] John was not oblivious of the public about him.[3]

Luke seems to have a sense of the fulness of the time that he shows in connection with the coming of the Holy Spirit on the Day of Pentecost.[4] Greek philosophy had issued in cynical pride or reckless abandon. Roman power was on the principle that might is right. "The idea of conscience, as we understand it, was unknown to heathenism. Absolute right did not exist."[5] Hellenism had pressed

[1] John 18 : 13, 19.
[2] John 1 : 19.
[3] Tiberius "was a malicious and furious man, unwilling to do anything that he thought would please his subjects" (Philo, "Leg.," 1033). Cf. Geike, "Life and Words of Christ," vol. I, p. 381.
[4] Acts 2 : 1.
[5] Edersheim, "Life and Times of Jesus," vol. I, p. 259.

the Jews into a corner. The more devout and patriotic spirits had made a noble and (for a time) successful stand against the Hellenizers. The glories of the Maccabean struggle were as noble traditions as Judaism had. But even the Maccabees fell under the spell of Greece. Pharisaism was the hard protest of a resentful people who clung to their traditions.[1] The time had come for a change. The darkest hour is just before the dawn. Luke's interest in the date of John's appearance is not simply because of John. It is due to the fact that John was the Forerunner of Jesus. It is the revolution wrought by Christianity which concerns Luke. "It was indeed a striking coincidence that just where Israel of old had entered the Land of Promise, the door of the Kingdom of Heaven should in those last days be opened." [2]

2. *The Place.*—Mark[3] has simply "in the wilderness," but that is clear enough. Matthew[4] adds "of Judea," while Luke[5] explains that "he came into all the region round about Jordan." [6] He was already in the desert when the word of the Lord came to him. So he began preaching where he was to the few passers by or cenobites. The news rapidly spread that a real prophet had appeared, the first since Malachi (c. 460–430 B. C.). But it is an itinerant ministry. The people came to John, but he moved on to the Jordan. The term wilderness included all the Jordan valley, or El-Ghor. He probably began in the south and

[1] "All real belief in a personal continuance after death must have ceased among the educated classes" (*ibid.*, p. 257).
[2] Smith, "In the Days of His Flesh," p. 26.
[3] 1 : 4. [4] 3 : 1. [5] 3 : 3. [6] περίχωρον. Cf. Gen. 13 : 10 f.

moved on north, and was now on one side of the Jordan, now on the other.[1] He finally went near the border of the Sea of Galilee.[2]

"His selection of the valley of the Jordan as his sphere of work was partly determined by the need of water for immersion." [3] In the early stages of his ministry we may think of him as in the lower Jordan valley, a little above the Dead Sea. He would move up the river. Bruce[4] thinks that he found a place by the river convenient for baptism, and then settled there. The Jordan ("the descender") has many memories (Joshua, Naaman, Elisha, etc), but its fame rests mainly on the work of John in this ministry. To the Jordan Jesus came for baptism. In a true sense the Jordan was John's river. Its principal source was on Mount Hermon, seventeen hundred feet above the sea, and it sank into the Dead Sea twelve hundred and ninety-two feet below the sea. The Dead Sea itself was some thirteen hundred feet deep.[5] The valley between the Sea of Galilee and the Dead Sea varied from two to six miles in width." "Winding about in this long, narrow valley is another depressed valley (forty to one hundred and fifty feet deeper), of several hundred yards in width; and within this the actual bed of the river sinks deeper still."[6] The one is El-Ghor, the other is El-Zor. It is only sixty-five miles between the Sea of Galilee and

[1] Plummer, "Luke," p. 85. Cf. John 1 : 28; 10 : 40.

[2] John 3 : 23.

[3] Plummer, "Luke," pp. 85 f. Cf. Stanley, "Sinai and Palestine," p. 312.

[4] "Luke," *in loco.*

[5] Broadus, "Commentary on Matthew," p. 43.

[6] *Ibid.*, p. 43.

the Dead Sea, but the actual winding of the river here is some two hundred miles. The amount of water in the river varies in different places and at different seasons of the year. There are numerous fords up and down the river. When the snows of Hermon melt in the spring, the water is high. In places it will be seventy-five feet wide and ten feet deep. At the rapids it would be only a few inches deep. But there is no place on the Jordan where we know certainly that John was save Bethany, beyond Jordan,[1] and Enon, near to Salim.[2] This latter was probably some distance from the Jordan, where were many pools.[3] But the people could find John even in the wilderness.

3. *The First Glimpse of the Man.*—"Now John himself."[4] After all, the man is more interesting and important than his surroundings. His dress was striking and would at once arrest attention. It was like that of Banus, described by Josephus.[5] But it was more like that of the prophets. It was probably the coarse, rude garment woven of camel's hair.[6] It is worth noting that the Oriental people did not care for this camel's hair cloth as much as Westerners do now.[7] Elijah, indeed, wore a sheepskin mantle[8] as some writers think was true of John.[9] But the Greek idiom is against it. Some of the saints in times of

[1] John 1 : 28. On the eastern side.
[2] John 3 : 23. On the western side.
[3] *ὕδατα πολλά.*
[4] Matt. 3 : 4; *αὐτὸς δὲ ὁ Ἰωάνης.*
[5] "Life," § 2.
[6] *απὸ τριχῶν καμήλου* (Matt. 3 : 4; Mark 1 : 6). Cf. Zech. 13 : 4.
[7] Holtzmann, "Life of Jesus," p. 113.
[8] I Kings 19 : 19.
[9] Cf. Cheyne, "Encycl. Bibl." D does read *δέρριν καμήλου* in Mark 3 : 6, probably from Zechariah. Cf. Swete on Mark 3 : 6.

emergency had worn sheepskins and goatskins.[1] It is possible, indeed, that John is consciously imitating in a general way the garb of Elijah.[2] It was probably a garment of sackcloth woven of camel's hair that John wore. The leathern girdle was also like that worn by Elijah[3] "in contrast with the metal girdles which the ancients preferred."[4] But this imitation of dress was not mere artificial copying. He had the mood of Elijah.[5] His very garb preached a lesson to that profligate age. His diet was as simple as his dress. The wild honey[6] was abundant in the clefts of the rocks. Some scholars think that it was tree honey that exuded from the palms and fig-trees. Bruce[7] holds to this idea on the ground that it was poorer food than the bee honey, which was nourishing and plentiful, if a luxury in some sections. But surely Swete[8] is right in holding to the natural meaning of bee honey (mountain honey). There is dispute as to the "locusts" also.[9] The notion that he ate the carob-bean is held by some. The Ebionites restricted John's diet to cakes made with honey or to honey alone.[10] There were clean locusts and unclean locusts. Four kinds of clean locusts are mentioned in Lev. 11 : 22 (Septuagint).[11] To-day the Bedouins eat many kinds of locusts. The legs and wings are stripped off and the rest is boiled, baked or roasted.

[1] Heb. 11 : 37.
[2] Plummer on Matthew, p. 27; Weiss, "Life of Christ," vol. I, p. 308.
[3] II Kings 1 : 8.
[4] Holtzmann, "Life of Jesus," p. 113.
[5] Bruce on Matthew, 3 : 4.
[6] *μέλι ἄγριον.* [7] Matt. 3 : 6. [8] Mark 1 : 6. [9] *ἀκρίδες.*
[10] Nicholson, "Gospel According to the Hebrews," p. 34.
[11] The Gemarists found eight hundred kinds of clean or edible locusts (Swete on Mark 1 : 6).

They are considered good food and sold in the market.[1] Evidently John was not a vegetarian if he ate these locusts and bee honey. At any rate he had plenty of good food, if it was decidedly monotonous. One may compare the use of Irish potatoes by the poor in Ireland and porridge by the poor in Scotland, not to mention fish and rice in Japan. But John's personal attraction was even more remarkable than his dress.[2] John's powerful personality was most impressive. It is a mere silhouette that Mark (and Matthew) has drawn for us. The lines are sharply cut and John stands out boldly and clearly. He was no charlatan, no trickster, no oddity. In reality, his dress and food comported well with the sturdiness of his nature, the courage of his message, the purity of his look, the directness of his speech, the elevation of his spirit. Alexander Maclaren[3] says: "John leaps, as it were, into the arena full grown and full armed." He springs forward with the same startling suddenness with which Elijah enters the scene.[4] Those who saw him would never forget him. They would be sure to tell others about him. Soon he was the talk of all Judea. But what did it all mean? What did he claim about himself?

4. *The Scriptural Similitude.*—John himself originated the idea that he was the Forerunner of the Messiah, the Voice crying in the wilderness, for he

[1] Bruce on Matt. 3 : 4.

[2] Holtzmann, "Life of Jesus," p. 114. "In the east such externals are supposed to lend a higher significance to the appearance" (Weiss, "Life of Christ," vol. I, p. 308).

[3] As quoted by Plummer on Matthew, p. 27.

[4] I Kings 17 : 1. Cf. Plummer on Matthew, p. 27; Didon, "Jésus Christ," pp. 191, 196.

quotes Isa. 40 : 3 to the embassy from Jerusalem,[1] and applies it to himself. It is possible that in Matt. 3 : 3 we have the language of John also, but it is more probable that it is that of the Evangelist.[2] All four gospels thus bear witness to this "primitive interpretation"[3] that John is the Forerunner described by Isaiah. Mr. W. P. Bradley[4] makes a curious argument to prove that while John did claim to be the Forerunner, he did not admit Jesus to be the Messiah. He notes properly that Mark is the earliest gospel and John the latest. Mark[5] and Matthew[6] state that John was Elijah that was to come, while John's gospel[7] represents the Baptist as denying it. What John's disclaimer really means will be discussed directly. But Mr. Bradley makes much of the fact that Mark and Luke do not represent John the Baptist as identifying Jesus with the Messiah. Therefore he did not really believe Jesus to be the Messiah. It is hard to take such straining after novelty as serious criticism. But, this aside, it is clear that as John stepped forth upon his mission, he is fully conscious that he is the Forerunner predicted long ago, who was to be the Herald[8] of the New Dispensation. In the prophetic picture the Forerunner has a place by the side of the Messiah.[9]

In what sense was John Elijah? "Everything in

[1] John 1 : 23. [2] "For this is he."

[3] Plummer, "Luke," p. 86. Mark (1 : 2) quotes from Mal. 3 : 1 and (in the best MSS.) attributes the whole to Isaiah as the greater and more prominent of the two prophets whose words are here combined.

[4] *Biblical World*, May and June, 1910.

[5] 9 : 11 f. [6] 11 : 14; 17 : 10–13. [7] 1 : 19–24.

[8] κηρύσσων (κήρυξ) Matt. 3 : 1.

[9] Godet, "Luke," p. 110.

him recalled the great prophet of action. Elijah did not write a single page in the Book of God; his book was himself, his prophecy was his life; it was enough for him to appear, to call up before degenerate Israel the living image of holiness."[1] There runs a real parallel between the careers of the two men. It is strikingly put by Edersheim.[2] "John came suddenly out of the wilderness of Judea, as Elijah from the wilds of Gilead. John bore the same ascetic appearance as his predecessor; the message of John was the counterpart of that of Elijah; his baptism that of Elijah's novel rite on Carmel." It is true that John pointedly disclaimed being Elijah,[3] but what he denied was the exaggerated expectations of the people,[4] not the real promise of the prophet.[5] Indeed, it was probably some word of John about this very matter that had led the Sanhedrin to make this inquiry, a word which had been misunderstood and which John now bluntly corrects. Jesus expressly says that John was the real fulfilment of the prophecy, he was the Elijah that was to come,[6] in the spirit and power of Elijah as Gabriel had said.[7] That is all that was ever meant, but it had been grossly misunderstood again.[8]

The Jewish expectations about Elijah as Forerunner were varied. It is probable that many teachers before John were asked, "Art thou Elijah?" The expectation was general that Elijah would come before

[1] Pressensé, "Jesus Christ," p. 238.
[2] "Life and Times of Jesus Christ," vol. I, p. 255.
[3] John 1 : 21–23.
[4] Westcott on John, vol. I, p. 34.
[5] Mal. 4 : 5.
[6] Mark 9 : 11 f.; Matt. 11 : 14; 17 : 12.
[7] Luke 1 : 17.
[8] Matt. 17 : 10.

the Messiah appeared. The "scribes" of Christ's day said that he "must"[1] come first. It became the custom at circumcisions for a chair to be placed for Elijah, as witness, and to cry, "Elias, come soon."[2] There would be the vague hope that the boy might prove to be Elijah who was going to come.[3] It is not clear that Jesus means that Elijah was to come still another time, because of the language in Matt. 17 : 11: "Elias comes and will restore all things." In Mark 9 : 11 it is "Elias comes first and restores all things." The present is rather from the point of view of the ancient prophecy. Jesus at once adds that Elijah has come.[4] The rabbis (scribes) expected that Elijah would come as a consoler, and to discriminate between things clean and unclean.[5] He was expected "three days" before the Messiah, and it was believed that "he would come in the mountains of Israel, weeping over the people, saying, O Land of Israel, how long will you remain arid and desolate?"[6] "His voice shall be heard from one end of the world to another."[7] The Jews kept on looking for the coming of Elijah. "Abdallah, the fierce lord of Acre, almost died of terror from a vision in which he believed himself to have seen Elijah sitting on the top of Carmel."[8] It was not clear to the rabbis how Elijah would come,

[1] Mark 9 : 11; Matt. 17 : 11. *δεῖ ἐλθεῖν πρῶτον.*

[2] Keim, "Jesus of Nazara," vol. II, p. 231. Cf. *Pirke R. Eliezer*, c. 29.

[3] *ὁ μέλλων ἔρχεσθαι.* Mark 11 : 15.

[4] *ἤδη ἦλθεν* in Mark 9 : 12 and *ἐλήλυθεν* in Matt. 17 : 13.

[5] Schoettgen, "De Messia, Hor. Hebr.," vol. II, p. 226.

[6] *Jalkut Sim.*, ii, fol. 53, 3 (Schoettgen), "Hor. Hebr.," pp. 534 ff. Cf. also J. Lightfoot for further collection of rabbinical passages.

[7] *Perikta Rabbathi*, fol. 62, 1. Cf. Reynolds, "John the Baptist," p. 223.

[8] Grove, Article "Elijah," in "Smith's B. D." Cf. Reynolds, "John the Baptist," p. 222.

but they distinguished between his coming and that of the Messiah as is seen in the question of the embassy to John.[1] "Whether the Tishbite himself was expected to return in his chariot of flame, from the unknown paradise into which he had been caught, or whether his spirit, by a metempsychosis, was to be re-embodied in the breast of some sage Pharisee or brave warrior, or whether the highest stage of Essenic culture was itself the possession of the Elijah-ship, did not seem to have been settled."[2] Indeed, according to the Talmud, as quoted by Lightfoot on Matt. 17 : 10, Elijah had frequently appeared to wise men in the past. The question of the three disciples about the coming of Elijah, as they came down from the Mount of Transfiguration, was a most natural and obvious one. There were popular expectations of the return of Jeremiah, the prophet foretold by Moses, or others of the prophets, and some even looked for several forerunners.[3] We think of Isaiah as the greatest of the prophets, but the Jews of our Lord's time held Elijah, Jeremiah, Daniel to be first. One may note the popular expectations about the return of Nero, Barbarossa, etc. Edersheim ("Life and Times of Jesus," vol. II, Appendix viii) gives a good sketch of rabbinic traditions about Elijah. The time of his coming will "be a time of genuine repentance by Israel."

What was the original meaning of Isaiah? The

[1] John 1 : 21.

[2] Reynolds, "John the Baptist," p. 222. But "John had no sympathy with the popular superstition that the spirit of the Tishbite was hovering on the hills of Judea, waiting for a new embodiment" (*ibid*, p. 226).

[3] Matt. 11 : 3; 16 : 4; John 1 : 21 f.

usual interpretation of Isa. 40 : 3–5 quoted by Luke[1] is that the picture is that of the return of the Jews from exile with Jehovah at the head of the people as they enter Jerusalem.[2] The custom of preparing the road for the Eastern king to travel is probably the basis for the image in Isaiah. But Godet[3] challenges the ordinary application to the return from exile. It is, he holds, rather God who comes to the people in their cities. The people are called upon by the courier to make ready the road by which the monarch is to enter. There is something to be said for this view. "Say unto the cities of Judah, Behold, your God! Behold, the Lord Jehovah will come a mighty one, and his arm will rule for him. He will feed his flock like a shepherd, he will gather the lambs in his arms, and carry them in his bosom, and will gently lead those that have their young." [4]

Jehovah is getting ready to visit the cities of Israel. "Prepare ye in the wilderness the way of Jehovah," the way which he is to travel. It is a picture of grading on mountain and in valley. John seizes upon this bold picture and applies it to himself. It was a perfectly natural use of it. In Isaiah "in the wilderness" goes with "prepare," and that is possible in the synoptics, though the editors generally connect it with "crying." Both points are true. The preparation was to be made in the wilderness, and the crying was the beginning of the preparation. "The voice of one

[1] Matthew and Mark quote only Isa. 40 : 3.
[2] Broadus, "Commentary on Matthew," p. 37.
[3] "Commentary on Luke," p. 111.
[4] Isa. 40 : 10 f.

saying, Cry. And one said, What shall I cry?"[1] The fire was in John's bones. He had to cry. "Behold, the day cometh, it burneth as a furnace."[2] Judgment was at hand. "Behold, I send my messenger, and he shall prepare the way before me: and the Lord, whom ye seek, will suddenly come to his temple."[3] "Behold, I will send Elijah the prophet before the great and terrible day of Jehovah come. And he shall turn the heart of the fathers to the children, and the heart of the children to their fathers; lest I come and smite the earth with a curse."[4] The first word in the New Testament is the promise of Gabriel to Zacharias that this promise is to come true at once. The last word in the Old Testament prophecy is that about Elijah's return. Behind that promise hung suspended the impending curse, like a Damascus blade, over the people of Israel. Suddenly a voice was heard in the wilderness which claimed to be that of Elijah! Instantly all listened to that Voice. Was it true? Jesus said of John that he was Elijah "if ye are willing to receive it" (Matt. 11 : 14). But are the Jews willing to receive it?

Was a Forerunner necessary? If one is disposed to question the wisdom of the mission of John as a herald of the King, let him reflect on what would have been the reception accorded to Jesus without the preparation made by the Baptist. "He came unto his own[5] and his own[6] received him not."[7]

[1] Isa. 40 : 6. [2] Mal. 4 : 1. [3] Mal. 3 : 1. [4] Mal. 4 : 5 f.

[5] εἰς τὰ ἴδια. His own places, his own haunts, his home. Cf. εἰς τὰ ἴδια for "home," in John 19 : 27.

[6] οἱ ἴδιοι. His own people, the Jews. [7] John 1 : 11.

They rejected him after all? Yes, but John prepared some soil for the Messiah's sowing. Those who first responded to Jesus came from the group of John's disciples.[1] The people will go from John to Jesus.[2] The people will recognize and believe in Jesus as the Messiah because of what John had said.[3] We know how quick the authorities in Jerusalem were to resent the assumption of Jesus as it was.[4] Brief as was the ministry of Jesus, it probably lasted as long as it did, humanly speaking, because of the ministry of John. He in a sense held off the "hour" of Jesus till Christ had at least had a hearing by people and leaders. Besides the keenest interest was excited in the subject of the Messiah. The masses began to wonder wistfully in their hearts if haply John[5] were not the Messiah himself. He served to rekindle the flame of Messianic expectation that had burned very low. The Sadducees had given up all hope of a Messiah. During the glorious Maccabean rule the Pharisees had blazed with patriotic hopes of a political Messiah who should make a great Jewish kingdom all over the world.[6] But the heel of Rome now pressed upon the neck of the Jew. Already there was the smouldering fire that later burnt into lurid flame against Rome. The Zealots had vowed vengeance against Rome. The spiritual features of the Messiah as portrayed in the Old Testament had faded from the mind of most. The Jews were sunk in formalism and secularism. The hopelessness of the people at large concerning a

[1] John 1 : 35 ff.
[2] John 3 : 26.
[3] John 10 : 40–42.
[4] John 2 : 13–25.
[5] μή ποτε αὐτὸς εἴη ὁ χριστός.
[6] Cf. "The Psalms of Solomon."

Messiah is seen in the wailing note in I Maccabees, three times[1] to the effect that there was no prophet in Israel. So it was with most minds, till John's voice was heard in the wilderness; the Messianic hope was inoperative. The Zealots had given the world up as lost. There were a few, like Simeon and Anna,[2] who were waiting for the consolation of Israel.[3] The Christian movement began with John. The ground was made ready by him. Jesus may have had John in mind when he spoke of the one who sows and the one who reaps who have joy together.[4] John came not merely to prepare men's minds for the Messiah, but their lives also. If the Messiah comes, who is worthy to go forth to greet him?

5. *The Startling Proclamation.*—It may be said that it is not hard to set a nation on fire. One may recall Martin Luther, whose theses spread like wildfire, or John Wesley's preaching, which blazed like a torch all over England.[5] John did no miracle[6] with which to startle the people or attract attention. He probably came with some reputation for piety because of his life of seclusion in the desert, and some few may have known about his remarkable birth. But John's great impression was not due to any special predisposition on the part of the people to hear him nor to personal peculiarities. These matters chimed in with his claim to be the Forerunner.[7] It is a superficial view (Strauss)

[1] 4:46; 9:27; 14:41.

[2] Luke 2:23–38.

[3] Some were driven by the very miseries of the time to long for the Messiah (Smith, "Days of His Flesh," p. 27).

[4] *ἵνα ὁ σπείρων ὁμοῦ χαίρῃ καὶ ὁ θερίζων.* John 4:36.

[5] Lange, "Life of Christ," vol. II, pp. 9 f.

[6] John 10:41.

[7] Smith, "In the Days of His Flesh," p. 27.

to say that John shrewdly discerned the signs of the times, and proclaimed himself the Forerunner because he saw that the people were eager for the Messianic era.[1] It was the preaching of John that drew the crowds, that startled the people of his time. He had a message that always wins "a response in the human heart—*sin and judgment, repentance and forgiveness.*"[2] We have only scraps and fragments of that message, hardly two pages in all. But that cry of John is still heard wherever the gospel goes. We shall need to study a little more in detail the elements of his power as a preacher and the various doctrines enunciated by him. Just here we are concerned with his fundamental proclamation: "Repent ye; for the kingdom of heaven is at hand."[3] The words rang out sharp and clear and echoed throughout Judea. Jesus himself[4] will take up the same watchword as he begins the Galilean ministry. The watchword of Jesus[5] was "believe," it is true, but none the less he took up this great word of John and passed it on. It was a more virile word[6] than our translation "repent." It was really, "Change your mind (life)." We shall need to return to this word in the next chapter. The call to repent challenged attention at once. John had the moral earnestness to demand a new life on the part of his audience. They listened with respect. But it was the second part of his proclamation that sent a thrill through the great crowds. "For the kingdom

[1] Weiss, "Life of Christ," vol. I, p. 312.
[2] Smith, "Days of His Flesh," p. 27.
[3] Matt. 3 : 2.
[4] Matt. 4 : 17; Mark 1 : 15.
[5] Bruce on Matt. 3 : 2.
[6] μετανοεῖτε.

of heaven[1] is at hand." He mentions this as a reason for instant repentance on the part of the people. The old prophets had urged repentance, but they had not been able to say that the kingdom of heaven had come nigh. The Talmud reports the rabbis as saying: "If Israel would repent but for a single day, forthwith the Redeemer will come."[2] Now at last the kingdom, the long-promised kingdom, is hovering near. Will the people repent? How near is the kingdom? John says literally: "Has drawn near."[3] It is more specious than true to say that John (and Jesus) felt that the kingdom was still in the future. Some aspects of the kingdom, the eschatological features, were still future. But the more vital and spiritual phases of the kingdom were felt by both John and Jesus to be already present. By "kingdom" John means "reign." The "reign of heaven has drawn near." A fuller treatment of "kingdom" will come later. Surely the note of warning is here sounded by John. The day of judgment for Israel has come. The only hope is in repentance. The destruction of Jerusalem throws a lurid light back on John's words. Jesus himself connected that dire calamity with the city's rejection of him.[4] What startled the people was not so much that the day of doom hung

[1] Matthew alone has this phrase. Mark and Luke have "Kingdom of God." Allen ("Commentary on Matthew") insists on a real difference of content. But he is pretty certainly wrong. "Heaven" seems to be "a reverential substitute of the later Jews for God" (Smith, "Days of His Flesh," p. 27). Cf. Bruce on Matt. 3:2; Dalman, "Words of Jesus," pp. 91 ff.; Lightfoot and Wetstein on Matt. 3:2.

[2] "Hieros. Taan.," 64, 1. Cf. Lightfoot on Matt. 3:2. Quoted by Smith, "Days of His Flesh," p. 28.

[3] ἤγγικεν. Cf. Matt. 26:45 f.

[4] Matt. 24 and 25.

in the background as that the Messianic era had arrived.[1] The wild delight of Andrew as he ran to Simon and cried:[2] "We have found the Messiah," helps us to understand the enthusiasm that was created by the wonderful words of John. Brother would tell brother what he had heard, neighbor would tell neighbor this real "news." Old men, like Simeon, would thank God that they had lived to see this day, this day so long in coming. They would gather in groups to talk it over. Each one felt that he must hear the new prophet for himself. In each heart "the kingdom of heaven" was interpreted to mean what he most wished. The rainbow of promise was stretched over each life. At first the intense curiosity excited probably served to divert attention from John's stern call to repent. He was the sensation of the time.[3] He was a "phenomenon" in the real sense of that much-abused term.

6. *Jerusalem at John's Feet.*—John, like Jeremiah and Ezekiel, was of a priestly family. But he made no appeal for more attention to the Levitical rites and sacrifices. He had caught the spirit of God in Hosea:[4] "I will have mercy, and not sacrifice." This was the figure of exaggerated contrast to emphasize the superiority of the spiritual over the ceremonial. This the rabbis and priests of Christ's time failed to understand. Jesus rebuked them for their ignorance on

[1] Nourse, in "Standard Bible Dictionary."

[2] John 1:41. Εὑρήκαμεν τὸν Μεσσίαν. Cf. 1:45, Philip to Nathanael.

[3] "John the Baptist, in his manifestation and energy, was like a burning torch; his public life was quite an earthquake—the whole man was a sermon" (Lange, "Life of Christ," vol. II, p. 11).

[4] 6:6.

this point. "Go ye and learn what this meaneth." John had learned. He stands out above his time because he had grasped spiritual values.

It perhaps does not seem strange, under all the circumstances, that great crowds thronged to hear the Baptist. Twenty thousand people would gather to hear George Whitfield and be melted to tears.[1] The excitable crowds in Palestine "gathered around Simon, Athronges, and Judas of Galilee, and even such a miserable impostor as Theudas."[2] Luke merely speaks of "the multitudes that kept going forth."[3] Mark notes that "all the country of Judea" joined in "this exodus to the Jordan."[4] Judea is personified. A living stream kept going forth[5] from all parts of the country. Matthew notes in particular that "all the region round about Jordan" came. This was most natural of all. The common people took John to be a prophet even long after his death.[6] They recognized the genuine[7] prophet in John. All classes came, including the most degraded, the publicans and harlots.[8] These "justified God"[9] because of the moral earnestness of John. "The chief need of the world is the death-defying courage of true

[1] Smith, "In the Days of His Flesh," p. 28.

[2] Farrar, "Life of Lives," pp. 167 f. "The multitude clung with convulsive hope or despairing frenzy to almost anyone who seemed to promise any form or possibility of emancipation—to Hyrcanus; to the beautiful young High Priest Aristobulus; to the impostor Alexander; to Agrippa I.; —some Jews even regarded Herod the Great as a divinely appointed Deliverer" (*ibid.*).

[3] τοῖς πορευομένοις ὄχλοις.

[4] Swete on Mark 1 : 5.

[5] ἐξεπορεύετο. Descriptive imperfect.

[6] Matt. 21 : 26, 32. Hence the rulers are afraid.

[7] Mark 11 : 32. The word ὄντως is added.

[8] Luke 7 : 29.

[9] ἐδικαίωσαν. Took John's side against the Pharisees and lawyers. Luke 7 : 30.

men."[1] The Jewish notion of a prophet was that of a fearless preacher more than that of a mere seer.[2] The truth shines forth from the true prophet as the light from the sun.[3] Josephus[4] bears testimony to the power of John with the people who "came in crowds about him, for they were very greatly moved [or pleased] by hearing his words," "for they seemed ready to do anything he should advise." Herod, Josephus adds, "feared lest the great influence John had over the people might put it into his power and inclination to raise a rebellion." Surely no greater tribute to the power of John over the people could be given.[5] There was in truth prodigious excitement. "From the days of John the Baptist until now the kingdom of heaven suffereth violence and men of violence take it by force."[6] It is not perfectly clear what this language of Jesus means, but he seems to have in mind the intense moral earnestness[7] of those who thronged around John, and later around himself. In Luke the bold figure is softened a bit,[8] and yet each man has a moral conflict who enters the kingdom.[9] "People no longer merely prophesy and dream about it, but they press to win entrance into it."[10] John himself was the noblest example of this moral enthusiasm, and it was contagious.

[1] Farrar, "Life of Lives," p. 171.
[2] Geike, "Life and Words of Christ," vol. I, p. 393.
[3] Clement of Alexandria, Hom. ii, 6.
[4] "Ant.," xviii, 5, 2.
[5] This testimony of Josephus to John is challenged by some, but on insufficient grounds. Its bearing on the gospel account of the death of John comes up later.
[6] Matt. 11 : 12.
[7] βιάζεται, καὶ βιασταὶ ἁρπάζουσιν αὐτήν.
[8] εὐαγγελίζεται.
[9] Luke 16 : 16. πᾶς εἰς αὐτὴν βιάζεται.
[10] Holtzmann, "Life of Jesus," p. 121.

But one must not think that all the people who came responded rightly to John's tremendous appeal. Luke, indeed, represents John as denouncing the multitudes who came as "offspring of vipers." [1] Matthew[2] probably more exactly defines "the Pharisees and Sadducees" as those to whom this fierce denunciation is addressed. But there were probably scoffers in the crowd then, as now, who shared with the leaders this hostile attitude toward the new prophet on the Jordan. "No doubt the effect on many of the people was superficial, and chiefly associated with secular conceptions of the Messianic reign. The ambitious began to dream of place and power ('Who shall be greatest in the kingdom of heaven?'), the self-indulgent to cherish hopes that the new king would 'destroy the law or the prophets,' and give new laws less severe, the poor to hope for better times somehow." [3] The effect on most of the crowd was electric. "Along the mountain terraces and rugged foot-tracks, the eager surging crowd were asking the question, What shall we do?" [4]

But the most astonishing thing remains to be discussed. "All they of Jerusalem" [5] went forth also. It was one thing for the *Am-ha-aretz,* the people from the county and the provinces, to go out to hear John. But "conservative, disdainful Jerusalem, slow to be touched by new popular influences," [6] was quite another matter. Bruce continues: "The remark-

[1] 3:7. [2] 3:7.
[3] John A. Broadus, in manuscript notes on John the Baptist.
[4] Reynolds, "John the Baptist," p. 254.
[5] Mark 1:5. Cf. Matt. 3:5.
[6] Bruce on Matt. 3:5.

able thing is that any came from that quarter." Proud, imperious Jerusalem was accustomed to have pilgrims come to her gates. But now the crowds swept out of her gates to the wilderness. "What went ye out into the wilderness to behold?"[1] Jesus will ask. There is fine irony in the question. He has in mind the point of view of the multitudes, to be sure, who in light-hearted curiosity tripped out to see the new sensation. John was anything but a reed shaken in the wind. He was not clad in soft raiment. He was a prophet and they were right in that, but he was a great deal more. He was a man. At bottom a real man is more than prophet or priest or king. Probably the people of Jerusalem were simply carried away with the tide. Many came with an apologetic air, half ashamed to be caught in such a motley crowd.

But why did the leaders go? John will himself demand an answer to that very question.[2] "Who warned you to flee from the wrath to come?" Doubtless they had come from no such motive. For one thing they wished to see what there was in this new prophet. They followed the crowd, which had left Jerusalem. They may have argued that they were responsible for the guidance of the people. In time[3] the Sanhedrin will come to take the work of John seriously as we shall see. They will be driven to it by the popular tide. But, at any rate, the religious teachers of the time are spectators in the prophet's great throng. The religious capital of Judea is no

[1] Matt. 11:7; Luke 7:24. [2] Matt. 3:7. [3] John 1:19 ff.

longer Jerusalem, but for the moment with John. His sceptre is his voice, and with it he sways the multitude.

Perhaps at first the leaders did not comprehend John. They were dazed and even for a time charmed by his power. Jesus later reminded the Jerusalem leaders of this fact. "Ye were willing to rejoice for a season in his light." [1] John was the popular idol and the leaders fell in with the drift of opinion. John had his "hour" [2] of glory even with the ecclesiastical authorities. Jesus reminds them also of the formal embassy[3] from the Sanhedrin. They were probably ashamed of that moment of weakness. But, before John had opened fire upon them, they basked in the light of his fame and power. Many a new pastor has John's experience. At first he is the lion of the town, the hero of the hour, but the tide turns against him and the powerful friends drop away. It was really "exulting joy" that the Jerusalem leaders once had in John.[4] There was in truth light enough in John for even Jerusalem to enjoy, if only Jerusalem had eyes to see. "He was the lamp that burneth and shineth." [5] Out in the wilderness this light blazed till it was seen in Jerusalem. It burned on after his death, burns, indeed, to-day. There was both heat and light in John. The impression on the rulers was temporary, but his light in the world of truth will never go out.

[1] John 5 : 35.
[2] πρὸς ὥραν.
[3] John 5 : 33, ἀπεστάλκατε. It was still a fact.
[4] Cf. Westcott on John 5 : 35, ἀγαλλιαθῆναι.
[5] John 5 : 35, ὁ λύχνος ὁ καιόμενος καὶ φαίνων.

7. *The Sins of the People Laid Bare.*—Luke[1] has preserved a specimen of John's preaching that goes far to explain the wonderful effect of his ministry. On two short pages can be printed all that has been preserved of the words of John. Luke is familiar with the fact that John made many other exhortations.[2] He probably had reports of some of them, and made these brief extracts as justly reflecting the style and temper of the man. They do this with remarkable effectiveness. There can be no doubt of the genuineness of these fragments. They ring true and fairly tingle with life and power. They are in reality words that breathe and burn. He preached "the good tidings unto the people," [3] but he did not confine himself to one particular line.[4] John challenged the life of the people along the whole line of its mere ceremonialism, its indifference to real religion, its corruption. He was a reformer, but more. With a prophet's tongue he lashed the sins of those in high stations as well as in low.

One day, when John had spoken with unusual vehemence and power, the multitudes[5] began to ask:[6] "What then must[7] we do?" The "then" (*οὖν*) points back to John's indictment. His words had cut

[1] 3 : 10–14. Not in Matthew, but still probably from Q (the logia), unless, indeed, there was a special document with sayings of the Baptist.

[2] 3 : 18. *πολλὰ καὶ ἕτερα* rather implies that they were not all just like these.

[3] *εὐηγγελίζετο.* In Luke 3 : 19 note *ἐλεγχόμενος.* He exhorted, he preached the good tidings, he reproved.

[4] *παρακαλῶν,* in Luke 3 : 18, is a difficult word to translate. It means, literally, to call to one's side (*παρά*).

[5] *οἱ ὄχλοι.* The plural shows how great the throngs were.

[6] *ἐπηρώτων* (3 : 10). Inchoative imperfect. Plummer takes it as repetition.

[7] *ποιήσωμεν.* Deliberative subjunctive.

to the quick. This "Incarnate Conscience" had reached the conscience of his hearers. That is a great moment in the preacher's life when he is called on to speak straight to the sin-smitten and conscience-stricken soul. But one must be sure not to misunderstand John's reply. He assumes that his hearers understand his teaching about repentance and the kingdom. The practical reply given about generosity is not to take the place of the grace of repentance, but is to be a proof of it. The same point applies to his reply to the publicans and the soldiers who likewise asked what they must do. It is reformation that John here demands as proof of repentance. He put his finger upon the besetting sin of each class that came before him. But John did not hesitate a moment to lay bare the sin that needed exposure. It was extortion with the publicans, violence and oppression with the soldiers. Travellers frequently wore two undergarments.[1] It is one of these that John suggests may be given to him who has none. The starving man is not to be left without help.[2] The publicans[3] were thoroughly detested by the Jews "as blood-suckers for a heathen conqueror."[4] Zacchæus admitted that he had robbed the people.[5] Those who collected for Herod Antipas were as much disliked as those who collected for Cæsar.[6] The soldiers were probably Jewish soldiers who may have been acting

[1] χιτών, not ἱμάτιον (the outer garment).

[2] Cf. the conduct of the priest and the Levite in the parable of the Good Samaritan (Luke 10 : 30–37). Cf. I Thess. 2 : 8.

[3] τελῶναι are *publicani*.

[4] Plummer on Luke, p. 91.

[5] Luke 19 : 8.

[6] Matt. 9 : 9 ff.

as police to assist the tax-collectors.[1] But intimidation ("do violence to no man" [2]) and false accusation ("neither exact anything wrongfully," marg. "accuse" [3]) were just the crimes that soldiers would be guilty of. Soldiers are notoriously prone to discontent with their wages.[4] John does not denounce the calling of publican and soldier *per se*. Taxes have to be collected. Soldiers have to defend their country so long as the horror of war exists. But he demanded morality in these men.

8. *Exposure of the Religious Teachers.*—Matthew[5] and Luke[6] both report this fragment of John's preaching. There may have been a document about John's ministry, or the original, virile preaching of John may have been handed down from mouth to mouth. Matthew is more specific than Luke in mentioning "many of the Pharisees and Sadducees" who came. These two religious parties disliked one another very much, but they are both deserving of John's condemnation.[7] They will later be found working hand in hand to compass the death of Jesus. For the moment they bury their theological differences and rivalry for place and power in the common curiosity about John.[8]

[1] *στρατευόμενοι.* Cf. Plummer, *in loco*. Schuerer thinks that they were heathen soldiers.

[2] *μηδένα διασείσηπε.* The aor. subj. with *μή* puts the matter delicately as if they were not yet guilty. Cf. III Macc. 3 : 21 for this verb with the sense of extortion.

[3] *συκοφαντήσητε.* Etymologically, "show figs by shaking the tree" (Plummer). The false accuser who wishes to obtain money. Cf. Zacchæus, in Luke 19 : 8, who uses this word of himself.

[4] *ὀψωνίοις* equals "rations" (*ὄψον, ὠνέομαι*). [5] 3 : 7–10. [6] 3 : 7–9.

[7] The single article *τῶν*, in Matt. 3 : 7, treats both classes as one.

[8] For discussion of the Pharisees and Sadducees, see Wellhausen, "Die Pharisäer und die Sadducäer; Schuerer," second division, vol. II, pp. 1–43 (where see Bibliography); Edersheim, "Life and Times of Jesus," vol. I, pp. 93 ff.; Broadus, "Commentary on Matthew," pp. 44 ff., etc.

"The formal piety of the Pharisees and the self-indulgent scepticism of the Sadducees would be equally hateful to him, and he meets them with indignant surprise."[1] Indeed, his sensitive spirit was troubled by their presence as is often the case with sincere natures like John. They instinctively recoil from such duplicity and craftiness as is seen in the Pharisees and Sadducees.[2] John himself was of priestly stock like the Sadducees; but he made no claims to recognition on that score. Some have wondered how John would know these pious ecclesiastics in the great crowds. He could tell partly by their dress, partly by their conduct, and partly by an instinctive feeling of hostility. It was John's business to know the life of his time which he had arraigned. He was no recluse in the sense that he held himself aloof from the currents of thought and shut his eyes to what was going on before him. He may have felt that these dignitaries had come to lay hands on him.[3] The authorities in Jerusalem may have wished to get control[4] of the movement, having sent deputies to spy upon it and report. Such an embassy was sent to John from Jerusalem according to the Fourth Gospel, though probably not at the time of this discourse.[5] However, it must be remembered that these fragments in Matthew and Luke have no notes of

[1] Plummer on Matthew, p. 27.
[2] Bruce on Matthew, p. 82. [3] Plummer, "Matthew," p. 27.
[4] Smith, "In the Days of His Flesh," p. 29. But Keim ("Jesus of Nazara," vol. II, p. 264) thinks that the hierarchy kept very quiet before John.
[5] Keim ("Jesus of Nazara," vol. II, p. 265) denies the value of the Fourth Gospel because the other gospels do not give it. But Matthew certainly shows that it was possible.

time at all save that it was during the six months before the baptism of Jesus.

John does not fear the religious leaders of the time. He turns on them with an indignant question: "Ye offspring of vipers, who warned you to flee from the wrath to come?" The point of the figure lies in the "fleeing," not in calling them "offspring of vipers." [1] Often John had seen the vipers run before the blazing dry-scrub[2] (like a prairie fire) as before the burning stubble in preparation for sowing.[3] There was a touch of grim humor[4] in the picture as well as of scorn. "The wrath to come" was judgment on Israel. The rabbis held that the judgment foretold as connected with the Messianic Dispensation was to be upon the heathen, but John saw that it was to include the Jews also.[5] How clear the content or nature of this judgment was to John's mind we do not know. But the destruction of Jerusalem is a natural fulfilment which itself is a type of the final judgment.[6] But it is not possible to soften the sting in the expression "offspring of vipers." [7] Jesus will twice use it concerning the Pharisees.[8] "These serpent-like characters" are "the crooked" [9] of Isaiah. John caught the metaphor fresh from the life of the wilderness and hurled it in the faces of the professional religionists of Jerusalem. It stung like the tail of a whip.

[1] Bruce on Matthew, p. 82.
[2] G. A. Smith, "Historical Geography of Palestine," p. 495.
[3] Furrer, "Zeitschrift für Miss. und. Rel.," 1890.
[4] Bruce on Matthew, p. 82.
[5] Plummer on Luke, p. 89. Cf. Joel 2 : 31; Mal. 3 : 2; 4 : 1; Isa. 13 : 9.
[6] Plummer, *ibid.*
[7] γεννήματα ἐχιδνῶν, broods of snakes.
[8] Matt. 12 : 34; 23 : 33.
[9] σκολιά (Isa. 40 : 4 f.). Cf. Plummer, "Luke," p. 89.

John is not entirely hopeless of the Pharisees and Sadducees, unlikely pupils as they are. There is an innuendo at their insincerity and hypocrisy.[1] They had heard John's word about repentance. John does not say that they must reform in order to repent. The Pharisees and Sadducees must prove their repentance by their life. That is true of all as a matter of fact, but John singles them out in this demand because of their prominence and their duplicity. It was virtually saying that in the eyes of men they were under suspicion. It was the appeal to life that was later made by Jesus,[2] by James,[3] by Paul,[4] by Peter,[5] by John the Apostle.[6]

The Baptist shows a masterful comprehension of the mental processes of the Pharisees and Sadducees. They would fall back upon privilege and station. Racial and ecclesiastical pride were combined in the Jew. John shows his knowledge of current rabbinism by this protest. The rabbis made much of the "merits of the fathers" and in particular of Abraham. Edersheim[7] has brought together an interesting set of quotations from the Talmud on the subject. The rain fell because of the merit of Abraham; the ships on the sea were preserved because of him; because of Abraham Moses received the law; for his sake Daniel was heard; for his sake every Israelite will have part in the world to come. John's stern rebuke against all the traditional nonsense was a reaffirmation of the

[1] Plummer on Matthew, p. 28; Bruce on Matthew, p. 83.
[2] Sermon on the Mount. [3] Epistle.
[4] Rom. 6–8; Gal. 4 and 5. [5] Epistles. [6] I John.
[7] "Life and Times of Jesus," vol. I, pp. 271 f.

eternal moral law.[1] He passed by all the myriad pettifogging rules and punctilios of the Pharisees and called them to a sense of their personal relation to God. Like the snail in the Hindoo proverb which sees nothing but its own shell and thinks it the grandest place in the universe,[2] so these self-satisfied Jews made continual boast of descent from Abraham.[3] It is probably true that the horizon of John the Baptist was narrower than that of Paul, but Paul himself never saw more clearly the distinction between the merely ceremonial and the spiritual and moral than did John on this occasion. Jesus, Stephen, Paul were all to sound this same note and meet the bitter hostility of the Pharisees.[4] There is a slight variation in Matthew's report of John's protest and that of Luke. Matthew says "Think not";[5] Luke has "Begin not"[6] to say. But the difference is merely verbal. One forbids the beginning of the utterance, the other the thought behind the utterance.

John leaves the Pharisees and Sadducees with a warning. "Even now is the axe laid unto the root of the trees."[7] The axe is then ready for use. The point lies in the "even now" (already), little as they think so. The axe is invisible (to them), but it is there. All that is needed is for the woodman to lift

[1] Farrar, "Life of Lives," p. 173. [2] *Ibid.*, p. 172.

[3] Cf. Josephus, "Ant.," iii, 5, 3; II Esdr. 6:56 ff.; Josh. 8:33, 53; James, 2:21; Wetstein on Matt. 3:9.

[4] Cf. Reynolds, "John the Baptist," pp. 253 f.

[5] μὴ δόξητε λέγειν. Moulton ("Prolegomena," p. 15) thinks that Luke made a deliberate improvement of the Aramaic original.

[6] μὴ ἄρξησθε λέγειν.

[7] ἤδη δὲ——κεῖται (Matt. 3:10). The two emphatic words are furthest apart. κεῖται is used as the perfect passive of τίθημι.

the axe and cut the tree. The chief value of a tree (olive or fig, for instance) in the East is the fruit which it bears. Jesus used the figure of the barren fig-tree to the same purpose.[1] The woodman had come and waited a little in hope of still obtaining fruit from the tree that merely cumbered the ground. The point is really the same as the demand for "fruits worthy of repentance." When it is clear that no fruit will be borne, the axe will fall. John has issued his challenge to the people at large, to the various classes in society, in particular to the religious leaders. The heart of his cry was for real manhood. He recoiled from the hollow shams in religion and society. "We know Diogenes went through the streets of Athens with a lantern, seeking for a *man;* and when some of the crowd came to him he beat them away with the contemptuous exclamation, 'I want men; ye are[2] *σκύβαλα.*'"[3]

"God give us men! A time like this demands
Great hearts, strong minds, true faith, and willing hands;
Men whom the lust of office does not kill,
Men whom the spoils of office cannot buy,
Men who possess conviction and a will,
Men who have honour, men who dare not lie."

[1] Luke 13 : 6–9.
[2] *σκύβαλα* equals rubbish. Cf. Phil. 3 : 8.
[3] Farrar, "Life of Lives," pp. 171 f.

CHAPTER III

REMEDY

"Preaching the baptism of repentance unto remission of sins" (Luke 3 : 3).

1. *John Not a Mere Iconoclast.*—One quite misses the force of John's mission who sees in him only the iconoclast. He was that as was Jesus when he appears in the temple at the beginning of his ministry as reported in the Fourth Gospel.[1] Geike[2] fails to grasp the fulness of John's message when he says: "He came to throw down, not to build; to startle, not to instruct; to use the axe, not the trowel." It is true that John made no breach with the law *per se*. He taught his disciples to fast as a regular observance much after the fashion of the Pharisees.[3] "The disciples of John fast often, and make supplications." [4] This praying, while spiritual in essence, probably conformed to the Jewish forms. John taught his disciples to pray.[5] The point to emphasize is that he had a positive programme to present to the people besides denunciation of their sins. The prophets of the Old Testament held out the promise of pardon as well as rebuke, "the flame which consumes and the light which consoles." [6] And John was the light that

[1] 2 : 13–22.
[2] "Life and Words of Christ," vol. I, p. 394.
[3] Mark 2 : 18. [4] Luke 5 : 33. [5] Luke 11 : 1.
[6] Farrar, "Life of Christ," vol. I, p. 114.

burns and shines.[1] He did not come to organize a new sect or separate community.[2] He may have had a special band of devoted followers gathered round him as Jesus had the twelve apostles,[3] but we do not know it to be true. We do know that disciples of John apparently lingered as a separate body long after his death.[4] We are justified in thinking that this was not in accordance with John's wish and plan.[5] Their loyalty to John in his trouble and death was beautiful,[6] but John rejoiced to see his disciples follow Jesus.[7] We know even from Josephus[8] that John "urged the Jews who were willing to live worthily, and to show uprightness one to another, and piety toward God, to be baptized." He did more than that, as we learn from the Fourth Gospel.[9] "There came a man, sent from God, whose name was John. The same came for witness, that he might bear witness of the light, that all might believe through him." What calls for comment in this passage is "that all might believe through[10] him." He was the intermediary who was to lead men to faith in the real light, which John saw and others did not. That was the heart of John's message.

2. *Submission to the Reign of God.*—This point is more implied than expressed in the brief words preserved to us in the gospel. John witnessed, as we have just seen, "that men might believe through him."

[1] John 5 : 35.
[2] Weiss, "Life of Christ," vol. I, p. 314.
[3] Geike, "Life and Words of Christ," vol. I, p. 407. Weiss, "Life of Christ," vol. I, p. 314.
[4] Acts 19 : 1–7.
[5] John 3 : 26–30.
[6] Matt. 14 : 12.
[7] John 3 : 28 f.
[8] "Ant.," xviii, 5, 2.
[9] John 1 : 6 f.
[10] δι' αὐτοῦ.

Believe what or whom? Paul explains in Acts[1] to some lingering, ill-informed disciples of John that John taught the people "that they should believe on him that should come after him, that is on Jesus." The element of faith, therefore, belonged to John's preaching. Edersheim[2] sees this clearly. "He came to call Israel to submit to the reign of God, about to be manifested in Christ." That was the goal before John. The term "kingdom" was by no means new in Jewish terminology. It has its roots in the prophetic writings,[3] in the righteous king of Isaiah[4] and Micah,[5] in the Davidic dynasty of Jeremiah[6] and Ezekiel.[7] In Psalm 89 the promise made to David [8] is expounded in language akin to that used by Jesus later.[9] Zacharias had heard the angel tell of John's mission "to make ready for the Lord a people prepared for him." [10] The people who followed Jesus to Jerusalem, and who "supposed that the kingdom of God was immediately to appear," [11] looked for some spectacular apocalyptic demonstration. But there were some of the Jews like Joseph of Arimathea "who was looking for the kingdom of God." [12] So, likewise, Simeon and Anna caught the vision of the spiritual nature of the kingdom. The one was "looking for the consolation of Israel," [13] the other "spoke of him

[1] 19 : 4.
[2] "Life and Times of Jesus," vol. I, p. 270.
[3] Broadus, "Commentary on Matthew," p. 35.
[4] 9 : 6, 7; 11 : 1–10.
[5] 4 : 1–8. [6] 23 : 5, 5. [7] 37 : 24. [8] II Sam. 7 : 13, 16.
[9] Matt. 16 : 18 f.; οἰκοδομήσω is used in II Sam. 7 : 13, 16; in Ps. 89 : 4; in Matt. 16 : 18. The figure of "house" is used as tantamount to "kingdom" (Hebrews 3 : 5 f.). [10] Luke 1 : 17. [11] Luke 19 : 11.
[12] Luke 23 : 51, προσεδέχετο (imperfect and so durative).
[13] Luke 2 : 25.

to all them that were looking for the redemption of Jerusalem."[1] It is quite gratuitous, therefore, to deny to John any comprehension of the spiritual aspects of this great word. He does use apocalyptic imagery more or less in accord with the ideas of the time. "The Jewish expectation was fantastic and superstitious"[2] on the point of the literal return of Elijah. But John the Baptist rose above that idea.[3] This matter of the apocalyptic language and hopes is one keenly debated at present. Schweitzer[4] seeks to explain thus the whole content of the term "kingdom" in the gospels. It is, with him, all futuristic and cataclysmic. "The futuristic aspect of the kingdom was certainly present to the mind of Jesus,"[5] but that is not saying that there was no other idea in the mind of Jesus. John caught the prophetic spirit of judgment for sin, and set that forth in apocalyptic language (as did Jesus).[6] Some have gone to the utmost extreme and have denied that John the Baptist was able to understand or believe in the spiritual sense of the kingdom as preached by Jesus.[7] It is clear that with Jesus the term kingdom was used in various senses. In the 119 passages in the New Testament where the word kingdom occurs, Edersheim[8] finds 34 where the

[1] Luke 2 : 38.
[2] Sanday, "The Life of Christ in Recent Research," p. 33.
[3] John 1 : 21 f.
[4] "The Quest of the Historical Jesus" (1910).
[5] Muirhead, "The Eschatology of Jesus," p. 85. For the ideas of the Jews, see the "Apocalypse of Baruch," lxxii, 4–6; "Assumption of Moses," x, 7–10.
[6] Burkitt, "The Eschatological Idea in the Gospel" ("Cambridge Bibl. Essays"), p. 204.
[7] Schweitzer, "Quest of the Historical Jesus," p. 205.
[8] "Life and Times of Jesus," vol. I, p. 270. See further, Dobschütz, "Eschatology of the Gospels" (1910).

idea is simply the rule of God, 17 where this rule of God is manifested in and through Christ, and one of these is Matt. 3 : 2, where the term is put into the mouth of the Baptist. The other passages tell how the kingdom of God is gradually developed, how it is triumphant at the second coming of Christ, how it is consummated in the world to come. Plummer[1] makes the point that Jesus gives no definition of the kingdom and that no definition can be made that is not partial and that does not leave out part of the truth. The "reign of God" is viewed now from one point of view, now from another. But when John the Baptist said: "The kingdom of heaven has drawn near," he had in mind the Messiah. He saw and described the Messiah as one who would baptize with the Holy Ghost.[2] It is thus beyond doubt that John had a clear grasp of the spiritual aspects of the kingdom of God, of the personal relation of each soul with God. The foremost thing in his programme was just this personal adjustment with God. He wished to prevent, if possible, the bursting of the cloud of divine wrath upon the Jewish people. That catastrophe could only be turned aside by the genuine conversion of the people as individuals brought face to face with God. Holtzmann[3] puts it well: "He is not content that they should merely gaze upon him with wondering curiosity; to every one who comes out to him must be communicated the same anxiety which has driven himself out into the desert."

[1] On Matthew, p. 25.
[2] Mark 1 : 8; Matt. 3 : 11; Luke 3 : 18.
[3] "Life of Jesus," p. 118.

3. *Repentance.*—This is John's great word,[1] and it is to-day a wofully misunderstood word. The trouble is not with the Greek[2] word. That is plain enough. In its etymological sense we have the substantive[3] in Heb. 12 : 17, "for he found no place for a change of mind *in his father.*" Elsewhere in the New Testament it has a moral quality. In Rev. 2 : 5 and 3 : 3 it is associated with memory.[4] The word in itself does not mean sorrow for sin, though that is, of course, involved. Another word [5] was used for that. Sorrow may bring about repentance,[6] and "godly sorrow" always does.[7] And contemplation of the goodness of God always leads to repentance.[8] Jesus came to call sinners to repentance.[9] It was directed toward God.[10] It is coupled with belief [11] and with conversion.[12] It is the trait in a sinner that causes joy in heaven.[13] It is essential to salvation.[14] It was commanded by Jesus[15] and by God.[16] It was a fundamental doctrine in the apostolic preaching.[17] Proof of repentance was demanded,[18] as was true of John the Baptist's preaching.[19]

So far so good. All the witnesses testify that John associated repentance with baptism.[20] Mark calls it

[1] Bruce on Matthew, p. 79.
[2] μετανοέω. Matt. 3 : 2.
[3] μετάνοια.
[4] μνημόνευε οὖν ——— καὶ μετανόησον.
[5] μεταμέλομαι. Cf. Matt. 21 : 30; 27 : 3; II Cor. 7 : 8.
[6] ἐλυπήθητε εἰς μετάνοιαν, II Cor. 7 : 9.
[7] II Cor. 7 : 10, ἡ κατὰ θεὸν λύπη.
[8] Rom. 2 : 4.
[9] Luke 5 : 32.
[10] Acts 20 : 21, εἰς θεόν.
[11] Mark 1 : 15, μετανοεῖτε και πιστεύετε.
[12] ἐπιστρέψῃ πρός σε λέγων Μετανοῶ. Luke 17 : 4.
[13] Luke 15 : 7, 10. ἐπὶ ἑνὶ ἁμαρτωλῷ μετανοοῦντι.
[14] Luke 13 : 3, 5.
[15] Matt. 4 : 17.
[16] Acts 17 : 30; 26 : 20.
[17] Mark 6 : 12; Acts 24 : 47; Heb. 6 : 1.
[18] Acts 26 : 20.
[19] Matt. 3 : 8; Luke 3 : 8.
[20] 1 : 4. βάπτισμα μετανόιας equals "repentance (kind of) baptism." The genitive case is the case of genus, kind, and describes the baptism.

"the baptism of repentance." Thus the relation is described by Luke[1] and Paul in Acts.[2] Matthew[3] uses another expression which is not clear in itself. The preposition *eis* here used is employed in Matt. 12 : 41 in connection with the repentance of the people of Nineveh, who "repented at the preaching of Jonah."[4] Hence Plummer[5] is justified in saying: "The repentance precedes the baptism, which seals it and reminds the baptized of his new obligations." Josephus[6] has this notion of John's teaching also. He says that John baptized "supposing still that the soul was thoroughly purified beforehand by righteousness." Repentance in the New Testament leads to forgiveness of sins and life.[7] It opens the door to full knowledge of the truth.[8]

The prophets of old were fond of sounding the note of repentance.[9] It is unfortunate that the English word "repent," from a Latin (late) compound, *re-poenitere* (cf. *poenitet me*) means to be sorry again. But the word is now so deeply rooted in English theology, literature and life that it is practically impossible to drop it. But one must never forget that John the Baptist did not urge men merely to be sorry, but to change their course of life. Indeed, "conversion"[10] is far more in accord with the real meaning of this word than "repentance." Least of all must it be

[1] 3 : 3.
[2] 13 : 24; 19 : 4.
[3] 3 : 11 (cf. Acts 2 : 38), εἰς μετάνοιαν.
[4] μετενόησαν εἰς τὸ κήρυγμα Ἰωνᾶ.
[5] On Luke, p. 86.
[6] "Ant.," xviii, 5, 2.
[7] Acts 15 : 31; 11 : 18; Luke 24 : 47.
[8] II Tim. 2 : 25.
[9] Isa. 1 : 16, 17; 55 : 7; Jer. 7 : 3, 7; Ezek. 18 : 19–32; 36 : 25–27; Joel 2 : 12, 13; Micah 6 : 8; Zech. 1 : 34.
[10] Stalker, "The Two St. Johns," p. 207.

imagined that the Baptist exhorted people to "do penance," as the Roman Catholic Vulgate has it.[1] John would be horrified beyond measure to find his trumpet-call for spiritual renewal turned into mediæval notions of earning salvation by paying money for it.[2]

4. *Remission of Sins.*[3]—It is not possible to treat these spiritual processes in natural order without entering the realm of controversy. Bruce[4] is not willing to admit that baptism is essential to forgiveness in John's teaching, though Plummer on Matthew[5] holds with Tertullian and Cyril of Jerusalem that baptism "bestows" forgiveness of sins. But Plummer[6] on Luke had taken the evangelical interpretation that the purpose was subjective, "assuring the penitent of forgiveness, and of deliverance from the burden, penalty, and bondage of sin"; Bruce[7] further refuses to consider "confession" as prerequisite to baptism. Broadus[8] sees that forgiveness is promised on condition of confession,[9] "though of course this is not the meritorious ground of forgiveness." Logically, and as a matter of fact, forgiveness or remission of sins turns fundamentally on the attitude of the heart toward God. When one comes to confession, he comes to see that his sins are already forgiven. It is a fine point and not to be pressed too far. A man who claimed forgiveness and yet refused confession and baptism justifies doubt of his forgiveness.

1 "Poenitentiam agite."
2 Cf. Broadus on Matthew, pp. 34 f.
3 ἄφεσις ἁμαρτιῶν, Mark 1 : 4; Luke 3 : 3.
4 On Mark, p. 342.
5 P. 22. 6 P. 86. 7 On Matthew, p. 81.
8 "Commentary on Matthew," p. 44.
9 Prov. 28 : 13; I John 1 : 9.

The term "forgiveness" or "remission"[1] is a beautiful word. God sends the sins away, out of sight, out of mind. It is objected that the Baptist was a poor theologian and had no doctrinal system, that, in a word, he knew nothing of the mediatorial work of Christ, that his notion of remission of sins was purely sacramental. It is easy to cite his great cry in John 1 : 29: "Behold the Lamb of God, that taketh away the sin of the world."[2] It is not necessary, in taking this to be a genuine *logion* of the Baptist, to attribute to him a theory of the atonement. John was doubtless familiar with Isa. 53 and its Messianic application. "There can be no doubt that the image is directly derived from Isa. 53 : 7 (cf. Acts 8 : 2)."[3] Why should not he have been familiar with the Paschal Lamb, since he was of priestly stock? He spoke this word after the baptism of Jesus, and in his moment of rapture at the fresh sight of the Messiah he gave expression to his deepest word about him. It is not necessary to explain this as an invention of the author of the Fourth Gospel dramatically put into the Baptist's mouth. It is "the sin of the world" in its collective aspect that John has in mind. But this work of Jesus as the Sin-Bearer makes possible, in John's view, the remission of sins in the case of the man who repents and turns to God. Thus John's theological stand-point does not differ greatly from that of the New Testament as a whole. We must remember also that we have only fragments of John's teaching.

[1] *ἄφεσις* from *ἀφίημι* equals send away.
[2] *Ἴδε ὁ ἀμνὸς τοῦ θεοῦ ὁ αἴρων τὴν ἁμαρτίαν τοῦ κόσμου.*
[3] Westcott on John, vol. I, p. 39.

The wonder is that we can piece out any system at all.

5. *Confession.*—This act was commanded by the Mosaic law.[1] It was often practised by the penitent.[2] It is public confession that is here meant by Matthew[3] and Mark.[4] Private confession to God is, of course, essential to salvation and is, in fact, done when one turns to God with a repentant heart. The case of the publican at worship is in point.[5] This public confession of sins by individuals was a new thing in Israel.[6] There had been, of course, collective confession like that on the Day of Atonement. "It must have been a stirring sight," Bruce adds, this breaking down of hearts before God and men. It is the greatest sight in all the world to see men coming out on the Lord's side. Confession followed as a matter of course when one had trusted God for his salvation.[7] Indeed, the act of baptism was itself[8] a confession of faith in the good news of the kingdom.

6. *Baptism.*—John's title, "the Baptist," shows how people regarded his baptism. The angel Gabriel had not said that he would have such a "nickname." He is not always so called. John was still his name and enough of itself.[9] Mark[10] probably gives the original form of the expression "John the man who

[1] Lev. 5 : 5; 16 : 21, etc.

[2] Cf. Broadus on Matthew, p. 44; Ps. 32 : 5; Acts 19 : 18.

[3] 3 : 6, ἐξομολογούμενοι. The ἐξ shows that it was a full and frank confession.

[4] 1 : 5.

[5] Luke 18 : 13, μοι τῷ ἁμαρτωλῷ.

[6] Bruce on Matthew, p. 81.

[7] Cf. Rom. 10 : 8 ff.

[8] Broadus on Matthew, p. 44; Köhler, Johannes der Täufer."

[9] Cf. Matt. 3 : 13 f.; Mark 1 : 9; Luke 3 : 2, 15; John 1 : 6, etc.

[10] ὁ βαπτίζων.

baptizes." That is probably the way people first began to speak of him. But it was easy to fasten upon him the epithet "the Baptist," as we find it[1] so frequently. Jesus himself[2] is quoted as calling John "the Baptist." Josephus[3] also so describes him. Matthew applies the term to John more often than the other gospels, but he does not always do so.[4] But John was also called a prophet[5] and teacher.[6] Hence he was not regarded as a mere ceremonialist. The novelty of his rite attracted attention, and it was easy for the title to arise. But with John the ordinance was secondary. The spiritual reality was first in his mind and in his message. There is danger to-day that John's striking ceremony in the Jordan may make some men misunderstand him and his mission.

What was the origin of John's baptism? The very title "the Baptist" argues the originality of John's baptism in some sense. Certainly it was new in its application.[7] The committee from Jerusalem were astonished that John should baptize[8] if he did not claim to be the Messiah nor Elias nor the prophet. There is no passage in the Old Testament that foretells baptism by these men.[9] The point of the question is that the Messiah would cause no astonishment if he were to introduce a new rite like this. But if

[1] *ὁ βαπτιστής.* [2] Matt. 11 : 11 f.
[3] "Ant.," xviii, 5, 2, *Ἰωάννου τοῦ ἐπικαλουμένου βαπτιστοῦ.*
[4] Cf. Matt. 9 : 14; 21 : 25 ff.
[5] Matt. 11 : 9; 21 : 26. [6] Luke 5 : 12.
[7] Edersheim, "Life and Times of Jesus," vol. I, p. 273.
[8] *τί οὖν βαπτίζεις;* John 1 : 25.
[9] Westcott on John, *in loco*, quotes Ezek. 36 : 25; Isa. 52 : 15; Zech. 13 : 1 for the notion of a Messianic "lustration." But no reference is here made to baptism.

John is nobody in particular, why had he done it? The question argues the novelty of John's baptism. To the same effect is the question of Jesus when he gave the rulers the dilemma about John's baptism: "The baptism of John, whence was it? Was it from heaven or from men?"[1] Jesus clearly implies that John's baptism had more than a mere human origin. "John came unto you in the way of righteousness and ye received him not."[2] But we are not to insist that ceremonial ablution was a new thing in the world. The Hindoo worship consists largely in lustral rites, the Greeks had their mystical lustrations, and the Romans had the custom of dipping the head in the Tiber to cleanse from sin.[3] The Jews had "divers baptisms"[4] and ceremonial ablutions.[5] "Those who had contracted Levitical defilement were to immerse before offering sacrifice."[6] "He that washeth[7] himself because of a dead body, if he touch it again, what availeth his washing?"[8] The Pharisee, who invited Jesus to breakfast with him,[9] "marvelled that he had not first bathed himself before breakfast."[10] Some scholars think that the Jewish "proselyte baptism," about which so much is said in the Talmud, was already in existence before the time of John.[11] There is no doubt whatever of the

[1] Matt. 21 : 25. [2] Matt. 21 : 32.

[3] Reynolds, "John the Baptist," pp. 277 f.

[4] *διαφόροις βαπτισμοῖς.* Heb. 9 : 10. [5] Cf. Lev. 11–15; Num. 19.

[6] Edersheim, "Life and Times of Jesus," vol. I, p. 273.

[7] *βαπτιζόμενος.* [8] Sirach, xxxiv, 25. [9] *ὅπως ἀριστήσῃ.*

[10] Luke 11 : 38. *ἐβαπτίσθη.*

[11] Cf. in favor of the early origin of proselyte baptism, Schuerer, "Jewish People," etc., second division, II. pp. 319 ff.; Lambert, "Hastings's D. C. G." Edersheim, "Life and Times of Jesus," vol. I, pp. 273 f.; vol. II, Appendix XII. Against this view, see Godet, "Luke," p. 110; Bruce, "Matthew," p. 79; Broadus, "Matthew," pp. 41 f.

existence of "proselyte baptism" from A. D. 200 onward. Edersheim[1] quotes a remarkable passage from the Talmud: "To a man who has in his hand a defiling reptile, who, even if he immerses in all the waters of the world, his baptism avails him nothing; but let him cast it from his hand, and if he immerses in only forty seah of water, immediately his baptism avails him." But we do not feel sure that this proselyte baptism existed before the time of John. There is nothing quoted from the Talmud to prove it. The dispute alleged to have existed between the schools of Hillel and Schammai rests on precarious evidence.[2] Arrian may allude to it.[3] If so, the proselyte baptism existed in the first half of the second century A. D. In itself there is no real objection from any standpoint to the idea that John was familiar with proselyte baptism. It was wholly new in Israel for a prophet like John to call for wholesale baptisms on the part of the people in proof of a spiritual and moral revolution. It was, indeed, a new ordinance, equivalent to a vow, and essentially different from the ceremonial washings with which the Jews were familiar.[4] If the people were familiar with proselyte baptism, then John was treating the Jews themselves as heathen in calling them to submit to a rite which they required of proselytes from pagan peoples.[5] The heathen were unclean *per se*, and this is an argument used for the

[1] "Life and Times of Jesus," vol. I, p. 273.
[2] Edersheim, "Life and Times of Jesus," vol. II, p. 747.
[3] "Dissert. Epicteti," ii, 9, in *τοῦ βεβαμμένου καὶ ᾐρημένου* as a description of one called "Jew."
[4] Holtzmann, "Life of Jesus," p. 119.
[5] Geike, "Life and Words of Christ," vol. I, p. 396.

early existence of proselyte baptism. The case of Naaman, who dipped himself[1] seven times in the Jordan, is not exactly parallel, as this was not an ordinance. Besides the Pharisees and the Essenes, who practised such frequent ablutions, there was the sect of the Sabeans, who practised immersions.[2] But there was something about the rite of John that was new and wonderful, whatever historical antecedents existed. In a real and true sense his baptism was of God, and it summoned the people to their knees in repentance. There was the hush of reverence in the great crowds when John stepped into the Jordan.

What was the significance of John's baptism? It is clear that John's baptism had no connection with ceremonial uncleanness. As a matter of fact, the doctors of the law thought the Jordan too impure for sacred uses.[3] Josephus,[4] while he naturally gives an inadequate description of the meaning of John's baptism, makes it plain that it was not connected with the sacramental purification of the Jews for the washing away of sin. He "commanded the Jews to exercise virtue, both as to righteousness toward one another, and piety toward God, and so to come to baptism; for that the washing would be acceptable to him, if they made use of it, not in order to the demanding pardon of some sins, but for the purification of the body; supposing still that the soul was thoroughly purified beforehand by righteousness."[5]

[1] ἐβαπτίσατο. Lxx II Kings, 5 : 14.
[2] Reynolds, "John the Baptist," p. 283. Cf. Chowlson, "Die Sabier."
[3] Cheyne, "Encycl. Biblica."
[4] "Ant.," xviii, 5, 2.
[5] Margoliouth's revision of Whiston's translation of Josephus, 1906.

The obvious point in Josephus's account is that John required spiritual renewal *before* the baptism. With John there was no sacramental or magical power in the ordinance. It did not convey righteousness nor set one right with God. Josephus mentions no symbolic significance for the ordinance. He is not giving a theological exposition of John's baptism, but the popular impression produced by the ordinance. It is not clear what Josephus means by the phrase "purification of the body." The Jewish ablutions were repeated as occasion (ceremonial defilement) demanded. But that is not the point here. It is interesting to note that the disciples of John have a dispute[1] with a Jew (probably Pharisee) concerning "purification"[2] (Josephus's word). The proximity of John to Jesus and the concurrent baptizing by John and by the disciples[3] of Jesus was the occasion of the argument. Probably this Jew (Pharisee) was seeking baptism of Jesus, and the disciples of John wanted to know why the baptism of John was not sufficient.[4] The disciples of John regarded the new rite as their master's prerogative, and resented the new work begun by Jesus. John was not himself baptized, but he had instituted the ordinance. Thus arose a discussion concerning the relative merits and significance of the baptism of John, of Jesus, and of the Pharisees. Unfortunately we have no report of the arguments advanced in this first debate on the meaning of baptism. It was, in truth, a humbling rite that was demanded

[1] ζήτησις (questioning). John 3 : 25.
[2] περὶ καθαρισμοῦ.
[3] John 4 : 1 f.
[4] Cf. John 3 : 26; Dods on John, *in loco*.

of those who had turned from their sins. It was not a confession and turning from this or that sin, but "it represented a complete purification; it was, as it were, a lustration carried to the second power."[1] John demanded of the people "to seal their repentance by immersion in the Jordan."[2] The matter is clearly put by Plummer on Matthew:[3] "It is his office to bind them to a new life, symbolized by immersion in water." It is a new kind of "proselytes of righteousness" that John is seeking to make, men of real righteousness in heart and life. No others were invited to his baptism except those who had, with repentance and confession, already entered upon this new life. The Jew had to fling away pride of inheritance and privilege and come as a repentant individual, confessing his sins and turning to a new life of righteousness. John was thus consecrating a "new Israel"[4] of spiritual reality in contrast to the old one of birth and ceremonial propriety. The public baptism was a public confession of sin and a public pledge to lead a new life. In a real sense, therefore, the baptism came to stand for the whole work of John. It was the outward sign that stood for the inward reality. A constant[5] stream of people went forth and were baptized of John. It was a wonderful spectacle, "so new, so mighty, so terrific."[6] They all "went out to be baptized of him."[7] They were certainly not all sincere. Some probably wished the baptism as a sub-

[1] Godet, "Luke," p. 110.
[2] Weiss, "Life of Christ," vol. I, p. 313.
[3] P. 28.
[4] Bebb, in "Hastings's D. B."
[5] Mark 1 : 5, ἐξεπορεύετο, ἐβαπτίζοντο.
[6] Keim, "Jesus of Nazara," vol. I, p. 257.
[7] Luke 3 : 7.

stitute for repentance or as a means of securing forgiveness of sins.[1] "Supercilious Rabbis, long-robed Pharisees, cold and courtly Sadducees, dignified high-priests, circumspect Levites, grey-haired elders of the people; the rich farmer with full barns, and the poor peasant; soldiers of the Tetrarch Antipas, from Perea; perhaps, also, proselytes from the Roman garrison at Jerusalem, more disposed to accept baptism in the Jordan than circumcision; publicans—born Jews, but despised and hated, alike for their calling and their unjust exactions,—found themselves together." [2] Small wonder that John indignantly demanded of the Pharisees and Sadducees why they had come to his baptism. Some had come to scoff. The Pharisees and lawyers as a whole refused to be baptized by John. They were not willing, these theologians and custodians of current orthodoxy, to admit that they needed to repent. To accept John's baptism, they held, would be to admit that they were not competent leaders of the religious thought of the time, would be to put themselves on a level with the *am-ha-aretz,* who were accepting John's baptism. The publicans and sinners came readily, but the theological lights "frustrated the counsel of God concerning themselves." [3] John's baptism came to be regarded as a rebuke to the leaders. It was a call to repentance that was heard by some and was disregarded by others. John made it plain also that those who came to his baptism confessed their faith in the coming Messiah, as Paul

[1] Plummer on Luke, *in loco.*
[2] Geike, "Life and Words of Christ," vol. I, p. 397.
[3] Plummer on Luke 7 : 29 f. τὴν βουλὴν τοῦ θεοῦ ἠθέτησαν εἰς ἑαυτούς.

(Acts 19 : 4) explained. This point is clear in John's own words, preserved in Matt. 3 : 11 f.; Mark 1 : 7 f.; Luke 3 : 16 f. Another point to note in John's baptism is that it brought men to decision (Stalker, "The Two St. Johns," p. 212).

What was the relation of John's baptism to Christian baptism? There has been a good deal of needless misunderstanding on the exact relation between the baptizing done by John and that done by the disciples of Jesus and commanded by him.[1] Jesus himself did not baptize, but his disciples.[2] It seems, in fact, that after the imprisonment of the Baptist the disciples of Jesus ceased to baptize, perhaps to avoid the excitement unavoidable to the ordinance at that time, as shown by the experience of the Baptist and the early baptizing of Christ's disciples. It was renewed on a large scale at Pentecost, after Christ's resurrection.[3] It is not to be supposed that the early baptizing by Christ's disciples[4] included the rebaptizing of those already baptized by John. Jesus was carrying on the work of John, not doing it over again. The first disciples of Jesus were disciples of John, and there is no evidence that they were baptized again.[5] The case of the twelve so-called disciples of John at Ephesus, who were baptized by Paul,[6] is not pertinent. These men had missed the essential points in the preaching of John (repentance, faith in the coming Messiah). They had the baptism of John only in form, not in essence. They were remnants of

[1] Matt. 28 : 19. Genuine in spite of recent efforts to discredit the verse.
[2] John 4 : 1 f. [3] Acts 2 : 38, 41. [4] John 3 : 26. [5] John 1 : 35 ff.
[6] Acts 19 : 1–10. See closing chapter of this book.

the disciples of John who had lingered on distinct from the Christians, and did not really represent John's work. Apollos had also only the baptism of John,[1] but he was not rebaptized. Besides, the Lord Jesus himself received John's baptism.[2] What was good enough for Jesus was good enough for his disciples. In broad outline, therefore, the baptism of John was essentially the same as that of Christian baptism.[3] The matter might be allowed to drop right here but for the difficulty felt by some over the words of Jesus concerning John: "He that is least in the kingdom of heaven is greater than he."[4] Whatever this means, it casts no reflection on John's baptism. It may be said in passing that Jesus does not mean to exclude John from the kingdom in reality, for he had just called him the greatest of those born of women. He means to emphasize the opportunity offered to those who come after John with the fuller light of the new dispensation, of which John was the harbinger. It is urged by some that John himself draws a sharp distinction between his baptism and that by Christ.[5] That is true. But the baptizing[6] by Christ is figurative, not literal. John does not here discuss the water baptism commanded by Jesus in Matt. 28 : 19, and at first practised by the disciples of Jesus.[7] What exactly John has in mind by the figurative baptism to be performed by the Messiah is matter for future discussion, but it is not pertinent

[1] Acts 18 : 25.
[2] Matt. 3 : 13 ff.; Mark 1 : 9 f.; Luke 3 : 21 f.
[3] Broadus on Matthew, pp. 240 f.
[4] Matt. 11 : 11.
[5] Matt. 3 : 11 f.; Mark 1 : 7 f.; Luke 3 : 16 f.
[6] ἐν πνεύματι ἁγίῳ καὶ πυρί.
[7] John 3 : 26.

here. It is beyond doubt true that Jesus saw a symbolic meaning in his baptism at the hands of John not seen by John himself.[1] That symbolic content is clearly set forth by Paul in its relation both to Jesus and the believer.[2] It is not necessary to suppose, nor is it likely, that John saw the fulness of this symbolism. But the essence of Paul's thought (the death to sin and the pledge to newness of life) is involved in John's doctrine of repentance in relation to baptism. The form of expression is changed, but the heart of the idea is the same. Jesus himself endorsed the baptism of John by submitting to it himself. He accepted its validity for his disciples. He agreed that it came from heaven and had God's authority. But, like the work of John as a whole, it was not to go on save in that of Christ. For a while John kept on baptizing after he baptized Jesus, but that could not go on indefinitely.

7. *Reformation.*—John was a practical reformer. His mission as herald[3] included vigorous handling of ethical problems. He had no time for mere Levitical ceremonial. His work as Forerunner of the Messiah called for a general toning up of the life of the people. But John did not make the mistake of putting reformation to the front as the main thing. He did demand fruit[4] of the Pharisees and Sadducees who came to his baptism, fruit before the baptism, as proof of repent-

[1] Matt. 3 : 14 f.; Luke 18 : 38 f.

[2] Rom. 6 : 1–6. Cf. "John's Baptism," by J. R. Graves (1891), and "Christic and Patristic Baptism," by J. W. Dale (1874), for controversial aspects of the matter.

[3] κήρυξ.

[4] καρπόν (Matt. 3 : 7) in the collective sense. But Luke (3 : 8) has καρπούς in connection with the multitudes.

ance. John preached reformation in detail to the various classes who came to him, yet not reformation in place of the spiritual renewal out of which righteousness comes. "It was Jesus who proclaimed the inwardness of true morality"[1] in the beatitudes, for instance. But one must not make the mistake of supposing that John also did not grasp this conception. His word "repentance" disproves that notion. With John reformation follows repentance as result, does not precede it as cause. The "fruit worthy of repentance"[2] is fruit that proves the profession of repentance to be genuine. In a word, if they were not hypocrites, their life would show it. Josephus[3] did not grasp clearly John's spiritual insight, and spoke of the soul's being "thoroughly purified beforehand by righteousness," *i. e.*, before coming to baptism. Josephus probably meant that morality caused the purification. He says also that John commanded the exercise of "righteousness toward one another." It cannot be expected that Josephus would, at all points, comprehend John's message. The people to whom John was addressing such plain words had heard his insistence on repentance and had come "to be baptized."[4] Hence, since John had reason to doubt the sincerity of the profession of these classes, he was justified in explaining to them that the new life symbolized by baptism meant quitting the old sins. The baptized life was on the other side of the river of baptism. The old life must be left behind. Indeed,

[1] Bruce on Matthew, p. 83.
[2] Matt. 3 : 7. [3] "Ant.," xviii, 5, 2. [4] Luke 3 : 7, 12.

three classes "asked"[1] John what particular sins they had to give up. These special queries from the common people, the publicans, and the soldiers are echoes of John's demand for "fruit worthy of repentance." This sort of repentance people could understand. It would pass muster with the man on the street and was current in the court of heaven. It was the appeal to life, to life as the source of moral action, to life as proof of spiritual renewal. Like every reformer, John's work was not wholly successful. But he lifted up his standard and exposed the shortcomings of the people of his time. He had, at any rate, made his protest. He made no ill-considered social propaganda for the uplift of the people *en masse* without spiritual regeneration as individuals. He denounced the evils of classes as classes when it was necessary, but more especially he touched the individual life as the best way to raise the general level of human happiness. The great masses of those who heard John went away with their curiosity satisfied but the moral nature unmoved. But many were brought to new life. John did "turn the hearts of the fathers to the children, and the disobedient to walk in the wisdom of the just."[2]

8. *John's Power as a Preacher.*—We have preserved just a few scraps of John's preaching, but they bear the stamp of originality and enable us to form a reasonably adequate conception of his power as a preacher. That is, of course, always a composite result. Often a sermon that shook the multitude is

[1] Luke 3 : 10, 12, 14.

[2] Luke 1 : 17.

cold and lifeless on the printed page. The magnetism of the eye, the penetrating voice, the dominating right hand, the masterful personality, the force of the human will, the touch of soul upon soul are absent. Robert Hall was a preacher of this type, whom Sir W. Robertson Nicoll calls "perhaps the supreme preacher of the last century." "We have no fit record of Hall's sermons, and there is none probably which could fitly represent the dazzling miracles of his eloquence" (*British Weekly*, October 6, 1910). And yet some men have the gift of projecting a large part of their personality into the mere speech so that, if written down, these words throb with life. They breathe and burn. That was pre-eminently true of Jesus. His words are spirit and life.[1] It was true of John the Baptist. This is the highest form of eloquence. Some men attract attention by dress[2] or mannerisms. But John was dependent on no externals like these for a hearing. He was a "field-preacher" like Antony of Padua, like Whitfield. But so was Jesus, who preached in street or common, as he could get a hearing, as well as in the synagogues of worship. John, like Jesus, was a young preacher, but he did not pose as a young preacher nor was that the thing which attracted attention. Indeed, the wonderful maturity of his powers is what is most striking about him. He has a consummate grasp of the great issues of his day, due to prolonged reflection and study.

John was endowed with gifts of a high order. That

[1] John 6 : 63.

[2] False prophets had tried to imitate Elijah (Zech. 13 : 4). "Neither shall they wear a garment of hair to deceive."

is manifest in the ringing words that we have in the Synoptic Gospels. He had a lambent imagination that played around his theme and lighted it up with illustrations from the Old Testament and from the life of the desert. He had an original way of putting things, that peculiar thing called style, which stamps all that a man says with his own individuality and makes it recognizable anywhere. He had the gift of speech in the best sense, not a fatal fluency of words, but the power to pick the telling word. His sermons hit the centre. They were not "orations," but talks straight from the shoulder. There are few preachers, if any, in the history of the world of whom it would be true that just a few pages chosen from their published writings would make the vivid, powerful impression on the modern reader that is created by these fragments from John the Baptist.

John had a great message, it is true. That is a large part of the preacher's power, his message. A preacher who has no message is no herald. He has no call from God or man. No one wishes to hear him and few will endure him. John was a man sent from God, and he never forgot that fact.[1] He never went far away from God's side. The word of the Lord came[2] unto John. He joyfully received it and believed it. He believed his message which he preached in the wilderness when no one else did. He had faith and he had courage. No preacher can be a coward and succeed. No preacher can be a sceptic and succeed. Faith and courage are essentials in the

[1] John 1 : 6. ἀπεσταλμένος παρὰ θεοῦ.

[2] Luke 3 : 2.

preacher. John had them both in a pre-eminent degree. He had a passion for righteousness that blazed like the flame of the Lord. It is curious to find Ruegg[1] saying that the trend of the Baptist's preaching was Pharisaical. He had called the Pharisees a "brood of vipers."

But John had also the spiritual qualification. He had the Holy Spirit with him from his birth. He had the fellowship of the Spirit. He had communion with God. There is nothing that can take the place of this in the prophet,[2] the "for-speaker" for God. Thus John had spiritual insight into his message and his world. Thus it was that he was able to use his great powers for the crisis which he faced. It is no wonder, therefore, that this man was able to rise above the fog of Pharisaism to the clear air of reality. He had a new voice because he had a clear eye. He had lived with God and had seen things as they were.

His words rang like peals of thunder over the mountains and reverberated down the wadys to the Dead Sea. They echo yet through the centuries, the words of this Voice in the Wilderness. It was mighty preaching that smote the hearts of men. Some were superficial, as always, and the words passed over their heads. Others had only a secular notion of the kingdom and began to dream of place and power in that kingdom. The self-indulgent began to hope for change, for a new king who would destroy the law and the prophets. The poor and down-trodden would hope for better times somehow. But the devout and

[1] New Schaff-Herzog Encycl.

[2] προ-φήτης.

deeply spiritual were stirred to the very heart. Men and women talked religion under the trees, by the river brink, on the rocks of the desert, by the roadside, at home. A new day had come to Israel. A real preacher of righteousness had spoken again.

CHAPTER IV

VISION

"The latchet of whose shoes I am not worthy to stoop down and unloose" (Mark 1 : 7).

1. *The Wonder About John.*—The now famous preacher was known all over Palestine. His name was upon every lip. Within the space of six months he had sprung from absolute retirement into the boldest publicity. John had become the sensation of the year by reason of the novelty of his message and the power of its delivery. He had thus far apparently held back one aspect of his message. He had made it plain that the kingdom of heaven had come nigh. They were just on the eve of the greatest event in Jewish history, yea, of human history. The air was big with destiny. "The people were in expectation." [1] The word suggests eager expectancy, on the tiptoe of interest with the flutter of excitement. It was used of the attitude of the people when they waited for Zacharias to come out of the temple.[2] It is the word employed about the people who eagerly awaited the return of Jesus from Decapolis to Capernaum.[3] It is the term that Luke selects to picture the hopeful look

[1] προσδοκῶντος δὲ τοῦ λαοῦ. Luke 3 : 15. The verb is peculiar to Luke outside of Matt. 11 : 3 (the word used by John in the embassy to Jesus); 24 : 50 (used of the second coming); II Peter 3 : 12, 14 (second coming also).

[2] Luke 1 : 21.

[3] Luke 2 : 40.

of the beggar at the Beautiful Gate when Peter and John said, "Look on us."[1] The eyes of all were turned on John the Baptist.

"And all men reasoned[2] in their hearts concerning John." It was inevitable that the question should occur to many, Luke says, "all," what John really was. He wrought no miracles, he made no claims about himself. He had fearlessly denounced the sins of the people, even of the hierarchy in Jerusalem. He had spared none, high or low. The very tenseness of his preaching had wrought upon the people so that they had to work the matter out. If the Messianic Dispensation was at hand, as constantly announced by John, who was the Messiah? Who more likely than this fearless preacher himself. As yet this query was in the hush of the heart. But John either read their hearts or overheard a whispered discussion between two earnest souls. It was at best a surmise "whether haply he were the Christ."[3] The use of "answered" by Luke[4] shows that John all of a sudden realized that the popular mind had taken this turn about him. Evidently the time had come for him to speak plainly on the subject. This he did, probably on an occasion when there was a great crowd, so that as many as possible could hear his words. To be silent now would be to be disloyal to the Messiah, whose Forerunner only John knew

[1] Acts 3 : 5.

[2] διαλογιζομένων Cf. our *dialogue.* But note the middle voice. This "dialogue" was in the heart, not yet uttered.

[3] μή ποτε αὐτὸς εἴη ὁ χριστός. The optative is due to the indirect question. Note the article with χριστός, the Anointed One, the Messiah. The μή ποτε puts it delicately with a shade of doubt.

[4] 3 : 16.

himself to be. Matthew and Mark do not give this reason for John's utterance on this point, but the point is really implied in the very distinction which John here draws between himself and the Messiah. Mark[1] says that "he preached, saying." We must understand that John had purposely held back a more particular description of the Messiah himself until now. The excitement was great enough as it was. John probably had no definite idea as to how soon the Messiah would appear. He knew that he was nigh. He had announced that fact. It was in all likelihood a sore disappointment to John to find that his own preaching had turned people's thoughts to himself rather than to his Lord. Many a true minister is subjected to like mortification. These hints about John's personality come at the very height of his reputation. He is on the very crest of popular esteem. The lamp was burning and shining with resplendent light, so that even the Jerusalem ecclesiastics were willing to rejoice in the brilliance of the new luminary.[2] But only for a season. They will indeed soon send a formal embassy to John on the subject of his claims,[3] showing thereby that John's present disclaimer was not accepted at once by all. But the nobility of John comes out finely here. He was not willing to sail under false colors. He wished no reputation for what he was not. He did not hesitate a moment.[4] "Whom do you take me to be?" Paul (Acts 13 : 25) represents John as saying to the people.

[1] 1 : 7. ἐκήρυσσεν λέγων. This imperfect may be merely descriptive, or it may be inchoative. Cf. Luke's reason.
[2] John 5 : 35. [3] John 1 : 19 ff. [4] Bruce on Matt. 3 : 11.

2. *The Mightier than John.*—"John was perfectly aware of the impression produced by his words. He knew that they were breaking stony hearts and crushing strong men. Soldiers were crying for mercy and feeling the sharp edge of the sword of his mouth. Harlots were weeping and penitent."[1] John had brought the people "face to face with the Unseen" and had made them "realize the grandeur of God, and feel the supremacy of righteousness and true holiness."[2] But John was not deceived by all the magnetism and manifestation of his preaching.[3] He was always able to take his own measure. The popular excitement did not mislead him in the least. The troubles concerning the false Samaritan Messiah[4] may have been partly due to the "tension of mind caused by John's teaching."[5] John had something in his experience to counterbalance the boundless enthusiasm of the masses. The teachers of the law scouted his claims to be the Forerunner and refused his baptism.[6] Some of the crowd sneered that John had a demon.[7] That was the true explanation of his peculiarities of dress and diet as well as of his power with the people. But John cared little for all this. It was a matter of indifference[8] to him what people thought of him till he found that many were mistaking him for the Messiah. This knowledge brought John in his consciousness face to face with the Coming One.

[1] Reynolds, "John the Baptist," p. 261.
[2] Farrar, "Life of Lives," p. 177.
[3] Holtzmann, "Life of Jesus," p. 119.
[4] Josephus, "Ant.," xviii, 4, 1 and 2.
[5] Farrar, "Life of Lives," p. 177.
[6] Luke 7 : 30.
[7] Matt. 11 : 18; Luke 7 : 33.
[8] Holtzmann, "Life of Jesus," p. 119.

The people needed a clear word about the King. "There cometh after me he that is mightier than I."[1] The term "the Coming One" occurs in the New Testament as a description of the promised Messiah.[2] Mark and Luke represent John as describing the Messiah as "the mightier than I,"[3] while Matthew turns the expression round: "The One coming after me[4] is mightier than I." In the one case the predicate is "cometh" and accents the near advent of the Mighty One. In the other case the predicate equals "is mighty" and accents the strength of the Coming One. The Jews, according to the Talmud, frequently spoke of the Messiah as *Habba,* the Coming One.[5] The phrase in itself is future in sense though the present participle is used. But in the mind of John the idea is that of near future, one just coming.[6] John knew that the time was near from the moral condition of the period. His own intuition led him to see this much.[7] But Luke[8] expressly tells us that the word of the Lord had come to John. It is not scientific to exclude the guidance of the Holy Spirit from John's vision in this crucial point in his message. He had already said repeatedly that the kingdom of heaven had drawn near.[9] John instinctively feels that the King is now very near.

[1] Mark 1 : 7; Matt. 3 : 11; Luke 3 : 16.

[2] Cf. John 11 : 27. The confession of Martha ὁ χριστὸς ὁ υἱὸς τοῦ θεοῦ εἰς τὸν κόσμον ἐρχόμενος. Cf. John 1 : 9 (probable interpretation). So John 3 : 31.

[3] ὁ ἰσχυρότερός μου.

[4] ὁ δὲ ὀπίσω μου ἐρχόμενος.

[5] Broadus on Matthew, p. 50. Cf. Ps. 118 : 26; Zech. 9 : 9; Mal. 3 : 1.

[6] Bruce on Matthew, p. 83 f.

[7] *Ibid.*

[8] Luke 3 : 2; 1 : 15.

[9] The perfect tense ἤγγικεν is used by Jesus in Matt. 26 : 45 f. for the approach of Judas in the garden and the hour of betrayal.

John here depicts the Messiah as the Mighty One, mightier than himself. It is no mock humility. As already noted John knew his power over the people. Jesus has added his word about John's real greatness.[1] But John is perfectly sincere when he compares himself to one of the lowest slaves in the house of the Messiah. The humblest menial would meet the Master of the house at the door, "stoop down and unloose"[2] the latchet of his shoes.[3] Matthew[4] adds "to bear" the shoes on into the house. He does not feel qualified[5] to act in this humble capacity in the presence of the Coming One.

The use of the term "mightier than" John leads Bruce[6] to think that John had a false conception of the Messiah as one whose chief attribute was strength (and dignity). But surely John is not thinking of mere prowess. It is rather force of character that must enter into John's notion of the Mighty One.[7] The term is used of moral and spiritual energy also.[8] It is the moral grandeur of the Messiah that causes John to feel his own insignificance so keenly. It is the conception of the greatness of the Strong Son of God that fills his heart rather than the Good Shepherd or the Prince of Peace.[9] The vision which John has is indeed inadequate, but not erroneous. It is not yet

[1] Matt. 11 : 11; Luke 7 : 28.

[2] Mark 1 : 7, *κύψας λῦσαι*. Note punctiliar act (aorist). Not even once.

[3] *ὑποδήματα* (bound under the foot), not *σανδάλια* (Matt. 6 : 9; Acts 12 : 8).

[4] *βαστάσαι*. Aorist also. Single act.

[5] *ἱκανός*. "Not fit to carry" (Broadus, "Matthew," p. 50).

[6] "Matthew," p. 84.

[7] *ὁ ἰσχυρότερός μου*.

[8] Cf. Heb. 5 : 7; 6 : 18. Indeed, *ἰσχύς* is confined to the moral sense in the New Testament. Cf. Mark 12 : 30; Eph. 1 : 19; Rev. 5 : 12, etc.

[9] Reynolds, "John the Baptist," p. 267.

based on personal knowledge, but is more than "religious preconception." [1]

The use of the article (the Coming One, the Mightier One) suggests that he ought to be known after he comes. John will later testify of him that he was before him as well as after him.[2]

3. *The Messianic Baptism.*—The baptism of John was the outstanding characteristic of his ministry. John therefore naturally uses that to show the superiority of the Coming One. He will surpass John in the very matter in which the people thought John to be supreme. There is, of course, no contrast drawn between the water-baptism performed by John and that performed by the disciples of Jesus.[3] John cannot be understood as reflecting on water-baptism, for he continued to practise it and did so after the disciples of the Messiah were doing the same.[4] John uses his literal baptism as the figure for the entire work of the coming Messiah and, indeed, for the Messianic Dispensation.[5] The report in Matthew[6] of John's words adds the explanation of the nature of his baptism: "I indeed baptize you in water unto repentance." [7] His baptism was a "repentance-baptism," a baptism marked by, or preceded by repentance.[8] John's baptism bound the baptized to lead

[1] Bruce, "Matthew," p. 84.

[2] John 1 : 15. He has gone ahead of John in rank (ἔμπροσθέν μου) as he was before him in essential superiority (πρῶτός μου). At the manifestation of the Messiah he took the place ahead of John, which belonged to him by his nature. Cf. Westcott on John 1 : 15.

[3] Broadus on Matthew, p. 48.

[4] John 3 : 23–26.

[5] Broadus on Matthew, p. 48.

[6] 3 : 11.

[7] ἐγὼ μὲν ὑμᾶς βαπτιζω ἐν ὕδατι εἰς μετάνοιαν.

[8] Mark 1 : 4; Luke 3 : 3.

a life worthy of the repentance already professed.[1] John's baptism was a symbol of repentance, a picture of the spiritual change wrought by the Holy Spirit. "The Messiah, will steep in the Holy Ghost those who have been baptized by John."[2] The Coming One, the Messiah, "is coming to immerse them in an element far more potent—the Holy Spirit and fire."[3] The Messiah will bring the spiritual baptism symbolized by the water-baptism. John does not, of course, mean to say that those baptized by him have not had the spiritual renewal. But the Messiah is to be endowed with the Holy Spirit in an especial sense.[4] It is the power[5] of the Messiah that John has in mind. Jesus himself after his resurrection used the same image of baptism for what is to take place on the great day of Pentecost.[6] The great importance of this word of John about the Messiah is seen in the fact that it is reported by the three Synoptic Gospels,[7] by the Fourth Gospel[8] as repeated by the Baptist on a later occasion, by Simon Peter[9] in the report at Jerusalem of his experience at Cæsarea, in the house of Cornelius, by Paul at Antioch in Pisidia,[10] who mentions John's "baptism of repentance," and explains that John pointed to the one who was to come after him. So at Ephesus[11] Paul explained that John preached the baptism of the Holy Spirit which was

[1] Luke 3 : 8. [2] Holtzmann, "Life of Jesus," p. 120.
[3] Plummer on Matthew, p. 28.
[4] Cf. Isa. 11 : 2. So Enoch 49 : 3; 62 : 2; Psalms of Solomon 17 : 42; Test. of the Twelve Pat. (Levi 18, Juda 24). Cf. Allen on Matthew, p. 25 f.
[5] αὐτὸς δέ Mark 1 : 8. [6] Acts 1 : 5.
[7] Matt. 3 : 11; Mark 1 : 8; Luke 3 : 16.
[8] John 1 : 33. [9] Acts 11 : 16. [10] Acts 13 : 24 ff.
[11] Acts 19 : 2 ff.

symbolized by his baptism of repentance. Jesus himself will not literally immerse men in water, nor burn them with fire. It is the great spiritual energy of the Messiah that John sees.[1] The language of the Baptist here, before he sees the Messiah, is well illustrated by the words of Peter on the Day of Pentecost, when the fulness of the Spirit's power has come upon the disciples.[2] Mark[3] has "I baptized you," a single look at John's work.

Matthew[4] and Luke[5] add "and in fire," which point is not reported by Mark. The addition is remarkable and it looks like a mixture of images. The allusion remains obscure, and we may probably never know exactly what was John's idea.[6] Bruce takes both Holy Spirit and fire to refer to the judicial function of the Messiah. "The whole baptism of the Messiah, as John conceives it, is a baptism of judgment. . . . I think that the grace of Christ is not here at all." [7] Bruce takes "spirit" in the sense of "wind." The three destructive elements (water, wind, fire) all come in judgment on the people. But, attractive as this looks, it is not conclusive. In support of this idea it is urged that "fire" in Matt. 3 : 10 (Luke 3 : 9) undoubtedly means Messianic judgment. The same thing is true of "unquenchable fire" in Matt. 3 : 12 (Luke 3 : 17). It appears natural to take fire in Matt. 3 : 11 and Luke 3 : 16 in the same sense. But if that be granted (for the moment) it does not follow

[1] Cf. John 44 : 3; Ezek. 36 : 25–27; Joel 2 : 28; 3 : 1.
[2] Acts 2 : 16–24.
[3] 1 : 8, ἐβάπτισα. Punctiliar.
[4] 3 : 11. καὶ πυρί.
[5] 3 : 16.
[6] Plummer on Luke, p. 95.
[7] On Matthew, p. 84.

that "Holy Spirit" refers to judgment also. That is to make an arbitrary limitation of John's language and horizon to fit a theory. John did himself preach "repentance," the work of the Holy Spirit. Broadus[1] agrees with Bruce as to "fire," but refuses to limit the "Holy Spirit" to the work of judgment. This view requires the "you" to include both classes, the penitent and the impenitent. Plummer once[2] held this to be "very improbable," but he has come to see it to be possible,[3] for "in the next verse the two classes are clearly distinguished." This is the common view among commentators, as Bruce admits.[4] Another view takes both the Holy Spirit and fire to refer to the cleansing and purifying work of grace. Appeal is made to Mal. 3 : 2 f., where the Messiah is compared to the refiner's fire which illuminates and purifies.[5] By this view the baptism of fire is the baptism of the Holy Spirit. The refiner's fire purifies the silver and the gold,[6] but this refining fire is also likened to a furnace which consumes all who do evil.[7] Still others take the figure to picture the fiery trials which Jesus and his followers must pass through.[8] The matter must be left an open one, but the startling image was doubtless expanded by John so that his hearers understood what he meant by the allusion.

[1] On Matthew, p. 51 f.
[2] "Luke," p. 95.
[3] "Matthew," p. 29. Plummer ("Luke," p. 95) rightly considers a reference to the tongues of fire on the Day of Pentecost unlikely. Cf. Acts 1 : 5.
[4] "Matthew," p. 84.
[5] Cf. Bengel, *in loco*.
[6] Holtzmann, "Life of Jesus," p. 120.
[7] Mal. 3 : 19; 4 : 1.
[8] Luke 12 : 50; Mark 10 : 38 f.; I Pet. 1 : 4.

4. *The Messianic Judgment.*—There is no doubt of the element of judgment in John's picture of the Messiah in Matt. 3 : 12 and Luke 3 : 17. But the image here is not that of baptism. It is that of the winnowing shovel.[1] It is a bold and impressive picture. The Messiah steps forth with the winnowing shovel in his hand. The grain and chaff together are cast up before the wind. The grain falls down together, while the chaff is blown farther away. The grain and the chaff are thus separated by the Messiah. The grain is gathered into the garners.[2] The chaff the Messiah will burn up with unquenchable fire.[3] The adjective is used either of a fierce fire that cannot be extinguished or of an endless fire that will never go out.[4] It is not clear which is John's idea.[5] It is never safe to press figurative language too far. It is not clear whether the apocalyptic language of John is to be interpreted of eternal punishment of the individual or the terrible judgments upon the people of Israel who will reject the Messiah (cf. the destruction of Jerusalem). The destructive force of fire is one of the most powerful agents in nature. The terrible forest-fires of modern times sweep all before them, driving men and wild beasts in common flight to a place of refuge. The conflagrations at Baltimore and San Francisco have left a deep mark upon the modern mind. John had said before to the Pharisees

[1] πτύον.

[2] ἀποθήκη, place of deposit (ἀποτίθημι). Cf. Matt. 6 : 26; 13 : 30. Cf. παραθήκη, in I Tim. 6 : 20.

[3] πυρὶ ἀσβέστῳ (cf. *asbestos*). Cf. Lev. 6 : 12 f.; Isa. 34 : 8–10, etc.

[4] Plummer on Luke, p. 95 f.

[5] κατακαύσει (cf. Matt. 13 : 30) has the "perfective" use of the preposition κατά that argues for inextinguishable fire.

and Sadducees that the Messiah was like the woodman with his axe at the root of the tree, to fell it if it be found without fruit. Here he is depicted as the thresher to find out if the harvest has come to aught. John's preaching is not for light-minded and dissolute people.[1] He has a word for the earnest and the sincere. The use of the apocalyptic imagery of Joel by Peter on the Day of Pentecost is a good example of the manner in which apocalyptic language is to be interpreted. The words of Jesus in Matt. 24 and 25 furnish another parallel. John wished to leave the people with a picture of the Messiah's power. He has turned their minds away from flippant thoughts about himself. They need to have searching of heart in the approaching presence of the Messiah of Israel. "Behold, the day cometh that shall burn as an oven, and all that do wickedly shall be stubble: and the day that cometh shall burn them up, saith the Lord of Hosts, that it shall leave them neither root nor branch."[2] One can imagine the hush of solemn awe that swept over John's audience as he spoke of the burning of the chaff in language that recalled the terrible picture of Malachi.

5. *The Sign of the Messiah.*—Perhaps some of the crowd turned round to see if the Messiah had not really appeared. The Messianic hope had died down a good deal before John revived it. It had ceased to be an active one in the popular consciousness.[3] It was not, indeed, entirely lost with the people. In the

[1] Holtzmann, "Life of Jesus," p. 121. [2] Mal. 4:1.
[3] Schuerer, "Jewish People," etc., sec. div., II, p. 136.

prophets it was "an essential element of their religious consciousness."[1] It had at first been a better hope for the nation and then for the world. It had also given a better hope for the individual. Under the Maccabees the Pharisees and scribes had revived the national hope of a great Messianic empire for the Jews.[2] But Roman power had dashed those hopes of earthly power. Still the Pharisees cherished the dream of throwing off the hated Roman yoke. When the Messiah comes he will do that. The people who heard John's burning words did not all agree in their notions of the Messiah. Some felt that, when the Messiah comes, no one will know whence he comes.[3] The scribes understood from Micah 5 : 2 that the Messiah would be born in Bethlehem.[4] "There is more than enough to show that the people generally were expecting a sublime yet lurid blending of heaven and earth; a vengeance upon the enemies of Israel, a new heir and occupant of the throne of David, a political Leader, a great Prophet, a resistless King, who should use his supernatural powers to promote his interests, to judge the nations, and to place others in a position of civil, intellectual, and political supremacy."[5] The rabbis had formed a picture of the Messiah quite different from that of the Old Testament, and far other than the reality as seen in Jesus of Nazareth.[6] They thought more of him as King and Deliverer, and less as Prophet and Priest.[7] One

[1] *Ibid.*, p. 129.
[2] Cf. "The Psalms of Solomon."
[3] John 7 : 27, 31.
[4] Cf. Matt. 2 : 4 f.; John 7 : 41 f.
[5] Reynolds, "John the Baptist," p. 266.
[6] Edersheim, "Life and Times," vol. I, p. 160.
[7] *Ibid.*, p. 167.

may turn to the Psalter of Solomon and to the Jewish portion of the Book of Enoch and of the Sybilline Oracles for the rabbinical notion of the Messiah. The Talmud also preserves to some extent the pre-Christian point of view. The gospels reveal also the Pharisaic idea of the Messiah. The repeated desire of the Pharisees for a sign from heaven shows how they looked for a heavenly portent in connection with his coming.

But it is an injustice to John the Baptist to limit his conception of the Messiah to the Pharisaic standpoint. He saw in dim outline, but he saw clearly what he saw. On the other hand,[1] we need not set John above his times entirely, nor beyond the great Day of Pentecost. The disciples of Jesus could not grasp clearly the idea of a spiritual kingdom till that day of illumination. Just before Christ's ascension the disciples still look for a temporal kingdom.[2] Indeed John has not made it perfectly clear in the words preserved to us what his idea of the Messiah was in all respects. He pulled back the veil far enough to see the presence of the Messiah. He felt the presence of the Messiah though he could not now see him. His baptizing, he will later explain, was for the purpose of manifesting the Messiah to Israel.[3] "And I knew him not; but that he should be made manifest to Israel, for this cause came I baptizing with water." John had been used of God to create the conditions under which the Messiah would appear.[4] John may

[1] Geike, "Life and Words of Christ," vol. I, p. 406.
[2] Acts 1 : 6.
[3] John 1 : 31 f.
[4] Weiss, "Life of Christ," vol. I, p. 319.

or may not have seen the boy Jesus in his early days. There is no proof that he did. But certainly he had no personal acquaintance with Jesus at this time, when he is on the lookout for the Messiah. He had a sign given him by God. Note how John speaks of his relation to God: "He that sent me to baptize with water, he said unto me."[1] This word lets us into John's own consciousness of his mission. He had received his commission from God, and the Father still communicated with him. In a word, he claims revelation as the Fourth Gospel reports him. The sign of the Messiah was for John's own personal benefit. The Holy Spirit will descend on the Messiah. When John sees that event, he will know that he has met the Messiah.[2] John mentions here also[3] the fact that the Messiah will baptize with the Holy Ghost. This point he had quite laid to heart. John knew that the Messiah was near. He knew what the proof would be.

6. *Where is the Messiah?*—The Talmud not only admitted that the Messiah might be among the living, but actually tells the strange story that he had been born in the royal palace at Bethlehem, had been discovered by Rabbi Judan and had been carried away in a storm.[4] Jewish tradition was busy with the notion of the Messiah's concealment. Where was the Messiah? Did not John scan carefully the face of every man who came to him for baptism? He may have had many a flutter of expectation, but the sign

[1] John 1 : 33. [2] *Ibid.* [3] *Ibid.*
[4] Edersheim, "Life and Times," vol. I, p. 175.

did not come. What will the Messiah look like? How long will John have to wait before he comes? His mission was to manifest[1] the Messiah. Till that had been accomplished he had not done his work. He must be able to say to the people: "There is the Messiah!" Did he have his moments of doubt as the Messiah still did not come? The strain was great upon John. The crowds came and went. John preached and baptized as usual. But his heart went out in his look of expectant hope as he turned to each new-comer. Where is the Messiah? John is loyal to his vision, but he longs for the reality. He still utters his cry: "Repent, for the kingdom of heaven is at hand," but a change seems to have come over him when it has become his solemn function to discover and proclaim the King himself.[2]

[1] John 1 : 31. ἵνα φανερωθῇ τῷ Ἰσραήλ.
[2] Reynolds, "John the Baptist," p. 312.

CHAPTER V

REALITY

I have need to be baptized of thee, and comest thou to me?" (Matt. 3 : 14).

1. *The Coming of Jesus to the Jordan.*—The news of what John had been doing came to Jesus, the carpenter, in Nazareth. The two men seem to have been unacquainted. Mary may have told Jesus of the kinship between them. Her heart must have been stirred afresh by what she heard of John. The slow years of waiting had gone by and now at last the Forerunner had lifted up his voice. The veil of silence rests upon the thoughts of Mary till she appears at the wedding in Cana, and bids the servants do what Jesus commands.[1] Had Mary kept all the things known to her in her heart[2] all the time? She pondered them often through the years and watched the grace of God upon Jesus and his growing favor with the people of Nazareth.[3] But did she come to tell the great burden to her Son? On this point we have no light. But she knew long ago that the Boy had come to consciousness of his unique relation to the Father and to his house.[4]

[1] John 2 : 5. [2] Luke 2 : 19. [3] *Ibid.*, 2 : 52.
[4] Luke 2 : 50. Cf. Weiss, "Life of Christ," vol. I, p. 319. Weiss is sure that Mary told Jesus of her hopes about him, the promise of Gabriel to her.

Jesus is now probably thirty years old.[1] John has apparently been preaching some six months. If John began in the spring, it would be autumn when Jesus appears on the banks of the Jordan. This is all conjecture, as we have no notes of time at all. The year was probably A. D. 26. It was beyond doubt with great stirring of heart that Jesus left his humble home in Nazareth to go to the Jordan. He was not the first to come from Galilee, as some have wrongly inferred from Matthew's expression "from Galilee."[2] He apparently came alone, or at any rate he appears alone before John. He had made up his mind before coming that John was the Messianic Herald. He had probably heard the talk of the people about John, and the various opinions held concerning him. He may, indeed, have heard of John's disclaimer about being himself the Messiah and his proclamation that the Messiah was about to appear. In a sense the coming of Jesus to the Jordan was his response to John's description of the Coming One. It is not necessary to insist that Matthew's "then"[3] joins the visit of Jesus immediately on to the previous description of the Messiah by the Baptist. The term is a very general one and is often used in Matthew (some ninety times).[4] Mark merely says "in those days," while Luke[5] implies that the bulk of John's work was over (not of time, but of amount) "when all the people were baptized."[6] Jesus had waited long enough for

[1] *Ibid.*, 3 : 23. Cf. Num. 4 : 3, 23, 30, 43, 47.

[2] Cf. Plummer, "Matthew," p. 31.

[3] τότε Matt. 3 : 13. [4] 1 : 9. [5] 3 : 21.

[6] ἐν τῷ βαπτισθῆναι ἅπαντα τὸν λαόν. Strictly speaking, the aorist inf. has no necessary notion of precedence, but is merely punctiliar. The

the work of John to show its true nature and to prepare the people for his own ministry. He came at what he evidently considered a fit moment all round.[1] It was not that Jesus was carried away by the masses in their enthusiasm about John,[2] but the mighty impression of the work of John brought matters to an issue in the mind of Jesus and led him to break his silence and to enter upon his ministry. His visit was not in the nature of inspection, but rather of deep resolve to take up his work as Messiah. The glow and stir of mighty thoughts are in the heart of Jesus as he leaves Nazareth for the sixty-mile journey to the Jordan. We do not know the place of meeting. Later, John was at Bethany, beyond Jordan,[3] but even that point is unknown. Then again, John may not have been at Bethany when Jesus came. It is better not to try to decide the impossible. John probably had many baptizing places along the Jordan at the different fords. Jesus came to be baptized of John.[4] This was the object of his visit.

At last John and Jesus are face to face. Jesus[5] "appears before John." Out of the ages the two men of destiny meet. John had spent his years in preparation for this moment. It is the culmination of his life-work. It is the beginning of the ministry of Jesus. Silently this crisis for John has come.

present inf. is, of course, durative, equals while. Both are common in Luke. It is only by implication in the context that the aorist inf. with ἐν τῷ equals after. Cf. Plummer, *in loco*.

[1] Geike, "Life and Words of Christ," vol. I, p. 410.

[2] Keim, "Jesus of Nazara," vol. II, p. 267.

[3] John 1 : 28. Bethabara is without doubt erroneous. [4] Matt. 3 : 13.

[5] πρὸς τὸν Ἰωάνην. Matthew has the historical present παραγίνεται with vivid dramatic effect.

Like two stars the two men touch each other's path and move on.[1] They meet only this once. John sees Jesus on two other days,[2] but they have no converse. Jesus knows who John is, but John at first does not know who Jesus is. He was to him a stranger. What is there in this stranger different from the many others who had come to the baptism of John? John usually had a private interview with those who sought baptism at his hands.[3] It is probably at such a private meeting that the two men first see each other. Jesus is conscious of the significance of their meeting, but John knows only that here is another applicant for baptism.

2. *John Recognizes the Messiah.*—It is true that the Synoptics give John's preaching before the baptism of Jesus and the Fourth Gospel afterward.[4] But there is a retrospective allusion to the period before the baptism in John 1 : 31–33. There is no reason for disputing the express statement of the Baptist that he did not know Jesus till the baptism.[5] Besides, Jesus, though not a disciple of John,[6] was certain of the divine mission of John.[7] There is a rather unnecessary amount of trouble made over John's instinctive insight into the character of Jesus when he first greets him.[8] "The gravest perplexity

[1] Godet on Luke, p. 117 f. [2] John 1 : 29, 35.

[3] Plummer on Matthew, p. 30. [4] Bebb in "Hastings's D. B."

[5] οὐκ ᾔδειν αὐτόν equals no knowledge of him, not mere personal acquaintance (ἔγνων). Lange, "Life of Christ," vol. II, p. 23 f., curiously holds that John knew Jesus.

[6] Renan, "Vie de Jésus," p. 107.

[7] Lange, "Life of Christ," vol. II, p. 22.

[8] "The apparent inconsistency between Matt. 3 : 14 and John 1 : 33 has tested the sagacity of interpreters." Lange, "Life of Christ," vol. II, p. 24.

has been allowed to gather round this apparent discrepancy."[1] It is possible, indeed, that John may have heard something of the early history of his kinsman through Zacharias and Elizabeth.[2] In the private interview, when Jesus sought baptism, John may have learned his name and claims. The brief dialogue in Matthew may be the conclusion of the interview, not the whole of it. It may have been the profound impression made upon John by the powerful personality of Jesus that caused him to protest: "I have need to be baptized of thee, and comest thou to me?" John stood in the presence of the One Sinless Man. His baptism symbolized repentance from sin, but here was one who had no sin and whose baptism would be meaningless. Besides, John himself had not been baptized. Here was one qualified for that service. John had come to be an expert in reading the human face, for many thousands had asked baptism of him. But he had never looked into a face like that of this Stranger. John was face to face with the greatest personality of history, and felt a moral awakening in his own sensitive soul. Here was "the Christ of Reality"[3] standing before John, the Coming One of whom he had spoken and dreamed. In these brief moments of rapid intuition, of spiritual illumination, John may have gotten more light than he had ever received before.[4] The mind works quickly in such supreme moments. The purity and the greatness of the Stranger overawed John. "There

[1] Reynolds, "John the Baptist," p. 313.
[2] *Ibid.*, p. 314.
[3] Bruce on Matthew, p. 85.
[4] Nourse in "Standard Bible Dictionary."

was something in His look, something in the sinless beauty of His ways, something in the solemn majesty of His aspect which at once overawed and captivated the soul of John. . . . As when some unknown dread checks the flight of the eagle, and makes him settle with hushed scream and drooping plumage on the ground, so before the royalty of inward happiness, before the purity of sinless life, the wild prophet of the desert becomes like a submissive and timid child." [1] John tried to hinder[2] Jesus in his purpose to be baptized. He *knows* that he is standing before one who is superior in all moral and spiritual qualities. He can *feel* that. How much more John means by his protest we do not know. He has not yet seen the sign of the Messiah which will confirm his present intuitions. He had recently spoken of the one who was coming the latchet of whose shoes he was not worthy to stoop down and unloose. All unexpectedly John finds himself in the presence of One whose presence makes him feel just that way. Is he not the Coming One, the Messiah? It is no affectation with John, but the deepest reverence of his soul which he here offers to the One Supreme Man whom he has now met. Matthew alone gives this perplexity and reluctance of John to baptize Jesus. Mark merely mentions the fact of the baptism without any interpretation, while Luke puts the baptism of Jesus in a subordinate clause, "Jesus also having been baptized." [3] He seems to be mainly concerned with the

[1] Farrar, "Life of Christ," vol. I, p. 115.
[2] διεκώλυεν. Matt. 3 : 14. Conative imperfect and note δια also.
[3] 3 : 21.

divine recognition given Jesus. In John[1] the baptism is assumed as well known, and the Baptist states that he has seen the Holy Spirit come upon Jesus. This the Synoptics show took place at the baptism. Bruce[2] correctly notes that this order illustrates the order of the gospels from Mark to John, and the varying interest in the subject of the baptism of Jesus by John. But Bradley[3] labors hard to prove thereby that John did not recognize Jesus as the Messiah, did not baptize him, and that the followers of Jesus invented the baptism of Jesus by John to relieve the embarrassment from this awkward situation. This is surely a strained reversal of the known facts about John, an arrangement more ingenious than true. The fact that Matthew proceeds to give the sign of the Holy Spirit at the baptism shows that he did not consider what he has written to be inconsistent with that. The knowledge that would come at the baptism with the sign of the Messiah would be like a blaze of light bursting on John's[4] mind. But even now the Baptist stands a suppliant before the One who has come, who is the true light that was to come. It is John's mission to bathe in this light so as to give a clearer witness of it.[5]

3. *The Significance of the Baptism of Jesus.*—John was humble in the presence of Jesus, as was Peter, later, when he said: "Lord, dost thou wash my feet?"[6] That was the proper spirit in the presence

[1] 1 : 32.

[2] "Matthew," *in loco.*

[3] *Biblical World*, June, 1910, pp. 399 ff. Weiss ("Life of Christ," vol. I, p. 319) says that the question in Matt. 3 : 15 "cannot possibly involve a contradiction of John's declaration just alluded to (John 7 : 31, 33)."

[4] Reynolds, "John the Baptist," p. 315.

[5] John 1 : 7 ff.

[6] John 13 : 6. Cf. Smith, "In the Days of His Flesh," p. 31.

of the Messiah. But why had Jesus come to be baptized by John? Nothing in the career of John has given rise to more discussion. As already stated, some writers deny that Jesus was baptized by John. Others deny that John acknowledged Jesus to be the Messiah. In Mark the narrative is objective and the baptism of Jesus by John relates the work of the Messiah to that of the Forerunner and furnishes proof of Messianic authority.[1] Luke accents the spiritual earnestness of Jesus on the occasion ("praying") and the divine endorsement of the Son as he enters on his work at the age of thirty.[2]

But Matthew seems concerned also with another question—that of the propriety of the baptism of Jesus by the Baptist. He had said that Jesus came "to be baptized of him." It is doubtless true that disciples of Jesus were puzzled over the fact that Christ had sought baptism at the hands of the Baptist just as the publicans and sinners had done. But the difficulty is a natural one, and could have occurred to John himself at the time of the baptism of Jesus. It is quite gratuitous to urge that Matthew has invented this reply of Jesus "to get rid of the difficulty of a sinless Messiah accepting repentance-baptism." [3] We have samples of such invention. Jerome[4] quotes the gospel according to the Hebrews as saying: "Behold the Mother of the Lord, and His brethren said to Him, John the Baptist baptizeth for the remission of sins; let us go and be baptized by him. But He said

[1] Allen, "Matthew," p. 28. Cf. Matt. 21 : 24 ff.
[2] Godet, "Luke," p. 118.
[3] Plummer, "Matthew," p. 31.
[4] "Adv. Pelag.," iii, 2.

to them, What sins have I committed, that I should go and be baptized by him? Except perchance this very thing that I have said is ignorance." The words of Jesus in Matthew belong to another world, and bear the stamp of originality.[1] Indeed, this very difficulty about the baptism of Jesus is itself strong evidence for its being historical.[2]

There are really two questions involved: the baptism of Jesus at all, the baptism by John. The reply of Jesus does not give, in general, the design of his baptism, a matter also worthy of discussion, but rather the reason why it should be done by one who was his inferior. This was the precise point raised by John in Matt. 3:14. He felt that he had nothing to offer Jesus. The rather he had much to receive from him. This is the exact point in the reply of Jesus: "Suffer it now: for thus it becometh us to fulfil all righteousness." Jesus means to say that, though superior to John, as John has just said, yet for the present[3] their real relations may properly[4] be reversed. Jesus does not say that he is under a necessity, or even obligation, to be baptized. He does not admit that he feels the "need" of baptism at John's hands felt by John toward Christ. The "us"[5] naturally refers to only John and Jesus, the two persons concerned in the matter.

It cannot be said that the purpose expressed by

[1] Cf. also the language in the "Preaching of Paul," in the *Tractatus de Rebaptismate*, 17 (Hartel, ii, p. 90), for another illustration.

[2] Plummer, "Matthew," p. 31.

[3] ἄφες ἄρτι. This particular juncture (ἄρτι), not νῦν.

[4] πρέπον ἐστίν, not δεῖ.

[5] ἡμῖν.

Jesus "to fulfil all righteousness"[1] covers the whole problem of the sinlessness of Christ and the baptism. It meets one aspect of the difficulty raised by John. The argument implied runs thus: John's baptism was from heaven in its origin and authority[2]; to accept John's baptism meant to welcome the reign of heaven proclaimed by it; therefore it was incumbent upon all good men to submit to it.[3] If Jesus did not submit to John's baptism, he at once placed himself in the attitude of the Pharisees and scribes who rejected the baptism of John.[4] There would then arise the anomalous situation of the Messiah, whom the Forerunner had proclaimed, standing apart from this Forerunner and apparently hostile to him. "It was impossible for such an one, on the ground of being the Messiah, or even on the ground of sinlessness, to treat John's baptism as a thing with which He had no concern. Love, not a sense of dignity or of moral faultlessness, must guide His actions. . . . Christ's baptism might create misunderstanding, just as His associating with publicans and sinners did. He was content to be misunderstood."[5] It was appropriate all around for Jesus to receive baptism at the hands of John. It not only avoided misunderstanding of one sort as the Messiah began his work. It gave the Messiah's sanction to the noble ministry of the Forerunner. It set the example for all men to follow the teaching of John and the example of Jesus. If Jesus had not

[1] πληρῶσαι πᾶσαν δικαιοσύνην. Note aorist (punctiliar) tense. Every righteous act.

[2] Matt. 21:25.

[3] Broadus on Matthew, p. 55.

[4] Luke 7:29.

[5] Bruce, "Matthew," p. 86.

himself submitted to baptism, a powerful argument against baptism by the disciples of Jesus would have existed. The later command by Jesus to baptize would have lacked the force of the Master's own example.

All this seems obvious enough. It is when we seek to find the full significance of the baptism of Jesus that trouble comes. Some of the ideas offered may be waved aside. The baptism did not consecrate Jesus as a priest. He was not a priest in the ceremonial sense at all. He was not connected with the priestly line and was a priest after the order of Melchizedek.[1] It was not a vicarious purification as the representative of a guilty people. It was not the Messianic consecration. The descent of the Holy Spirit was that. It was not the public introduction by John of Jesus to the multitude. Apparently the multitude did not witness the baptism. All these views may be put to one side.[2]

Edersheim is impatient with all such ideas. He holds that Jesus had no ulterior motive at all. It may be questioned if the matter is quite so simple as that. Kirtley[3] considers it to be the symbolical fulfilment of all righteousness. That is certainly not all that is meant, but it is possible that this idea may be latent in the act of Jesus. Weiss[4] urges that the symbolical character of the act must be kept in view.

[1] Cf. Broadus on Matthew, p. 55.

[2] Cf. Reynolds, "John the Baptist," pp. 316 ff.; Weiss, "Life of Christ," vol. I, pp. 322 f.; Farrar, "Life of Christ," vol. I, pp. 116 f.; Edersheim, "Life and Times," vol. I, pp. 279 ff.; Broadus, "Matthew," pp. 55 f.

[3] "Design of Baptism,"

[4] "Life of Christ," vol. I, pp. 322 f.

True, Jesus had no sins to confess nor to be symbolized by the act of immersion, but he entered upon a new phase of his life-work. In a fuller sense it is true that the baptism prefigured Christ's own death and resurrection as afterward explained by Paul.[1] In a sense, also, Jesus put himself on a par with other men. The solidarity of the race was illustrated by this act of Christ. It was, in truth, a vow of devotion to the Messianic kingdom on Christ's part, an oath of allegiance, as it is with all who are baptized. He came like any other man and submitted to John's baptism, though the act did not have the same symbolism for him that it did for others. It was, besides, his duty to follow the command of God, as already stated. This last is the only point made by Jesus with John, though these others just mentioned may have been involved more or less. Jesus was in no mood for controversy. He mentions the most obvious reason. It satisfies John and he baptizes him in the Jordan. This was, in truth, the climax of John's own work, but Jesus did not submit to baptism for that reason. The practical aspect of the matter for the Christian to-day is that of the example of Jesus. If he submitted to baptism, is the disciple above his Lord?

4. *The Sign from Heaven.*—After the baptism Jesus "went up straightway from the water."[2] Luke[3] adds that he was praying. It was with Jesus

[1] Rom. 6:2–6.

[2] Matt. 3:16. Out of the water, Mark (1:10) has it, ἐκ τοῦ ὕδατος. More graphic than Matthew.

[3] 3:21. Lange ("Life of Christ," vol. II, p. 25) says: "Jesus had immersed himself by the prayer of the heart in the abyss of Deity, even while He was being immersed in the stream."

no mere ceremonial rite. He had no sins of his own to be praying about, it is true, but he had the sin of the world on his heart. The Messianic consciousness of Jesus is a theme that has called forth much discussion. Jesus at twelve years of age revealed signs of his consciousness of a peculiar relation to the Father.[1] In the temptations which follow the baptism, as told in the Synoptic Gospels, Jesus is fully conscious of the mission which he has undertaken. It is not attributing premature conceptions to Christ to suppose that he himself saw a meaning in his baptism that was concealed from John and from us. In epitome, to him the baptism foreshadows the tragedy of the cross. "The extraordinary manifestations about to be related thus become God's answer to the prayer of Jesus, in which the sighs of His people and of mankind found utterance."[2]

It is a vision that Jesus has as he comes out of the water. The heavens "were opened"[3]; "rent asunder,"[4] according to Mark's more graphic phrase. Jesus will use the symbol of the rent heavens to Nathanael in his picture of the free intercourse between heaven and earth through the Son of man.[5] The vision was primarily for Christ,[6] but John the Baptist also saw it. "I have beheld the Spirit descending as a dove out of heaven, and it abode upon him."[7] John carried that vision with him as a permanent possession.[8] He can still see, as he later

[1] Luke 2 : 49.
[2] Godet, "Luke," p. 118.
[3] ἠνεῴχθησαν (Matthew and Luke).
[4] σχιζομένους.
[5] John 1 : 51.
[6] Swete, "Mark," p. 8.
[7] John 1 : 32.
[8] τεθέαμαι. Perfect tense (punctiliar plus linear).

described it, the Holy Spirit coming out of the opened heaven. This was the sign of the Messiah that had been promised the Baptist.[1] Whatever doubt had lingered in the mind of John was now completely swept away. He could ask no more. He had in deed and in truth baptized the Messiah. It was a high and holy moment with John, and the gospels are silent as to his emotions. Perhaps it was for this holy hour that Jesus had waited to be alone with John.[2] This was the real baptism, that of the Holy Spirit, which John had said the Messiah would bestow.[3] Now the Messiah himself had received in all fulness this baptism. "The contrast between this anointing of the Messiah, this coronation of the promised King, and the Herald's proclamation of the coming of the Kingdom is remarkable." [4] With John fire is the fitting symbol of the Spirit's baptism, or at least of one phase of the Messianic baptism. But the dove is the emblem of the descent of the Spirit upon Jesus. Both points of view are true. The fire searches and consumes; the dove is gentle as the Messiah is "meek and lowly in heart." [5] Though the heavens had been opened suddenly, the descent of the dove was gentle, hovering over Jesus and then resting upon him.[6]

We need not speculate on the question whether it was an actual dove or whether the vision just looked like a dove. Luke[7] alone has "in a bodily form."

[1] John 1 : 33. [2] Plummer, "Matthew," p. 32.
[3] Weiss, "Life of Christ," vol. I, p. 323.
[4] Plummer, "Matthew," p. 33.
[5] Matt. 11 : 29. Cf. Plummer, "Matthew," p. 33.
[6] Weiss, "Life of Christ," vol. I, p. 324.
[7] 3 : 24. σωματικῷ εἴδει.

That naturally suggests an actual dove. It is possible, of course, that there was nothing visible to the eye, that John and Jesus saw with the eye of the soul. The words, however, naturally suggest a visible manifestation. Symbolical visions had been granted to Moses and the other Old Testament prophets. The purpose of this vision was twofold. It gave the Baptist the promised proof of the Messiah, and it marked the official entrance of the Messiah on his mission, like the anointing of the King.[1] This was the heavenly anointing. Jesus was, of course, in closest fellowship with the Holy Spirit all of his earthly life from his very birth.[2] The Cerinthian Gnostics held that this coming of the Holy Spirit on Jesus was the descent of the Messiah on the man Jesus. What is true is that this is the official endowment of Christ for his mission. It is a great moment for Jesus and for John. John had said that the Messiah was nigh. Now he can say that the Coming One has come. The hour of destiny has struck. John has much to think of now, but more is to come.

5. *The Father's Approval.*—John heard the Voice out of the heavens. Indeed, in the correct text in Matt. 3 : 17, the Voice is addressed to John : "This is my beloved Son, in whom I am well pleased." This is the form in which the words are spoken on the Mount of Transfiguration, in all three Synoptics.[3] There the Voice speaks to Peter, James and John : "Hear ye him." In John 12 : 28 a third time the

[1] Plummer, "Luke," p. 99.
[2] Luke 1 : 35.
[3] Matt. 17 : 5; Mark 9 : 7; Luke 9 : 35.

Father speaks in audible voice, but here it is for the comfort of the Son, who has cried out for light. Each of the three times the Son has been praying, and the Father answers his prayers. The form of the words in Mark[1] and Luke[2] is an address to Jesus: "Thou art my beloved Son; in thee I am well pleased." The form in Mark and Luke represents the Voice after the baptism as spoken for the cheer of Jesus. That in Matthew is for the benefit of John. Both objects were accomplished, whatever was the original form of the language. It is, of course, abstractly possible that the words were repeated in the two ways.

The Voice is not designed to convince the Baptist of the Messiahship of Jesus. That function was performed by the descent of the Holy Spirit. The Messiahship is not mentioned, but the Sonship. Whether to John this meant the full deity of Jesus is more than doubtful.[3] We need not credit John with a developed system of theology like that of Paul. But the words will remain in his mind and heart and will help to clarify his ideas about the Messiah in coming days. Now that he has actually seen the Messiah, the vagueness will disappear, and John will have a positive note of identification to sound. He will soon call Jesus "the Son of God."

The Father has good pleasure in the Son. "Behold my servant, I uphold him; my chosen one, my soul delights in him. I have put my Spirit upon him."[4]

[1] 1:11. Note εὐδόκησα. Sort of timeless aorist indicative.

[2] 3:22. Cf. Ps. 2:7. In Luke a Western reading substitutes the words of the Psalm.

[3] Plummer, "Matthew," p. 34. Cf. Briggs, "Messiah of the Gospels," p. 77.

[4] Isa. 42:1. Cf. Matt. 12:18.

One can well understand how gracious words of approval from the Father were to Jesus. He may have had some natural shrinking from the formal entrance upon his world task. The soul of Jesus will cry out in Gethsemane, and even here the dim shadow of the Cross may have come, the long shadow of the morning. He had not yet turned to the people. How will they receive him and his message? But most important of all to Jesus at this juncture was the consciousness of the Father's presence and approval. Nothing else really mattered if that was true. "Thou lovedst me, before the foundation of the world." [1] How vivid a consciousness of his pre-existence[2] Christ had we do not know. The day will come when he will pray about "the glory which I had [3] with thee before the foundation of the world." Into that Holy of Holies we may not go. But here is fellowship between Father, Son and Spirit at the very beginning of the Messiah's work. The heaven is opened, and it was never closed for Jesus save for one brief moment when the Father's presence was withdrawn as he hung on the Cross.[4] But Jesus can go forth in the strength of this hour to meet the Tempter in the wilderness, to meet the world which he has come to save.

John leaves Jesus. Or did Jesus leave John? Did he cast another glance at the Messiah as he faded from view? Now that he is gone, is it all true? We cherish the smallest details of our great experiences. The world is never the same for the Baptist again. He

[1] John 17 : 24.
[2] Cf. John 17 : 5.
[3] εἶχον. Imperfect (durative).
[4] Matt. 27 : 46.

has had his day, a glorious day. True, the people still flock about him and clamor for baptism as before. But there is a wistful look in John's eye never there before. He is glad with a strange joy. Will the people believe him if he unfolds to them what has come into his life? That is now his task, to make plain to the people that the Messiah has already come. He knows full well what it will signify to himself and his ministry. It will mean the setting of his sun. The people will turn from the Forerunner to see the Messiah himself. There is need for mental readjustment on John's part. But John feels in his heart that all is well. He has seen the Lord's Anointed. He was in truth not worthy to stoop down and unloose his shoes. And yet he had baptized him. That was honor enough for any man. He had seen the Spirit like a dove rest upon the Messiah. He had heard the Father's word of identification. He had fulfilled his mission in life.

CHAPTER VI

TEMPTATION

"Behold the Lamb of God, which taketh away the sin of the world" (John 1 : 29).

1. *A Month of Reflection.*—Jesus went his way to the wilderness out of which John had come. It is no invention nor artificial parallelism to which we owe the wilderness preparation of Moses in Midian (forty years), of John the Baptist in Judea (several years), of Jesus in Judea (forty days) and of Paul in Arabia (about three years). A period of self-adjustment in each case was demanded and was wise. The baptism of Jesus marked an epoch in his life. "It was the true moment of His entrance on a new life. Past years had been buried in the waters of Jordan. He entered them as Jesus, the Son of Man; He rose from them, The Christ of God." [1] These words of Geike are rhetorical, and yet they contain a large element of truth. The baptism in water had linked Jesus in a formal way to John's campaign for righteousness. He had acknowledged to John that he was the Messiah. The baptism of the Spirit had set him apart for his Messianic work. The Voice of the Father had proclaimed him as the Son of God. He now had in audible words

[1] Geike, "Life and Words of Christ," vol. I, p. 414.

the Father's endorsement for his work. So Jesus went to the wilderness in the strength of the Holy Spirit to meet the Tempter. No one can conquer men for God who cannot first conquer the devil with the Spirit of God. The devil stands between the Redeemer and man.

Meanwhile the Baptist goes on with his work. Apparently as yet the crowds know nothing of the great event between John and Jesus. As there were, so it seems, no witnesses of their interview, John took some time for reflection before he made formal announcement that the Messiah had actually come. That was a fateful word, not to be recalled when once he had let it go. There is one thing that he must have felt at once: Now that he had seen the Messiah, how did his former ideas and statements correspond with the reality? He had tried to expound the Old Testament teaching concerning the Messiah. John probably made a careful examination of this teaching in the light of his great experience. At some points he probably found occasion for revision of his form of statement. A natural modification[1] of his words would come, in clarification of his vision, a widening of his horizon, a deeper grasp of the essential elements in the Messiah's work. We shall watch his words. The apocalyptic language is less prominent in the messages of John that are preserved for us after the baptism of Jesus. The note of wrath and judgment had been dominant in John's teaching about the Messiah before that event. Now the note of love and redemption

[1] Nourse in "Standard Bible Dictionary."

comes to the fore. It had not been absent before (cf. repentance, baptism of the Holy Spirit). Now it naturally is uppermost. John did not have to make a fundamental revision of his teaching about the Messiah. It is rather a fuller emphasis on the spiritual and redemptive side of his work. He may, indeed, have been puzzled by what he had just seen and heard. The truth was so much richer than he had imagined. But John was not a man to dodge issues or to hedge. With the new light in his possession he continues to preach and to grapple with his fresh problems. When he speaks on this phase of the subject again, he must have a clear word and a sure word. When we recall how it took the entire ministry of Jesus and the coming of the Holy Spirit at Pentecost to illumine the mind of Peter on the significance of Christ's person and work, we can have the more sympathy with the struggles of the Baptist at this period. The night was passed and the day had dawned, but he was not yet accustomed to the light, and more light was coming.

We owe our knowledge of the attitude of John to Jesus, during the period following Christ's baptism, to the Fourth Gospel. This Gospel assumes and implies the baptism of Jesus by John in various ways, and once expressly mentions it.[1] The frequent echoes of the words of John in the teaching of Jesus demand a connection of Jesus with John such as the synoptic account of the baptism reveals.[2] The attitude of cer-

[1] John 3 : 26.
[2] Keim, "Jesus of Nazara," vol. II, p. 273.

tain critics[1] toward the Fourth Gospel makes some men timid in the use of this book as an historical document. But I do not hesitate to avow my own conviction that John the Apostle is the author of the Fourth Gospel, and that he wrote out of fulness of personal knowledge, with the exalted spiritual interpretation of an old man who looked across the long years to the first days of the kingdom of heaven on earth. He has his own peculiar style and spirit, but the historical reality is present, and the essential elements of his conception of Christ occur in the Synoptic Gospels. The events given in John's Gospel for the most part supplement those narrated in the Synoptic Gospels. The description of the Baptist given in the Fourth Gospel not only demands the synoptic account, but it harmonizes with it, fills it out, interprets it, when allowed to have its natural meaning.[2]

2. *The Committee from Jerusalem.*—Farrar[3] is very precise as to the time of the embassy, fixing it "the day previous to our Lord's return from the wilderness." That is possible, of course, if Jesus came directly to Bethany,[4] where John was now baptizing. The location of this Bethany beyond Jordan, as already stated, is unknown. It was somewhere on the eastern side of the river, probably about half-way between the Dead Sea and the Sea of Galilee. We do not at all know that John had remained in the same place during the

[1] Cf., for instance, Bacon, "The Fourth Gospel in Research and Debate" (1910). *Per contra*, among recent defenders of the Johannine authorship, note Drummond, "An Inquiry into the Character and Authorship of the Fourth Gospel" (1904), and Sanday, "Criticism of the Fourth Gospel" (1905).

[2] Cf. Edersheim, "Life and Times," vol. I, p. 309.

[3] "Life of Christ," vol. I, p. 143.

[4] John 1 : 28.

forty days while Jesus was in the wilderness. It is more than probable that John had kept moving up the river, having crossed over to the eastern side.

"*Who art thou?*"—The news of John's work by the Jordan had already reached Jerusalem, as we know from the Synoptic Gospels.[1] The Pharisees and Sadducees had themselves come in large numbers to make a personal investigation of the Baptist and his work.[2] They had received a decided rebuff, but apparently did not make a hostile report concerning John on their return to Jerusalem. These leaders were manifestly powerfully impressed by the hold of John on the masses, many of whom had actually come to wonder[3] if John himself were not the Messiah of whom he spoke so graphically. They probably reported this perplexity of the multitude to Jerusalem. It must be borne in mind that, so far as we know, the scene between John and Jesus at the Jordan was still a secret between these two. Neither the public nor the rulers in Jerusalem were aware of the sudden new turn in the whole situation.

It is not certain that the formal committee sent back to John was directly from the Sanhedrin. Edersheim[4] is quite positive that this was not the case, since such a question as the status of John the Baptist could hardly come before the Sanhedrin in an official capacity. That is probably true, but all the same the members of the Sanhedrin were the recognized leaders of Jewish thought and life in Jerusalem,

[1] Matt. 3 : 5; Mark 1 : 5. [2] Matt. 3 : 7. [3] Luke 3 : 15.
[4] "Life and Times," vol. I, p. 309.

and it is quite probable that as individuals these members of the Sanhedrin sent the committee to John. We do not know that the committee was sent from an evil purpose.[1] The motives may, in fact, have been varied, though it is difficult, in view of all that we know, to consider the deputation as wholly friendly.[2] The Pharisees[3] were the prime movers in the matter of sending this embassy to John, though they shrewdly managed to see to it that only Sadducees were on the committee. "Priests and Levites"[4] alone were sent, and they were Sadducees. The point was probably made that "the colleagues of John the Priest"[5] should be chosen for this purpose rather than the rabbis, since the priests and Levites, if going alone without the Pharisees, might avoid another denunciation from John, and might, in general, be more acceptable to him. The general term "the Jews," in John 1 : 19, is introductory, and is explained by "the Pharisees" in 1 : 28. The Pharisees were, of course, the more numerous party, and often had their way against their powerful rivals in the councils of the Sanhedrin.[6]

The event justified this piece of worldly wisdom on the part of the Pharisees. They were received with courtesy and with frankness.[7] They go directly at

[1] Westcott, *in loco*.

[2] Smith, "In the Days of His Flesh," p. 42, holds that the committee was sent by the Sanhedrin officially. So Godet, *in loco*.

[3] John 1 : 25. Marcus Dods, *in loco*, seriously supposes that the deputation itself was strong in Pharisees.

[4] John 1 : 19.

[5] Edersheim, "Life and Times," vol. I, p. 310.

[6] Josephus, "Ant.," xviii, 1, 4.

[7] Smith, "In the Days of His Flesh," p. 43.

the point of their mission with the rather blunt query:[1] "Who art thou?" "As for thyself—thou that excitest the people and stirrest vain hopes [Luke 3 : 15] —who art thou?"[2] John had met this temptation once before, when it came to him from the people like sweet murmur of applause to the orator. But it came in a new form, in a most flattering form if he chose to regard it so. Here was a formal committee composed of Sadducees and sent by Pharisees—the very men whom he had formerly denounced, who now seemed to imply that they were half disposed to agree with the popular notion that he was the Messiah. It was a wonderful tribute to John's power and marked the very acme of his fame. "It may be regarded as being, in some sense, a temptation of John corresponding to the (simultaneous) temptation of Christ."[3] With many men this supreme flattery would have turned their heads. But John never faltered for a moment in his loyalty to Jesus. The devil by flattery and insinuation had sought to dazzle Jesus with the vision of "the kingdoms of the world and the glory of them."[4] Now this temptation to glory and power not rightly John's had come to him through the medium of the official ecclesiastics, but ultimately from the devil also. If a breach could be made between John and Jesus, it would forebode evil for the kingdom of God. Two rival Messiahs would neutralize each other. It was a temptation for John to allow himself to be considered to be more than he really

[1] John 1 : 20. Σὺ τίς εἶ; The order in the Greek is interesting.
[2] Westcott, *in loco*. [3] *Ibid.* [4] Matt. 4 : 8.

was, and in a matter that vitally affected the very essence of his mission. If John had proven false here, he would have been false everywhere. It was a severe test of his manhood, but he was ready to meet it.

"And he confessed, and denied not; and he confessed, I am not the Christ."[1] No formal charge had been made by the committee. It was only a query, but it stung John to the quick that he could be thought capable of claiming to be the Messiah himself, especially after his recent interview with Jesus. The repetition in the gospel here serves "to bring out the earnestness, almost horror, with which John disclaimed the ascription to him of such an honor."[2] John puts it positively and negatively. He eagerly confessed, nor did he for a moment yield to the temptation offered him. His confession, in short, was frank and categorical.[3] "I am not the Messiah."[4] John evidently felt that he was in the presence of men who were willing to give him a dignity to which he was not entitled. "We can feel what the trial was to take the lower place in the crisis of highest popularity."[5] But he took it instantly and with vehemence. John was not a fanatic[6] in any sense. It is possible that his clear-cut denial brought a sense of relief to the Sadducees. They would not then have to report such a claim to the Pharisees with all the accompanying embarrassment. They had once cowered before the boldness of this mighty preacher. "His confession had divested

[1] John 1 : 20. [2] Marcus Dods on John, *in loco.*
[3] Godet on John, *in loco.* Cf. Josephus, "Ant.," vi, 7, 4.
[4] ἐγὼ οὐκ εἰμὶ ὁ χριστός. [5] Westcott, *in loco.*
[6] Smith, "In the Days of His Flesh," p. 43.

him of his terrors, and they might now deal with him as they listed." [1] They press this advantage with a question somewhat more imperious in tone: "What then? [2] Art thou Elijah?" What function do you fulfil if not the Messiah? The committee probably knew that John had claimed to be the Forerunner of the Messiah. The Jews expected Elijah to come in person, and this is the question that the committee put to John. They do not ask his interpretation of Mal. 4:5 ("Behold, I will send you Elijah the prophet before the coming of the great and dreadful day of the Lord"). The question later put to Christ[3] about the coming of Elijah shows that John could not have answered "yes" without being grossly misunderstood. The promise[4] of Gabriel had only been that he would come "in the spirit and power of Elijah." John is now in no mood to parley with these men, since he has probably noticed their altered tone. So he rather abruptly says: "I am not." [5] He will not split hairs over the rabbinical refinements. They can reconcile what he now says with his claim about being the Forerunner at their leisure. "If people need to question a great spiritual personality, replies in their own language will often mislead them." [6] The committee take his reply to be a denial that he is Elijah in any sense. So they push matters further while they have the opportunity. "Art thou the prophet?" Moses had said: "The Lord thy God will raise up

[1] *Ibid.*
[2] τί οὖν; John 1:21. Here alone in John, but common with Paul. Cf. Westcott.
[3] Matt. 17:10–13.
[4] Luke 1:17.
[5] οὐκ εἰμί.
[6] Marcus Dods, *in loco.*

unto thee a prophet from the midst of thee, like unto me." [1] Peter[2] and Stephen[3] take this prophecy to refer to the Messiah. But that was not the understanding of this committee. The Jews had a vague expectation of some prophet who would usher in the Messianic age, who was different from Elijah.[4] Jeremiah was also looked for, while some expected "one of the prophets." [5] The reply of John is bluntly monosyllabic, "No." [6] His answer was shorter each time.

But the committee will take nothing for granted, now that the question is raised. They repeat their original query, "Who art thou?" [7] Here the point is the office rather than the person of John that the question turns upon.[8] They feel called upon to apologize for their insistence and repetition. The excuse is "that we may give an answer to them that sent us." They then sharply ask: "What sayest thou of thyself?" So far John had dealt in negatives about himself. The committee call upon him to make a positive pronouncement about himself. There is a note of triumph and almost of condescension in this query, not to say a tone of pity. What was left for him to claim now that he has made so many renunciations? But they little understand John. He is greatest when he is most humble. His reply puzzled them and passed over their heads: "I am the Voice of one crying in the wilderness, Make straight the way of the

[1] Deut. 18 : 15. [2] Acts 3 : 22. [3] Acts 7 : 37.
[4] Cf. I Mac. 14 : 41; John 6 : 14; 7 : 40.
[5] Matt. 16 : 14. [6] οὔ. [7] τίς εἶ; John 1 : 22.
[8] Westcott, *in loco*.

Lord, as said Isaiah the prophet."[1] It is possible,[2] though not certain, that John had used this language of himself at the beginning of his ministry. But it adequately describes his true mission and relation to the Messiah. In reality John has thus in scriptural language claimed[3] to be the Forerunner of the Messiah which they had thought him to deny concerning Elijah. John does not here mention the element of judgment brought out before. For John the Messiah had already come, and he did not now need the apocalyptic imagery.[4] But the language of the Baptist was too vague to be understood by the committee.

> "Thou art to me
> No bird, but an invisible thing,
> A voice, a mystery."

The Evangelist pauses to explain that the committee had been sent by the Pharisees. Perhaps they wish that the Pharisees were now here to pursue this inquiry further. Indeed, this explanatory remark points forward rather than backward.

"*Why then baptizest thou?*"—The committee rallied. "They asked him, and said unto him." The question is probably on behalf of the Pharisees, who were so much concerned about ceremonial ablutions.[5] The Sadducees were more interested in John's claims concerning his person and office. The Pharisees had probably already had secret resentments against John's new rite, which they probably regarded as an inno-

[1] John 1 : 23 f.; Isa. 40 : 3.
[2] Matt. 3 : 3.
[3] Marcus Dodds, *in loco*.
[4] Westcott, *in loco*.
[5] Godet, *in loco*.

vation that bordered on the sacrilegious, since it did not have their sanction nor authorization.[1] "Why then baptizest thou?"[2] The condition which follows enumerates in order John's three denials and assumes that those points are now out of the way.[3] The "then" is significant. If John had admitted his identity with either the Messiah, Elijah or the prophet, there would have been no surprise expressed at his introduction of his new rite. As it was, by his own admission, did not the Pharisees have a ground of complaint against him? If John was just a priest, or even a rabbi, of unusual and undoubted gifts and popularity, there was no occasion nor authority for his challenge of the life of the people and the institution of a symbolic rite which called a nation to repentance at the Jordan. "The strictest guardians conceded, indeed, to the Messiah, or to one of his forerunners, the right of making innovations in the matter of observances."[4] If the committee expected to embarrass John with a quandary, they were much mistaken. He has no idea of making an apology for his baptism. That he admits as a well-known fact. "I baptize in water."[5] It is so generally understood that John has no further word on that subject. He does not seize the opportunity to make an exposition of the difference between his baptism and the ceremonial ablutions of the Pharisees. That would have been in the spirit and to the taste of the Pharisees. All men knew that John's

[1] *Ibid.*

[2] τί οὖν βαπτίζεις;

[3] εἰ plus indicative is a condition of the first class determined as fulfilled. Cf. Robertson, "Short Grammar of the Greek New Testament," pp. 161 f.

[4] Godet, *in loco.*

[5] ἐγὼ βαπτίζω ἐν ὕδατι.

baptism was a "repentance-baptism," but John does not say so here. There is something to be said concerning the reason why he as the Forerunner introduced baptism because of its relation to the manifestation[1] of the Messiah, but he will not make that point to these men at this juncture by way of apology. There is a greater and a more needed word to say. He will speak that.

"*In the midst of you standeth one whom ye know not.*"[2]—There is indeed an implied thought in the transition to the effect that, if they really understood the introductory nature of his baptism and its relation to the work of the Messiah, they would make no cavil. But that is all by the way. In reality, John now turns the tables on this committee who had turned prosecutor, so to speak, of John and his baptism. John now virtually says that but for their ignorance they would not have asked him the questions already asked. They would not have challenged John and his baptism if they knew what John knew. John had seen the Messiah, but he had not yet made proclamation of that fact. He feels that he can no longer delay this great announcement. But it is to a now hostile audience that John has to speak. However, his language is cautious and figurative. They had wished to know about the Messiah. He has already come, and they, the ecclesiastical leaders, do not know him. "He came unto his own and they that were his own received him not."[3] None are so blind as those who

[1] John 1 : 32.
[2] μέσος ὑμῶν στήκει ὃν ὑμεῖς οὐκ οἴδατε.
[3] John 1 : 11.

will not see. To be sure, as yet the Messiah had been manifested only to the Baptist, but his words are a parable and a prophecy of the attitude of the ecclesiastics toward Jesus when he does make himself known to them. They will have none of him then as they wish none of John now. The Unseen Christ has continued to walk through the ages in the midst of men who do not see him when he comes into the midst of them. This is his indictment of the committee. But he has a further word that bears upon John's relation to the Messiah, a matter also asked about by the committee. "He that cometh after me the latchet of whose shoes I am not worthy to unloose." This was language already used [1] by John in the presence of the multitudes, and correctly describes John's own sense of inferiority to the Messiah. "Every service which a servant will perform for his master, a disciple will do for his rabbi, except loosing his sandal thong." [2] Thus John has in his own way told the committee all that they had asked and more. They had not understood his replies, and on the whole probably felt more mystified than ever. The moment that they thought they understood him he said something else that left them at sea. We are not told the effect of all this upon the committee. They are at last silent, whatever their thoughts. Probably deeper questionings had come to them than they had ever had before. And what can they say to the Pharisees? [3]

[1] Luke 3 : 16. Cf. Mark 1 : 7.

[2] Talmud. Quoted by Marcus Dods on John, p. 694.

[3] Henderson ("Palestine," p. 154) thinks that "Bethany equals Batanea (Bashan). So Conder. Then Beth-abarah might thus be the place where John was. But even so, Bethany is the correct text in John 1 : 28.

3. *The Second Glimpse of the Messiah.*—John and Jesus have both come out triumphant from their temptations, and they meet again. On the next day[1] after the interview with the committee from Jerusalem, Jesus comes to John, probably directly from his temptation. It is the first time that the Fourth Gospel has taken a definite notice of time. The author seems conscious that he is dealing with an epoch in history, and carefully singles out these days as the days of the Passion Week are described. In all probability John the Evangelist was present during these important days of crisis, and he has a vivid recollection through all the years of the significant details. Apparently the embassy from Jerusalem had departed without further inquiry concerning the One who was standing in the midst of them. If they had waited a day, they would have seen the Messiah himself, and have heard John's witness to him. They may have been really indifferent to John's figurative description of the Messiah or have affected unconcern.[2] But the inquiry from Jerusalem doubtless created fresh interest[3] among John's disciples, and there was probably a buzz of suppressed excitement as a result of the dialogue.

(a) *John's Identification of the Messiah.*—If the Messiah had already come, where was he? He might appear any day by the side of John. It was only fitting that the Messiah should receive public identification and endorsement from his Herald and Fore-

[1] John 1 : 29.

[2] Godet, "John," p. 310.

[3] Westcott, *in loco.*

runner.[1] From every point of view it was natural for Jesus to come to John. The private recognition already received would not suffice for the people. We may not attribute to Jesus an artificial plan of procedure in his work as Messiah, but it was surely wise for Jesus to give John the opportunity of doing as he wished about the matter of a public identification. In the circle of John's disciples Jesus would be more likely to find a sympathetic reception. Once more John and Jesus are face to face.[2] We are not told that Jesus spoke aught to John. But he looked at John. "There was something unearthly in His look, and John gazed at him." [3] The marks of struggle and of victory were perhaps still on the face of Jesus as he confronted John. Was John still satisfied that he was the Messiah? I pass by for the moment John's great word about the Lamb of God. That is in the nature of theological interpretation, and will be discussed presently in its logical order. "This is he," said John, "of whom I spoke." [4] That is identification. John looks on Jesus[5] with eager gaze and identifies him in his presence to the crowd of bystanders. Jesus hears the words and they are gracious unto his ears. John adds in the presence of Jesus also that he is inferior to the Messiah. He does not use the word Messiah, whether because of the political meaning connected with that term in the minds of the Jews we do not know. On the day before John had

[1] Westcott, *in loco*. [2] πρὸς αὐτόν.
[3] Smith, "Days of His Flesh," p. 44.
[4] John 1:30. ὑπὲρ οὗ, in behalf of whom, vindicating his glorious office, Westcott. [5] βλέπει τὸν Ἰησοῦν.

said to the committee that this one of whom he spoke came "after" [1] him. He now repeats that statement. Jesus was after him in order of time, for John was his messenger (forerunner); but he was before him in dignity, office and worth.[2] It is not necessary to think that John meant the pre-existence of Jesus, though that was, of course, true also. Marcus Dods (*in loco*) considers it more than probable that John did have in mind the pre-existence of the Messiah, "a thought which may have been derived from the apocalyptic books." But Jesus, as soon as he is manifested, steps in front of John because of his essential priority.[3] The second "before me" really implies absolute priority and is a remarkable expression.[4] It is a metaphorical line that John has in mind, but a very real superiority is meant by John.

John seems to feel that he must explain why he had not pointed out the Messiah before. The explanation is very simple. He had not known him as the Messiah.[5] John may have known of Jesus through Zacharias and Elizabeth. But there is no evidence that he had been thrown with him. What John here means is that till he met Jesus at his baptism, he did not know that he was the Messiah, and may not have had any personal relations or acquaintanceship with him. He had foretold the Messiah in general terms. He had stated that he was near at hand.[6] On yester-

[1] John 1: 26. *ὀπίσω μου*. John is ahead in time.
[2] Cf. John 1: 15. Here also we have *ἔμπροσθέν μου* and *πρῶτός μου*.
[3] Westcott on John 1: 15.
[4] *πρῶτός μου* (ablative of comparison with superlative). Cf. Westcott.
[5] *οὐκ ᾔδειν αὐτόν*. John 1: 31.
[6] Matt. 3: 10.

day he had said that he had come.[1] He does not feel called upon to explain why he had remained silent for a month after he had met and baptized Jesus. In reality no explanation was needed, as the time had not been long. He may have waited for the return of Jesus. But he does say[2] that the public aspect of his work of baptizing had to do with the manifestation of the Messiah to Israel. He will presently explain that he had seen the proof of the Messiahship of Jesus at his baptism. It was, in truth, through John's work as the baptizer that he had discovered the Messiah whom he now proclaimed and pointed out. It was the divine ordaining that had made it so. His prophetic presentiment[3] at the first sight of Jesus was confirmed by the sign of the Messiah. This was another great hour[4] in John's life when he was able to point to Jesus as the Messiah. On yesterday he had said: "He is there." To-day he says: "There he is." [5] He had done his duty as he met it from day to day in the unfolding providence of God. His own ministry, like that of Jesus,[6] had revealed thoughts out of many hearts. The deepening of the sense of sin on the part of the people made it easier for them to grasp the truth about Christ's atoning and redeeming work, while the confessions of the masses were rounded out by the self-surrender of Jesus.[7] But John seems to be deeply conscious of the fact that he had not fully portrayed the riches of the Messiah. The half had not been told. The reality had gone

[1] John 1 : 26. [2] John 1 : 31 f. [3] Meyer on John, *in loco.*
[4] Smith, "Days of His Flesh," p. 44.
[5] Godet, *in loco.* [6] Luke 2 : 35. [7] Westcott, *in loco.*

far beyond what he had foreseen. "The gift which John possessed, of seeing over and beyond his own work, is one of the most remarkable, and can only be found where there exist a rare self-knowledge and a rare humility."[1] John was able to understand his own relation to the world, a thing that few men can do. He had a sensitive soul that responded to the best and highest in men. He understood Jesus, a thing that few men of Christ's time did. It was glory enough[2] to have baptized Jesus. Then he had been permitted to point him out.

(b) *John's Interpretation of Jesus.*—I have reversed the order of John's words on purpose. In order of time his interpretation comes first, and then his identification. But it was all over in a moment. It suits my purpose better here to follow the identification by the interpretation. But what John did was dramatic enough. "When he came suddenly again into the circle where the Baptist was standing, the first look at him sent through the Forerunner's soul a revealing shock; whereupon, with out-stretched finger pointed at him, he cried: 'Behold the Lamb of God, that taketh away the sin of the world!'"[3] The words are exclamatory[4] and are not addressed to Jesus. Critics like Strauss and Holtzmann reject these words as those of the Baptist, on the ground that this sacrificial view of the death of Jesus could not have been held till after Jesus had died, and that John, or the child of his age, could not have grasped such a theological

[1] Stalker, "The Two St. Johns," p. 227.
[2] John 1:32.
[3] Stalker, "The Two St. Johns," p. 229.
[4] ἴδε ὁ ἀμνὸς τοῦ θεοῦ.

conception, since John's eye "never ranged beyond a Jewish horizon." [1] It is an easy way to settle difficulties by "could" and "could not." The Old Testament was open to John. He had spoken the day before of Isaiah.[2] Since the baptism of Jesus, John would naturally make a fresh investigation of the Old Testament passages concerning the Messiah. The fifty-third chapter of Isaiah was open to him. The older rabbis, "before the polemic against the Christians had driven the Jewish interpreters to another explanation," [3] did not hesitate to apply this passage to the Messiah. "But he was wounded for our transgressions, he was bruised for our iniquities; the chastisement of our peace was upon him; and with his stripes we are healed. . . . As a lamb that is led to the slaughter, and as a sheep that before its shearers is dumb, so he opened not his mouth . . . because he poured out his soul unto death, and was numbered with the trangressors: yet he bare the sin of many, and made intercession for the transgressors." [4] The mention of Isaiah and John's announcement on the day before that the Messiah had at last come may well have started talk between John and his disciples about the prerogatives and general scope of the Messiah.[5] It is possible that John and Jesus may have had converse about the real nature of his work. before they parted at the baptism and after the vision and the Voice.[6] But it is enough that one with John's

[1] Marcus Dods, *in loco.*
[2] John 1 : 24.
[3] Godet, *in loco.*
[4] Isa. 53 : 5, 7, 12.
[5] Westcott, *in loco.*
[6] Marcus Dods. *in loco.*

keen and penetrating insight had faced long and earnestly the problem of the Messiah.

Some of the critics are hard to satisfy about John. They find fault with him because he was narrow and Jewish in his conceptions of a Messiah who would bring only judgment and wrath. Then, when passages like this are met which do reveal a knowledge of the spiritual and redemptive work of the Messiah, they are promptly rejected just because they do not give the deeper insight into the Messiah's mission. Simeon is credited with prophetic insight into the sufferings of Jesus.[1] If he had that gift, why not John the Forerunner? Who more than he was likely to gain real knowledge of the true nature of the Messiah's work? The fact that scales covered the eyes of the disciples[2] on this very point proves nothing for certain concerning John, one of the rare spiritual souls of the ages. John himself will later have a time of gloom, but that fact does not disprove his present grasp of the truth. His specific mission was to "bear witness of the light."[3] Jesus will say to the Jerusalem authorities: "Ye have sent unto John, and he hath borne witness unto the truth."[4] John had knowledge of the truth that is in Christ not possessed by the men of his day. Else he had no power to rise above his time and teach it. It is puerile to try to put every genius that arises back into the leading-strings of his time. John shook off the dust of rabbinism and blazed as a bright and shining lamp.

It is possible that by the term "Lamb of God"

[1] Luke 2: 25 ff. [2] Matt. 16: 21 ff. [3] John 1: 8. [4] John 5: 33.

John (cf. Isaiah) recognized the meekness and gentleness of the Messiah and the peril of Jesus as he came into inevitable conflict with the generation of vipers.[1] But certainly this was not all. John was of a priestly family, and it was natural for him to think of the lamb as sacrifice, in particular, the paschal lamb. We do not know how clearly the language of John was apprehended by the people who heard it.[2] But a man's knowledge of his words is not always to be determined by the ignorance of his audience. In Isa. 53 the idea of patient endurance and vicarious sacrifice both occur. Both may have been in the mind of John on this occasion. But certainly he had that of sacrifice, for he says, "which taketh away the sin of the world."[3] It is sin (singular, not plural), "regarded in its unity as the common corruption of humanity,"[4] that John has in mind. It is the prophetic, not the legal, conception of Christ's work, and John vividly describes it as present.[5] It is the world-conception of Christ's work also. John's horizon is here that of the whole world in sin that needed a savior. The Jewish Messiah is the world's Redeemer. The boldness and originality of this interpretation of Jesus argue for the genuineness of this testimony. John the Apostle heard John the Baptist, whose disciple he then was, say these wonderful words. They made such a deep mark upon his mind that he never forgot them. John the Baptist has grown mightily in these few weeks in his appre-

[1] Stalker, "The Two St. Johns," p. 229.
[2] Godet, *in loco.*
[3] ὁ αἴρων τὴν ἁμαρτίαν τοῦ κόσμου.
[4] Westcott, *in loco.*
[5] Meyer, *in loco.*

hension of the Messiah. He has had great experiences. His mind was keenly alert to seize every new item about the Messiah. That was John's passion, the Messiah. He has come out upon the high plane of the world vision of the Messiah's mission. But there is a higher plane yet and he will come to that.

(c) *John's New Testimony: "This is the Son of God."*—He speaks from experience. "I have beheld the Spirit descending as a dove out of heaven; and it abode upon him." [1] He can never get away from that experience. It was the fulfilment of the sign that God, who sent him to baptize, had given him. "The same is he that baptizeth in the Holy Spirit." [2] John had, as they recalled, spoken of this as the difference[3] between the Messiah and himself. He cannot doubt that day in the river when the heavens opened and the Spirit as a dove came and rested upon Jesus. John here assumes the baptism of Jesus as well known by his disciples. Probably, since his mention on yesterday of the presence of the Messiah, he had told them the details of that great event.[4] He sees no reason for rehearsing the story here, but assumes it as known, and appeals to the coming of the Holy Spirit at that time as proof of the Messiahship of Jesus. John has a holy confidence that is past all speculation and theorizing. "And I have seen," [5] he says.

[1] John 1 : 32. τεθέαμαι. He still sees that picture (perfect tense).
[2] John 1 : 33. [3] Matt. 3 : 11.
[4] Meyer, *in loco*. Cf. Edersheim, "Life and Times," vol. I, p. 337. Keim has shown that John's preaching was steeped in the language of Isaiah. Edersheim laments that Keim did not understand Jesus as well as he did John.
[5] κἀγὼ ἑώρακα. John 1 : 34. The vision is with him yet.

He is glad to repeat that point for emphasis. But that is not all: "and have borne witness that this is the Son of God."[1] We have no record of a previous testimony from John to this effect. It was true by implication, to be sure, from what John had already said about Jesus as the Lamb of God. It is but a step further. God's Lamb is God's Son. It is, perhaps, in this climacteric[2] sense of the perfect tense that he uses the word, "I have borne witness." He has come to the place where he can say it and stand by it: This man Jesus here before you is the Son of God. The Old Testament[3] called the Messiah the Son of God. The term in the Old Testament does not always have its highest meaning. It is used even of kings.[4] In one sense all men are sons of God. But John means only the highest content of the phrase.[5] It is idle to cavil that this is a height to which even John could not climb. John had heard the Father's voice at the baptism expressly call Jesus "my beloved Son."[6] He evidently has that fact in mind. He had pondered deeply on the significance of that voice. Now he interprets that message to the people without express mention of the miracle as he had done concerning the descent of the Holy Spirit. Thus John has shown in his bold stand vivid recollection of the two great miracles at the baptism of Jesus. John has accomplished his work. He has predicted, baptized, borne witness to the Messiah. He has pointed out Jesus as the Messiah to the men of his

[1] *και μεμαρτύρηκα ὅτι οὗτός ἐστιν ο υἱὸς τοῦ θεοῦ.*

[2] Linear plus punctiliar action in the perfect.

[3] Cf. Ps. 2:7, 12; Dan. 3:25.

[4] Cf. Ps. 82:6.

[5] Note the two articles *ὁ υἱὸς τοῦ θεοῦ.*

[6] Matt. 3:17.

generation. His work is over. He stands upon the top of the mountain. To go on he must go down the other side. He will go on, go with a glad heart. The Messiah has come and it has been John's glory to have seen his coming from afar, to have gone forth to greet him, to welcome him to his great work, to make his path somewhat easier. He has made ready the way for the King. Now the King has come. There is naught for him to do but to step aside and let the King have the highway. He will not sulk. He will help on the work as he may. But no more will he call men to himself. He will tell men to go to Jesus. Will they go? Are they ready now that the Messiah has actually appeared? That question time alone can answer. Will John live long enough to see the glory of the Messianic days?

4. *The Last Sight of Jesus.*—There is an element of pathos in the fact that John, whose life centred in that of the Messiah, saw Jesus only three times. But they were rich and gracious days and his soul fed on the memory of them.

(a) *John Standing and Looking at Jesus.*—The day before had been a great day for all. The hearts of many were now full of "holy impressions, great thoughts, and unutterable expectation."[1] On this, the following day, there was the atmosphere of silent waiting. John stood[2] with "two of his disciples," probably in conversation about the great events of these days. They were the days long looked for by

[1] Godet, *in loco.*
[2] ἱστήκει. John 1:35. Past perfect, but used as imperfect.

the Jewish people. Prophets had sought out and searched out[1] this time, but they could not find the day. At last it had come. One of these disciples of the Baptist was Andrew, as we are told.[2] The other was almost certainly John the Apostle and the writer of this narrative. John the Baptist soon catches sight of Jesus again and is filled with rapture at the sight. "He looked upon Jesus as he walked."[3] It is a beautiful spectacle to us, that of John entranced with the vision of Jesus. But it was more beautiful to John than we can imagine. His heart went out into that look. He feasted his soul upon Jesus, who was to him the one altogether lovely. The word for "looking" in the Greek means a penetrating glance.[4] It is the look of the mystic, for John was a true mystic. Jesus is not this time coming toward John. We do not know that Jesus saw John on this occasion. But John sees Jesus, and that is enough for him. He may not know that this will be his last glimpse of the Messiah. But he will drink in the glory of this vision.

(b) *John Repeats His Interpretation.*—He merely says this time: "Behold the Lamb of God."[5] It is not that John has changed his mind since yesterday about the redemptive work of the Messiah. But it is simply not necessary to give the whole description, since these frequent words will call up the testimony already given.[6] John stands by his interpretation of Jesus as the Lamb of God, with all that the term justly signifies. Perhaps his remark the day before had

[1] ἐξεζήτησαν· καὶ ἐξεραύνησαν. 1 Peter 1 : 10. [2] John 1 : 40.
[3] John 1 : 36. ἐμβλέψας τῷ Ἰησοῦ περιπατοῦντι.
[4] Westcott, *in loco.* [5] John 1 : 36. [6] Westcott, *in loco.*

provoked discussion. It is to the credit of the Baptist that he was the first man to rise to the height of calling Jesus the Son of God. He had penetrated the mystical nature of the Messiah that far. "He was dazzled with the mystery of this new life."[1] It was not the Oriental pantheism that John had in mind. He would not have applied these words to himself. "In no loose or indefinite sense did he persist in the conviction"[2] that Jesus was the Lamb of God, the Son of God. This second witness of John is crisp and pointed. Apparently it did not attract the attention of Jesus. It has been suggested that Jesus wished to avoid the appearance of a private understanding with the Baptist.[3] But John has now twice publicly pointed out Jesus as the Messiah whose coming he had proclaimed. That is all that he can do. Jesus will go his way and John will go his. Many a preacher has had the joy of discovering a young man who can really preach. But John has laid his hand upon the Hope of Israel.

(c) *The First Fruits of John's Testimony.*—Apparently Jesus had been walking alone. As yet he had no following. No one but John had avowed faith in Jesus as the Messiah. Jesus had come from the fierce conflict with the Tempter into the warm, sympathetic atmosphere of the Baptist's presence. On yesterday the heart of Jesus had been made glad by strong, clear witness of John. But no one had come out in open allegiance to Jesus. When would a be-

[1] Reynolds, "John the Baptist," p. 360.
[2] *Ibid.*, p. 362.
[3] Meyer, *in loco*.

ginning be made and where? Who will be the first to own Jesus as the Messiah?

The two disciples of John had listened with eager attention to the renewed testimony of their master to Jesus. There is power in repetition. John did not say that they should leave him to follow Jesus, but the repetition of his witness might bear that interpretation. The earnest look of John also added emphasis to his words. They recalled what John had said about his own inferiority to the Messiah, "the latchet of whose shoes he was not worthy to stoop down and unloose." They had loved John and his teaching. But he himself had brought them up to this point and now practically suggested that they go to the New Teacher, who could teach them what John could not. They were to pass up to a higher school, to become the first pupils in that school of Christ which has been growing in numbers and power ever since. The moment of decision has come. They look at John again and they left him and "followed Jesus."[1] They made their choice once for all. "The circumstance has a significance for all time. Christ's first disciples were made by the practical interpretation of a phrase which might have been disregarded."[2] They were not driven from John, but were drawn to Jesus. It was the positive attraction of this magnet of the ages who was "set for the falling and the rising up of many in Israel."[3]

It was as it should be. The first disciples of Jesus

[1] ἠκολούθησαν τῷ Ἰησοῦ. John 1:37. The aorist (punctiliar) tense marks the crisis.

[2] Westcott, *in loco*.

[3] Luke 2:34.

came from the circle of John's followers. That of itself was a comfort to the Baptist. He had not labored in vain. He had come to make ready the way of the Messiah. The soil was ready in places, at any rate. The seed sown had now sprung up and had borne some fruit. There were doubtless many more who would follow the example of these two. "One soweth and another reapeth,"[1] Jesus will himself joyfully say one day when he has seen a Samaritan woman saved. It was a proverb, and it was true of John and Jesus. It was with tender thoughts and a moved heart that John watched Andrew and John, who was to become the Beloved Disciple of Jesus, walk away from him. The last sight that John had of Jesus was in the nature of the triumph of Jesus. But there was no sting of regret in John. He had a holy satisfaction in seeing the two men leave him for what was better. They had only taken him at his word. John will go on preparing more soil for Jesus, sowing more seed for the kingdom. John has done his work well at Bethany, beyond Jordan. Some two or three years afterward Jesus will be here again. The people will recall John's witness and say: "All things whatsoever John spake of this man were true."[2]

"Jesus turned"[3] rather suddenly, for he had heard their steps. Evidently Jesus had been walking past or away from the Baptist. He "beheld these following"[4] him. He probably stops and says somewhat abruptly, "What seek ye?" Jesus assumes that they

[1] John 4: 37. [2] John 10: 40–42.
[3] στραφείς. John 1: 38. Second aorist passive participle.
[4] θεασάμενος αὐτοὺς ἀκολουθοῦντας.

wish to see him. The point is, Why do you wish to see me? In reply they say that they wish to go to his present abode in Bethany and have an opportunity for private converse.[1] The matter is too grave for brief conversation by the way. They call Jesus "Rabbi" or "Master" (Teacher),[2] as was customary with teachers. The title does not mean that they have already become disciples of Jesus, but that they are willing to talk with him about the matter of his Messiahship. They are willing to learn from him. Jesus is gracious to them. "Come and ye shall see."[3] The comment of the Evangelist is laconic in its pith and brevity. "They came therefore and saw where he abode." Yes, "and they abode with him that day,"[4] all through that day. It was ten o'clock in the morning.[5] John the Apostle remembers all through the years when he and Andrew spent that first of the many glorious days with Jesus. There is nothing further told of the conversation with Jesus during that day. Perhaps it was too sacred for other ears. But actions speak louder than words. "He findeth first his own brother Simon, and saith unto him, We have found the Messiah."[6] The leaven of the kingdom was at work in Andrew, and apparently also in John the Evangelist. The best proof that one is a disciple of Jesus is just this, the effort to win others. We may not follow this story further. The heart of Jesus is

[1] Westcott, *in loco*.

[2] ῥαββεί, Διδάσκαλε.

[3] Ἔρχεσθε καὶ ὄψεσθε. John 1 : 39.

[4] καὶ παρ' αὐτῷ ἔμειναν τὴν ἐκείνην ἡμέραν.

[5] Roman time, as always in this gospel.

[6] John 1 : 41. Εὑρήκαμεν τὸν Μεσσίαν. He has made the greatest discovery of the ages. He can say "Eureka."

more than full of gratitude and hope. The beginning has been made. But where is John the Baptist? What thoughts are in his heart as he went on his way, an increasingly lonely way, down the hill whose summit he has now passed?

CHAPTER VII

JOY

"But the friend of the bridegroom, which standeth and heareth him, rejoiceth greatly because of the bridegroom's voice" (John 3 : 29).

1. *John Still at Work.*—There was nothing for John to do but to work. He was no shirker. He could help on the work of Jesus best by preaching and baptizing, not by quitting as in a sulk. He could tell of the Messiah with new power now. While John had been and was the Forerunner of the Messiah, he had no disposition to make suggestions to Jesus as to how to manage his affairs. He wished to give Jesus a free hand to work out his own destiny in his own way. The difference between the two men will soon be evident to all. They both leave Bethany, beyond Jordan, which "was no longer thronged by an eager multitude hanging on the prophet's lips." [1] John, indeed, may have been forced to leave because the rulers had declared against him.[2] Perhaps the committee had made their report to the Pharisees, who were soon to take note also of the work of Jesus in relation to that of John.[3] John's disclaimers about himself made it easier for the ecclesiastics to assume the aggressive

[1] Smith, "Days of His Flesh," p. 69.
[2] *Ibid.*
[3] John 4 : 1 ff.

against him. So John went on further north on the western side of the river. It is not clear where "Ænon near to Salim" was. Henderson[1] identifies it with Shalem of Gen. 33 : 18, some seven miles south of 'Ainûn Springs at the head of the Wady Far'ah in the northern part of Samaria. If so, he was near Galilee in case the rulers in Jerusalem became aggressive again. "Many waters"[2] were there, so that "even in summer baptism by immersion could be continued."[3] The people still came in great numbers to John and were baptized as before.[4] As yet there was no sign of loss of prestige or power on the part of the Baptist save the open hostility of the ecclesiastics.

When Jesus left Bethany with the half-dozen followers, he went to Cana of Galilee to a wedding-feast. At once it was manifest that Jesus was no ascetic; that he was not going to remain in the wilderness as John did; that he was going into the homes of the people; that he would seek men and not wait for men to come to him; that he would not hold himself from the life of men; that he would the rather enter into full sympathy with the joys and sorrows of men.[5] News of this festival at Cana probably came to John and would at once set him to thinking. Was he willing to take the Messiah as he revealed himself in his actual life? The incidents in Jerusalem at the first Passover[6] of Christ's ministry may have come to

1 "Palestine," p. 154. 2 ὕδατα πολλά. 3 Marcus Dods, *in loco.*

4 παρεγίνοντο καὶ ἐβαπτίζοντο. Imperfect (repetitive, iterative and descriptive).

5 Cf. Reynolds, "John the Baptist," p. 387.

6 John 2 : 23–3 : 21.

John's notice also. The breach between Jesus and the rulers in Jerusalem now placed both John and Jesus in the attitude of men whose teachings had been disapproved by the ecclesiastical leaders of the nation. John had been rejected as the Forerunner, Jesus as the Messiah. They would have none of either. Jesus is compelled, therefore, to go on with the work of prophetic preparation in much the same manner as John was doing, "in some sort, His own forerunner." [1] So he left Jerusalem for the land of Judea with his little band of six disciples, and preached while they baptized.[2] The place was probably down near the Jordan, where John had once preached and baptized. Here Jesus "tarried" some time, possibly some months. The same regions where John had once done such a mighty work are now the scene of the work of Jesus. He is again reaping where John has sown. Jesus in a real sense, therefore, takes up his work where John has left off. The work of Jesus and John went on *pari passu.*

"For John was not yet cast into prison." [3] This explanatory note is made in the narrative of the Fourth Gospel for two reasons. He soon was cast into prison when his active ministry ceased. This phase of John's ministry is not told in the Synoptic Gospels, though they do mention the arrest of John.[4] There is nothing in the account of the Fourth Gospel to call for the explanation. He seems to have the Synoptic Gospels in mind. He states what he does, not to correct the

[1] Godet, *in loco.* [2] John 3 : 22 ff.; 4 : 3. [3] John 3 : 24.
[4] Cf. Luke 3 : 19 f.; Matt. 4 : 12; Mark 1 : 14.

Synoptic Gospels, but to explain that the events recorded by him here come before that event took place. John alone records the early ministry of Jesus. He here dates it, or, as it were, relates it to the closing part of John's ministry. How long John labored before he was cast into prison we do not know. He may have continued a year after the baptism of Jesus before he was arrested, but certainly not more than that. It is pleasant to think of John and Jesus at work near each other, pushing on the work of the kingdom of God in the midst of tremendous difficulties. The religious atmosphere of Judea was cold and formal, unresponsive to the highest spiritual appeals. Jesus was finding, what John had learned by bitter experience, that he had to do his work in spite of the religious leaders of the nation. In fact, they were now the chief enemies of John and Jesus. The two teachers differed greatly in life and manner, but they both agreed in putting the chief accent on the inner life of the heart and on practical, not ceremonial, righteousness. In that matter they both incurred the active enmity of the Jerusalem ecclesiastics.

2. *The Discussion on the Significance of Baptism.* —At first it may seem strange that Jesus should have allowed his disciples to baptize so close to John. In a sense the discussion about baptism arose because of this apparent competition between John and Jesus.[1] The disciples of John start the question[2] with the Jew.[3] It is possible that they had challenged the Jew for

[1] Godet, *in loco.*
[2] ζήτησις. Cf. Acts 15 : 2; I Tim. 6 : 4; II Tim. 2 : 23; Titus 3 : 9.
[3] Correct text, not "Jews."

seeking baptism at the hands of Jesus.[1] The Jew may have ascribed greater efficacy to the baptism of Jesus.[2] It is more than probable that Jesus, when his disciples administered baptism, explained how it symbolized the new birth which they had experienced, the death to sin, the new life on which they had entered.[3] So, then, if this Jew was a disciple of Jesus, the disciples of John, being jealous for their master, spoke in his defence. This was the first[4] sacramental dispute, but by no means the last. The term "Jew," however, leads some to suppose that he was a Pharisee and hostile to both John and Jesus.[5] This is quite possible in itself. But if the controversy began from some remark by this Jewish caviller about the difference between the Jewish ceremonial baptisms,[6] the baptism of both Jesus and John was soon brought into the discussion, so that it became a triangular debate.[7] The origin and validity of John's baptism (he was not himself baptized) had been challenged by the Jerusalem committee.[8] The Jew probably raised the question again in an acute form. He probably "twitted them with the decline of their master's popularity, telling them of the stir which the new prophet was making in Galilee."[9] The relation between the baptism of John and that of Jesus has been the subject of sharp debate ever since.[10] The matter has been discussed al-

[1] Marcus Dods, *in loco*. [2] Godet, *in loco*. [3] Westcott, *in loco*.

[4] Reynolds, "John the Baptist," p. 389. Reynolds, p. 392, suggests that the Jew wished to stir them up against Jesus.

[5] So Godet, *in loco*. [6] Cf. Heb. 6 : 2; 9 : 10.

[7] Marcus Dods, *in loco;* Edersheim, "Life and Times," vol. I, p. 391.

[8] John 1 : 25.

[9] Smith, "Days of His Flesh," p. 70.

[10] Cf. Lange, "Life of Christ," vol. II, p. 327.

ready in this book at sufficient length. The point to note here is not the merits of the controversy, but the bitterness of tone which was manifested, as is presently plain. All the elements of partisan feeling are present. The intense conviction and prejudice of the Pharisee met the warm devotion of John's disciples to their great prophet, a devotion all the warmer because of the rising of the new star on the Jewish horizon, one whom they had come to feel was a rival to John. To be sure, neither Jesus nor John was involved in the matter. It was the heat of over-rash disciples of John and a Pharisee and possible disciple of Jesus. But it is with just such inflammable material that the fire usually starts. The sparks flash and the blaze grows. Can there come a cleavage between John and Jesus? That depends ultimately on John and Jesus, and first on John, for the trouble was started in his circle and is sure to come to his notice first.

3. *The Effort to Make John Jealous of Jesus.*—There is the sting of bitterness in their words when, probably in sore discomfiture[1] at the hands of the Jew, they come to John and say: "Rabbi, he that was with thee beyond Jordan, to whom thou hast borne witness, behold, the same baptizeth, and all men come to him."[2] The recital of the facts is well calculated to stir envy in the bosom of John. It is plain that these disciples find refuge from defeat in the determination to drive a wedge between John and Jesus. The method of their statement claims for John the precedence over Jesus. He had come to John beyond Jordan.

[1] Smith, "Days of His Flesh," p. 70. [2] John, 3: 26.

"Every word was bitter or charged with innuendo."[1] Reynolds puts this sharply: "*He that was with thee* (dependent on thee, apparently a humble disciple of thy message) *beyond Jordan* (in a better baptizing place than this, on a grand historic site, at a moment of thy greatest influence, when even the Sanhedrin sent to examine and endorse thy self-assertions), *to whom thou hast borne witness* (thus making his position dependent in some respects on thy influence with the people), *behold the same baptizeth, and all men come to him.* (Are there two baptismal communions to co-exist? Dost thou approve of the course taken by the new prophet?)" Every word is a poisoned arrow. The littleness of these disciples of John is shown by this story of bad temper. John had probably heard before of the great work of Jesus down by the Jordan in his old haunts. He had testified to Jesus nor had he taken it back.[2] They had, no doubt, exaggerated a good deal when they said "All men come to him." But they were putting it strongly on purpose. They felt deeply on the subject and wished to stir resentment in the breast of John toward Jesus. It was well and good to be sensitive for the honor of John, but had Jesus done aught to justify the anger of these defenders of John? What preacher of the gospel has not had his special admirers come to him with bitter talk in depreciation of some other preacher supposed to be a rival of their favorite? The devil had gone directly to Jesus for open combat. He came

[1] Reynolds, "John the Baptist," p. 392.

[2] *ᾧ σὺ μεμαρτύρηκας.* There is an implied reflection on John in the use of the perfect tense.

to John first in the guise of an ecclesiastical commission, full of flattery and palaver. He comes again to John in the person of his own disciples, who doubtless felt that they deserved the highest place in John's esteem by reason of their superior loyalty. They had championed his cause against a Pharisee. They had stood for John's cause against that of the new-comer at the Jordan, who owed all his prestige to the generous words, the too generous words, of John himself. "The suggestion was that Jesus had kicked away the ladder by which he had risen, and that his success was at the expense of his friend. It was such a speech as would have played havoc with a little mind and an unprincipled soul. Never are the suggestions of self-love so dangerous as when they are whispered in the ear by the flattering lips of sympathizers." [1] Many a man in high station has had his soul embittered by the foolish talk of fawning admirers who, once they saw that their envious tattle is relished, have a never-failing supply of fresh gossip at the expense of the great man's rivals. It is a severe testing to which John is here subjected. "When for a lifetime a man has stood on the pinnacle of influence, but at last his day is over and another appears to take his place, it is a miracle of grace if he is able to look on his successor with friendliness and genuine good-will." [2] Can John work that miracle? Will he be loyal to Jesus now?

4. *John's Noble Reply.*—Nowhere does the Baptist appear so well as in his response to the envious innu-

[1] Stalker, "The Two St. Johns," p. 232. [2] *Ibid.*, p. 233.

endoes of his disciples. The greatness of John rises far above their littleness of soul. He performs a miracle[1] of self-mastery, and with serene lucidity brushes aside their rancorous hints. He is genuinely humble, supremely humble and great, as with pathetic tenderness[2] he passes by the cause of their dispute and touches the really essential matter, his own relation and attitude toward Jesus.

(a) *The Hand of God Acknowledged by John.*—"A man can receive nothing, except it have been given him from heaven." [3] Thus he meets the jealous zeal of his disciples with a broad general principle of God's control over a man's life. This is no platitude with John, but his philosophy of life. The language is general [4] and does not refer directly to either John or Jesus. The critics have been much divided as to whether John means to describe Jesus. "The greater activity and success of Jesus was given Him of God." [5] Hence John has no ground to complain at the manifestation of God's power in the work of Jesus. On the other hand, Godet[6] argues that John is thinking of himself: "I cannot take that which God has not given me." Godet argues for this interpretation, since verses 27–30 seem to be a portrayal of the Baptist's work, and verses 31–36 that of Jesus. A plausible interpretation can be made from either standpoint. Westcott[7] holds that the principle is applicable to both John and Jesus, and probably was meant by

[1] Stalker, "The Two St. Johns," p. 233.
[2] Edersheim, "Life and Times," vol. I, p. 392
[3] John 3 : 27.
[4] ἄνθρωπος.
[5] Meyer, *in loco.*
[c] *In loco.*
[7] *In loco.*

John to have a double reference: "I cannot claim any new authority which has not been directly assigned to me; He, of whom you speak, cannot effectually exercise His power unless it be of divine origin." This is probably nearer the truth, though, as a matter of fact, John would naturally make the application first and mainly to himself. This general principle is a sufficient justification of Jesus in his work of preaching and baptizing. It also shows that it was not rivalry that prompted John to go on with his work after Jesus had begun his ministry.[1] From our point of view the difficulty is that John should have carried on a parallel ministry, but it is a superficial objection, which disappears upon reflection. Some of the disciples of Jesus may have wondered at the time why John did not quit baptizing and give way at once to the work of Jesus and enroll himself as a disciple of the Messiah. "But so long as John saw that men were led by his preaching to accept the Messiah he might well believe that he served Christ better thus than by following in His train."[2] John wishes to make it plain that in the nature of the case there is no ground for rivalry. "The message which was brought by his disciples as a complaint, in his eyes crowns his proper joy."[3] Success would not be success if it did not come from God. He is not arrogating anything to himself, when he simply receives[4] what is given him

[1] Cf. Marcus Dods, *in loco.*

[2] Marcus Dods, *in loco.*

[3] Westcott, *in loco.*

[4] λαμβάνειν. Cf. Meyer, *in loco.* The perfect passive subjunctive (periphrastic). ἐὰν μὴ ᾖ δεδομένον is rather awkwardly translated in the Revised Version. The gift is already made before it is received, made in God's plan.

from heaven as part of God's plan for him. Each man's life is a plan of God according to John. But it is only a great soul who can realize this truth in his own life when the tide of success is ebbing away from him. This is the greatness of John, that he can see God in his life when the sun has begun to go down. John was untainted by the artificialities of life. He went straight to the heart of things.

(b) *John Had Already Explained the Situation.*—"Ye yourselves bear me witness, that I said, I am not the Christ, but, that I am sent before him." [1] John not merely applies his general principle to himself, but he appeals to these querulous disciples[2] as witnesses to his previous teaching on this very subject of the relation between himself and the Messiah. They were mistaken in their zeal, and it was due to needless ignorance on their part. They cannot blame John for their error in the matter. They had heard him deny to the committee from Jerusalem (or had certainly heard of it) that he was the Messiah.[3] He had also expressly pointed out Jesus as the Messiah, and had done it publicly twice.[4] They had accused John of having borne testimony[5] to the work and mission of Jesus. In so doing they convicted themselves of knowledge of the fact that John is now bringing to their attention. He had plainly said: "I am not the Christ." He had also said that Jesus was the one of whom he had been speaking.[6] John reminds them

[1] John 1 : 28.
[2] αὐτοὶ ὑμεῖς. Emphatic intensive pronoun.
[3] John 1 : 19–30.
[4] John 1 : 32, 35.
[5] John 1 : 26.
[6] John 1 : 30.

that, while he has borne witness[1] to Jesus as they have charged, they are themselves bearing witness[2] against themselves. It is not a mere keen retort. It is a complete answer and exposure of their bad spirit in their suggestions. Certainly he is not responsible for the jealous humor which they have exhibited.[3] As to himself, John repeats, what he has previously explained, "I am sent before him." He is the Forerunner of Jesus the Messiah. He claims to be no more, but he does claim that. That is honor enough for him. He is willing now to stand aside and see Jesus do the work, if God so wills. Some men have to be second in God's plan. John is second while Jesus is first. He has no repining as he takes his divinely allotted place. "There is nothing more disastrous or ridiculous than for the second, instead of filling his own place and doing his own work, to be pining for the place and the work of the first." [4]

(c) *The Friend of the Bridegroom.*—"He that hath the bride is the bridegroom; but the friend of the bridegroom, which standeth and heareth him, rejoiceth greatly because of the bridegroom's voice: this my joy is fulfilled." [5] In the Old Testament the bride is a familiar figure for the people of God whose bridegroom is Jehovah himself.[6] The Messiah, therefore, as the bridegroom is the highest manifestation of Jehovah.[7] This mysterious language about the Mes-

[1] μεμαρτύρηκας. John 3 : 26.

[2] μαρτυρεῖτε. John 3 : 28.

[3] Godet, *in loco.*

[4] Stalker, "The Two St. Johns," p. 233.

[5] John 3 : 29.

[6] Ex. 34 : 15; Deut. 31 : 16; Ezek. 16; Isa. 54 : 5; Hosea 2 : 18; Ps. 45; 73 : 27; Mal. 2 : 11.

[7] Godet, *in loco.*

siah is in harmony with John's use of the phrase, "Lamb of God," about the Messiah. John stands "on the arch of the Old Testament" [1] in giving the interpretation of the system which he closes. Jesus himself will later speak of himself as the bridegroom[2] when the disciples of the Baptist come in company with the Pharisees to complain of the disciples of Jesus for not fasting. Once again, therefore, disciples of John will be jealous of Jesus and his followers, and will seek to fasten the clamps of an outworn Judaism upon Christianity, but a Christianity from which they still hold aloof. They will then be in company with Pharisees, not in controversy, as here. But we have no doubt as to the answer that the Baptist would have made. He did practise fasting, but he did not seek to bind Jewish ceremonialism upon the people. He sought to make them really spiritual in life. Jesus likewise uses the figure in Matt. 22 : 1 f. in the parable of the Marriage of the King's Son. He is the King's Son and the bride is the people of God. Once more in the Parable of the Ten Virgins[3] Jesus is the bridegroom. The figure is repeated by Paul [4] and John.[5] John shows his knowledge of the Old Testament in the use of the figure, and also his power in the use of happy illustrations. The parable throws a touch of beauty and of joy into the overstrained tension of the moment.

The bridegroom has[6] the bride. He is supreme at

[1] Westcott, *in loco.*
[2] Matt. 9 : 15; Mark 2 : 19 f.; Luke 5 : 34 f.
[3] Matt. 25 : 1–13.
[4] Eph. 5 : 32 f.; II Cor. 11 : 2.
[5] Rev. 19 : 7; 21 : 2, 9; 22 : 17. Cf. also James 4 : 4.
[6] ἔχων equals has and holds as wife. Cf. Marcus Dods, *in loco.*

the marriage feast. "There is only one in whom the people of God can find their permanent joy and rest; one who is the perennial spring of this happiness and life." [1] Jesus is the bridegroom[2] and is entitled to the happiness of the present hour. It is his hour of joy and he is entitled to the jubilation which comes with the setting up of the kingdom. As for John himself, he is "the friend of the bridegroom." But that is no mean function in a Hebrew wedding. He acts as a "go-between" in the wooing of the bride by the bridegroom, makes the arrangements for the wedding and acts as master of ceremonies at the feast.[3] When the bridegroom comes upon the scene, the friend of the bridegroom steps into the background, but not too far away. He stands "in the attitude of expectation and ready service" [4] and listens[5] for the further commands of the bridegroom. He has finished his work, but he tarries to see if there is aught more for him to do. There is joy in the ring of the bridegroom's voice, and because[6] of this fact the friend of the bridegroom rejoices exceedingly.[7] There is no alloy[8] in this joy. The full, clear joy of the bridegroom "causes the heart of his friend to leap for joy." [9] John's disciples need not think that he, the friend [10] of this bridegroom, is jealous or unhappy over the news from the Jordan. They have utterly misunderstood John and the whole

[1] Marcus Dods, *in loco*.
[2] ὁ νυμφίος *sponsus*.
[3] Cf. Buxtorf, "Lex. Rabb."
[4] Westcott, *in loco*. ὁ ἑστηκώς.
[5] ἀκούων.
[6] διὰ τὴν φωνὴν τοῦ νυμφίου.
[7] χαρᾷ χαίρει. Common in the LXX, but found in the ancient Greek.
[8] Westcott, *in loco*.
[9] Godet, *in loco*.
[10] ὁ φίλος τοῦ νυμφίου. Also called παρανύμφιος, νυμφάγωγος; the Hebrew *Shoshben*.

situation if they imagine that to be true. Instead of that he is shouting "Hallelujah."[1] "This my joy therefore is fulfilled." The joy of seeing my work as the friend of the bridegroom so well accomplished is mine. The news that the disciples bring of great crowds who attend the ministry of Jesus fills John's cup to the full. It is full and will stay full,[2] in spite of all their jealous talk. The song is in his heart. What has caused vexation in them is precisely the thing which raises his joy to the highest point.[3] There is no murmur to come from John at the success of Jesus. It is in truth the very object for which he has been striving all the time.[4] Here is generosity, here is real greatness of soul, a greatness of spirit that will lead Jesus to call John the greatest of those born of women.

(d) *John's Fading Light.*—"He must increase, but I must decrease."[5] "It is for Him to go on growing and for me to be ever getting less."[6] Paley adds that the language is solar. Dr. W. H. Whitsitt, sometime President of the Southern Baptist Theological Seminary, and long Professor of Church History, once remarked that in the church calendar the birthday of John the Baptist comes when the days begin to shorten and that of Jesus when they begin to lengthen. This is true in the calendar, though no one knows how it was in reality save that the two events were about six

[1] Reynolds, "John the Baptist," p. 397.

[2] πεπλήρωται. This perfect is durative plus punctiliar.

[3] Godet, *in loco.*

[4] Stalker, "The Two St. Johns," p. 234.

[5] John 3 : 30. 'Εκεῖνον δεῖ αὐξάνειν, ἐμὲ δὲ ἐλαττοῦσθαι. The tenses are present (durative).

[6] Paley, quoted by Marcus Dods.

months apart. Marcus Dods[1] denies that the arrangement in the church calendar had such a motive in view. But it is a noble renunciation that John here makes in plain language. It is said, not with the spirit of unwilling resignation, but it comes from the heart[2] of the Baptist. The shadow will soon begin to fall across John's path, the shadows of imprisonment, suspense, martyrdom,[3] but John will go steadily on his way with an upright head so long as he may. This may be the last word which we have from the Baptist[4] till doubt in the darkness of the dungeon at Machærus forces a cry from him for more light.[5] His sun will indeed go down, down into the night. The darkness is nearer at hand than John probably knew. But he has done a man's work in his short day. His public ministry could not have been more than eighteen months in length. But his sun has blazed with brilliance during that day, "a bright and shining lamp," indeed. He was no meteor, no comet, but the bright morning star.[6] He has seen the true[7] light come, the Sun of Righteousness with healing in his wings. He knew that he was not[8] the real light. But it had been his joy to bear witness[9] of that light. He has shone like the star in the early dawn. He has hailed with joy the coming of the full day. Now that day has come, he fades away. If these are the last

[1] *In loco.*
[2] Stalker, "The Two St. Johns," p. 234.
[3] Westcott, *in loco.*
[4] Unless the next section is from him.
[5] Matt. 11 : 2 f.; Luke 7 : 19.
[6] "Fidelis Lucifer." Bernard says: "Lucet ergo Johannes, tanto verius quanto minus appetit lucere." Cf. Marcus Dods.
[7] John 1 : 9.
[8] John 1 : 8.
[9] John 1 : 10.

words of John in public discourse, they "are the fullness of religious sacrifice, and fitly close his work, and with it the Old Dispensation."[1] The law and the prophets were until John. John is the link between the Old Covenant and the New. His work is finished, but it stands as its own monument. It can never be duplicated nor forgotten. He formed the bridge by which the first Jews passed over from Moses to Christ. We are on the other side of Jordan now, but let us never forget the bridge by which we crossed over.

(e) *In Praise of Jesus.*—It is a matter of keen dispute among scholars whether in John 3 : 31–36 we have the reflections of the Evangelist[2] or the final testimony of the Baptist[3] to Jesus. It is true that the Fourth Gospel rather often glides from discourse or dialogue into narrative in a manner difficult always to determine the point of departure. An instance has occurred in this very chapter of John (in the dialogue with Nicodemus).[4] Here it is not clear whether we have the words of Jesus or the reflections of the Evangelist. It is possible also that we have in John 3 : 31–36 a summary of the teaching of John[5] which may not have been spoken on this occasion. It is not easy to give a categorical answer in view of all the facts. The question of style can be argued both ways.[6] The use of "the Son" and "the Father" is like the language of Jesus at a later time, but John had heard the Father's voice at the baptism of Jesus, and had called Jesus the Son of God. It is possible that in

[1] Westcott, *in loco.*
[2] So Westcott, Marcus Dods, etc.
[3] Meyer, Godet, etc.
[4] Verses 16–21.
[5] Cf. John 12 : 44–50.
[6] Westcott, *in loco.*

this section we do not have so formal a reproduction of the very language of the Baptist, but his words adapted more freely to the language of the Evangelist. The passage may be expounded as substantially the language of the Baptist, but with an element of doubt remaining. Meyer[1] is quite positive: "We perceive how the Baptist, as with the mind of Jesus himself, unveils before his disciples, in whose narrower circle he speaks, with the growing inspiration of the last prophet, the full majesty of Jesus; and with this, as his swanlike song, completes his testimony before he vanishes from the history. Even the subsequent perplexity is not irreconcilable with this, simply because John is 'of the earth.'" It is not hard to see how the testimony here given is possible from John's standpoint. He would, in that case, rise to a somewhat higher level, but that is all. The Coming One is "from above" as John knew from the Voice at the baptism. He is in truth "above all," not merely John, but all men. John then makes a still wider cleavage between himself and Jesus. Jesus is above and speaks what he receives from above, while John is from the earth like other men, and receives his message through the medium of men. "No man receiveth his witness" sounds pessimistic in view of the report of the disciples of John about Jesus. But John knows that crowds and conversion are not synonymous terms. The vast multitude of men in the first century did not come to Christ. John qualifies his universal negative in the next sentence. God had sent Jesus

[1] *In loco.*

and had endowed him with the Holy Spirit without stint, as John had previously said. The Son has unlimited power. One's attitude to the Son of God determines his spiritual destiny. If John spoke these words, they have a reference once more to the jealous talk of the disciples of John. If they are the words of the Evangelist, they constitute a warning suggested by the last testimony of the Baptist, "the final peal of thunder from Sinai in the New Testament." [1]

In any case we have no more words of the Baptist to expound save his rebuke of Herod Antipas and that one cry in the night from Machærus. It is with regret that we must continue the narrative of the Baptist's career without his soul-revealing words. In a sense, John slips away from us now. We catch a glimpse of him now and then as he flits past us in the shadows. But we do not see his eye nor hear his voice. The echo of that voice that was first heard in the wilderness of Judea continues to reverberate. We know that John was not idle, though he no longer fills the centre of the stage. The very trouble that soon befalls him is due to his activity, not to his inactivity. He was not the kind of man to sit idly by, to mope, to lament opportunities for service now gone forever. He was not an old man. He probably had no very clear conception as to how the end would come to him, nor when. But he will die in harness if God so wills. In all probability the effect of John's earnest words, his last public testimony to Jesus as the Messiah, was to focus attention more than ever

[1] Lange, "Life of Christ," vol. II, p. 332.

on the work of Jesus. John may have witnessed more of his own disciples leaving him to join the Messiah. If so, his heart was glad. We do not know whether John's noble testimony was reported at once to Jesus or not. He must surely have heard of it in time. The light is turned down. The curtain is drawn. The Baptist bids us good-night.

CHAPTER VIII

PERIL

"But Herod the tetrarch, being reproved by him for Herodias his brother's wife, and for all the evil things which Herod had done, added yet this above all, that he shut up John in prison" (Luke 3 : 19 f.).

1. *The Sin of Herod and Herodias.*—The story of Herod the Great as told by Josephus[1] is one of the most shameful in human history. He was a man of great gifts, which he prostituted to selfish ambition and passion. At his death one of the worst of his sons, now that Antipater was dead, was the one named Antipas, his son by Malthace. Archelaus had a worse reputation than Antipas at the time, as is shown by the change in the plans of Joseph in Egypt on receipt of the news that Archelaus is reigning in Judea.[2] Archelaus was inefficient and incapable to such an extent that he lost his position in ten years. Antipas was Tetrarch of Galilee and Perea, and for a while his country (Perea) afforded an asylum for John the Baptist from the persecution of the Pharisees. Jesus also spent most of his active ministry in his dominion (Galilee). The vices of Herod Antipas were mainly of a private nature. He became proficient in his

[1] Cf. "Ant.," Books xiv–xvii.

[2] Matt. 2 : 22.

father's vices, "craft, cruelty, and licentiousness."[1] It is his private life that concerns our narrative because it is at this point that John's career touches his. "In point of character, Antipas was a genuine son of old Herod—sly, ambitious, and luxurious, only not so able as his father."[2] Jesus will call him "that fox."[3] He needed his craft in managing the Galileans, and made a political marriage with the daughter of Aretas, King of Arabia, in order to keep away the Arabians. On a visit to Rome to see his brother Herod Philip, son of Herod the Great by Mariamne (the high-priest's daughter), he fell in love with Philip's wife, Herodias, daughter of Aristobulus (son of Mariamne). She was thus the granddaughter of Herod the Great, and had married her uncle, Herod Philip. They had a daughter, Salome, named after the sister of Herod the Great. Herod Antipas, also her uncle, proposed to her that she leave Philip for him. She entertained his proposal and consented on condition that he divorce the daughter of Aretas. It was not necessary for Antipas to divorce his wife, since "the Jewish law allowed the king eighteen wives."[4] She would need a divorce from her husband, but her stipulation was doubtless occasioned by jealousy. The daughter of Aretas found out the agreement and wrote to her father, King Aretas, "to send for her to come to Machærus, which is a place in the borders of the

[1] Smith, "Days of His Flesh," p. 71.
[2] Schuerer, "Jewish People," div. I, vol. II, p. 18.
[3] Luke 13 : 32. "Herod Antipas—the pettiest, meanest, weakest, most contemptible of titular princelings" (Farrar, "Life of Christ," vol. I, p. 289).
[4] Smith, "Days of His Flesh," p. 71. Cf. Schuerer, "Jewish People," div. I, vol. I, p. 455.

dominions of Aretas and Herod."[1] This fortress soon passed into the hands of Herod Antipas. Antipas was glad for his wife to go. She fled not merely to Machærus, but to her father's home in Petra, and the result was that Aretas became hostile to Herod Antipas. Antipas went on and married Herodias, to the disgust of the public. He had flagrantly violated the Jewish law in this marriage.[2] His brother was still living and they had a living daughter. It was indeed "a monstrous transgression, combining heartlessness, treachery, adultery, and incest."[3] The Jews had now become familiar with wickedness in high places. It was the Roman fashion, as was seen in the lives of Julius Cæsar and Antony. The old Roman virtue in public men was gone. The Herods had caught the fashion of the times. People were expected to concern themselves with the public acts of rulers, not their private morals. Once Nathan had gone to David and said: "Thou art the man." Was there a prophet to-day who would denounce a Herod to his face for his sins? The people would talk in private and lament the sad lapses in public and private life. But the professional rabbis in Jerusalem could excuse themselves by saying that they lived in the jurisdiction of Pontius Pilate. Was there a voice willing to be the conscience of the people in this emergency?

2. *John's Denunciation.*—"For John said unto Herod, It is not lawful for thee to have thy brother's

[1] Josephus, "Ant.," xviii, 5, 1.
[2] Lev. 18:16; 20:21.
[3] Smith, "Days of His Flesh," pp. 71 f.

wife."[1] The ground for this condemnation is not that she was his niece,[2] but the fact that Herodias was his brother's wife, and his brother was still living and the daughter also. Herod had put away his wife, and Herodias had nominally divorced her husband Herod Philip. But "Herodias took upon her to confound the laws of our country, and divorced herself from her husband while he was alive, and was married to Herod."[3] Salome, the sister of Herod the Great, had also divorced her husband contrary to Jewish custom.[4] It was a Roman custom extremely common at this time and is mentioned once by Jesus.[5] The imperfect tense[6] ("said") in both Matthew and Mark may indicate that John had repeatedly expressed the opinion that Herod should put Herodias away.[7] It is not clear how John came to speak on this subject. He had not feared to upbraid the Pharisees and Sadducees (the religious leaders) to their faces.[8] John was not the kind of preacher to be blind to the sins of men in high places (ecclesiastical or civil). He was not a demagogue and would not appeal to the baser passions of the people against men in office. He had been fearless in the exposure of the sins of all classes of people in Palestine. John did not keep his ear to the ground for the applause of the groundlings. Never was man more absolutely indifferent to public

[1] Mark 6 : 18. Cf. Matt. 14 : 4.

[2] This was also apparently unlawful (cf. Lev. 18 : 12 ff.). Broadus, "Commentary on Matthew," p. 317.

[3] Josephus, "Ant.," xviii, 5, 4.

[4] *Ibid.*, xv, 8, 10.

[5] Mark 10 : 12.

[6] ἔλεγεν. Said repeatedly, had been saying. The form may indeed be an old second aorist also, but the imperfect idea suits best here.

[7] Broadus, "Commentary on Matthew," p. 317.

[8] Matt. 3 : 7.

opinion in itself. He would defy a nation or a king with equal readiness if occasion demanded it. When John was at Enon, near to Salem, he was not far from Tiberias, the capital of Herod Antipas. He was on the border of Galilee. Did Herod Antipas send for John to come and give his opinion of his marriage in the hope that it might be favorable in order to stem the tide of public discontent against him? That is possible in itself,[1] but on the whole hardly likely. It is possible that the Pharisees in John's audiences may have, from time to time, asked his opinion of Herod's marriage in order to inveigle John into imprudent remarks.[2] If it was a trap, John was not afraid to walk into it. He probably knew what the penalty would be. It seems clear that John finally spoke his opinion of Herod to his face. John was no frequenter of courts[3] and may have sent his message to Herod by his disciples.[4] But it is much more probable that John went himself. Herod did later have frequent personal intercourse with him.[5] It is likely that, after John had publicly denounced this marriage of Herod and Herodias that he received a message to come to Machærus to see Herod. The motive of Herod may have been to overawe John and make him take it back or to have absolute proof against him in case he stood by the reported condemnation.[6] It is hardly likely that John was asked to come to Tiberias. He may indeed have gone to Machærus several times and

[1] Broadus, "Commentary on Matthew," p. 317.
[2] Cf. John 4 : 1 f.; Luke 13 : 32.
[3] Matt. 11 : 8.
[4] Swete, "Mark," p. 116. Cf. Matt. 11 : 2.
[5] Mark 6 : 20.
[6] Broadus, "Matthew," p. 317.

have repeated his demand that Herod put away Herodias.[1] There are always people ready to say that a preacher is meddling in politics if he exposes the sins of men in public office. But John did not think of morality and public office as two wholly distinct spheres. With him public office was not a closed circle which he could not enter. The preacher is the public censor of morals. It may be prudence on the part of a preacher to be silent in the face of evil conduct in the lives of public men, but it is probably also cowardice. It is easy to retort that John ran the risk of losing his head by his course, but the reply is at hand. A preacher's head is not worth saving when his mouth is silent at the cost of his courage and his duty. It is not for the preacher to measure his words when righteousness is in peril. If the ruler can with impunity defy the laws of God and man, the common decencies of life, it is idle to exhort the people to obey them. John did not spare Herod. He dared to look Herod in the eye and tell him of all his sins.[2] It was a long list in simple truth. John laid chief emphasis on Herod's adulterous marriage. He rebuked [3] him with point and force. So Luther, at the Diet of Worms, defied the authorities. Knox faced Mary Queen of Scots.[4] Jesus himself one day turned upon the scribes and Pharisees with a denunciation the echoes of which will never die away.[5] John had refuge in the territory of Herod Antipas and now it

[1] Swete, "Mark," p. 116. Cf. I Kings 17 : 1; 18 : 1 f.; 21 : 17 ff.; II Kings 1 : 15.

[2] Luke 3 : 19. περὶ πάντων ὧν ἐποίησε πονηρῶν.

[3] ἐλεγχόμενος. Luke 3 : 19. Cf. I Tim. 5 : 20.

[4] Broadus, "Matthew," p. 317.

[5] Matt. 23.

had come to this.[1] But how will Herod and Herodias stand this open and repeated rebuke by the popular preacher from the wilderness? The fact that John voiced public sentiment in the matter will be no necessary safety to John, not when a Herod is concerned in the matter.

3. *The Resentment of Herod and Herodias.*—One day Herod himself "sent forth and laid hold upon John and bound him in prison for the sake of Herodias." [2] Did Herod send up to Aenon after John? A day came when Herod, prodded by Herodias, would stand John's rebukes no longer. Luke[3] says that Herod "added yet this above all, that he shut up John in prison." In Luke's opinion this was the crowning crime of his career. It was Herodias who cared most. Herod was a hardened sinner and man of the world, more ready to give and take. The very boldness of John in the matter had a sort of fascination for him. At times he "heard him gladly," [4] though this was not his normal mood. But there was no vacillation with Herodias. She "set herself against him" [5] with relentless and increasing hate. "Herod silenced the Baptist by sending him down to the dungeons, and dismissed the matter from his mind. Not so Herodias; her resentment could be satisfied only by the Baptist's death." [6] But that was not to

[1] Keim, "Jesus of Nazara," vol. II, p. 332.

[2] Mark 6 : 17. Cf. Matt. 14 : 3. ἀποστείλας ἐκρατησεν τὸν Ἰωάνην καὶ ἔδησεν ἐν φυλακῇ.

[3] 3 : 19.

[4] Mark 6 : 20.

[5] Mark 6 : 19. ἐνεῖχεν αὐτῷ. Cf. Gen. 49 : 23. Note imperfect (durative). There is ellipsis. The phrase is curiously like the modern slang, "had it in for him."

[6] Swete, "Mark," p. 116.

come as yet, for, though she desired to kill him, "she could not." [1] The reason why she could not was that Herod "feared John, knowing that he was a righteous man and a holy, and kept him safe." [2] There is power in goodness, and John awed Herod by mere force of character. The bad fear the good whom they affect to despise.[3] Ahab was stirred to anger against Elijah by Jezebel.[4] So Herod was impressed with the piety of John and regarded him as blameless in his relations to both man and God.[5] Hence, though Herodias raged like a tigress after her prey, she could not reach him. Herod kept him safe[6] from her. He was unwilling to put him to death, but he kept him in prison. He could not denounce him to the public while in the dungeon, and yet Herod allowed his disciples to come to see him.[7] Herod had in reality a mixture of reverence and superstitious dread toward John.[8] So Herod kept John for a time from the malice of Herodias. He seems to have made frequent visits to Machærus, and really found pleasure[9] in hearing John speak, perhaps, about the kingdom of heaven (cf. Paul and Felix). Herod was drawn two ways[10] about John. He had respect for John's goodness and yet could not rid himself wholly of the evil purpose of his wife, with which he at times partly

[1] Mark 6 : 19. [2] Mark 6 : 20. [3] Bengel, *in loco.*

[4] Broadus, "Matthew," p. 317.

[5] δίκαιον καὶ ἅγιον.

[6] συνετήρει. Imperfect (durative). Perfective force of συν. Cf. Matt. 9 : 17.

[7] Luke 3 : 19.

[8] Marcus Dods, *in loco.*

[9] ἡδέως αὐτοῦ ἤκουε. Iterative imperfect.

[10] A δίψυχος ἀνήρ (James 1 : 8). Marcus Dods, *in loco.*

sympathized. Hence he was "perplexed."[1] When driven hard by his wife's demoniacal vindictiveness he would flee to John, who braced "his jaded mind as with a whiff of desert air."[2] This psychological tangle is not only of interest to students of men, but it is intensely human and realistic. Herod could not as yet make his way[3] out of the tangle, but the Damascus blade of peril hung over John's head continually. There came moments when Herod went over wholly to the point of view of Herodias and gave way to his own resentment against him. Then "he would have put him to death," literally "wishing to kill him,"[4] and be done with the whole miserable business. At such times all that restrained him was the fact that he "feared the multitude."[5] He had such spells[6] of fright of the people as all demagogues have. The masses "counted him as a prophet."[7] There was no way to change popular opinion of John. To kill him would be to intrench him as a hero in the minds and hearts of the people and to enrage them still more against Herod. Even the Jewish religious leaders quailed before the reputation of John at a later time.[8] There is thus no real conflict between the motive given by Mark (respect for John) and that presented by Matthew (fear of the people). Herod was

[1] ἠπόρει correct text (Mark 6 : 20), not ἐποίει (Text. Receptus). Herod did do many things, but his perplexity is the point here. Note imperfect tense.

[2] Swete, "Mark," p. 117.

[3] ἠπόρει from ἀπορέω equals lose one's way.

[4] θέλων αὐτὸν ἀποκτεῖναι. Matt. 14 : 4. Note aorist (punctiliar) ἀποκτεῖναι.

[5] Matt. 14 : 4.

[6] ἐφοβήθη, aorist (punctiliar) tense.

[7] ὡς προφήτην αὐτὸν εἶχον. Note imperfect tense (durative).

[8] Matt. 21 : 25–27, 32.

influenced by both at different times, in different moods.

So John is left to languish in the prison at Machærus. The fortress is mentioned by Josephus:[1] "Accordingly he was sent a prisoner, out of Herod's suspicious temper, to Machærus, the castle I before mentioned." Josephus[2] also gives a description of this powerful fortress. This interesting description by Josephus has been confirmed by recent explorations.[3] It is on the eastern side of the Dead Sea toward the northern end, about seven miles from the sea. It was first fortified by one of the Maccabean princes about 100 B. C., then destroyed by the Romans, and rebuilt by Herod the Great.[4] It had for a time been held by Aretas, the King of Arabia, whose daughter Herod Antipas had divorced, but now it belonged again to Antipas. The fortress was on a high mountain loftier than those around Jerusalem. The citadel crowned a conical hill which was impregnable. Tristram found two dungeons in the ruins, in one of which John the Baptist was surely placed. They were dark and cold and dank like the inner prison[5] of Philippi in which Paul and Silas were confined, or the Mamertine Prison in Rome in which Paul was probably held during his second Roman imprisonment in loneliness and cold.[6] Near Machærus were springs, *Callirrhoe*, and it may have been

[1] "Ant.," xviii, 5, 2. [2] "War," vii, 6, 1.

[3] Cf. Tristram, "Land of Moab" (1873); Schuerer, "Jewish People," div. I, vol. II, p. 250; G. A. Smith, "Historical Geography of Palestine," pp. 569 f.

[4] Broadus, "Commentary on Matthew," p. 316.

[5] Acts 16 : 24. [6] II Tim. 4 : 10, 13, 21.

these springs that drew Herod Antipas, like his father before him, to Machærus. But we must leave John "in that remote and hopeless imprisonment, in one of those deep and dark dungeons which were so cold in winter and so hot in summer."[1] Here for about a year he is left. He has occasional visits from his followers who tell him bits of news from the outside world, with now and then a word about Jesus, the Messiah, whom he had announced, baptized and identified.[2] How strange a world it was now to John! Gone the great crowds that hung upon his words in the wilderness; gone the excitement and the enthusiasm of those wonderful days. Will the Messiah not set the Forerunner free?

4. *The Hand of the Pharisees.*—We must retrace our steps a bit. In the Synoptic Gospels we have only the personal aspects of the controversy between Herod (and Herodias) and John. But the Fourth Gospel[3] has a clear implication that the Pharisees had a hand in the arrest of John the Baptist, "when therefore the Lord knew that the Pharisees had heard that Jesus was making and baptizing more disciples than John." Jesus therefore left Judea to go into Galilee, not because he was afraid of Herod Antipas. Galilee was the country of Herod Antipas. Matthew[4] states that Jesus withdrew into Galilee "when he heard that John was delivered up." That was sad news for Jesus. Machærus was not far from the wilderness of Judea where Jesus was. Herod Antipas as yet had

[1] Broadus, "Matthew," p. 316.
[2] Broadus, "Matthew," p. 197.
[3] John 4 : 1 f.
[4] 4 : 12.

no reason to be hostile to Jesus. His hatred of John was a personal matter. He did not interfere with John because of his religious activity. But the Pharisees were already opposed to Jesus[1] as to John. The Pharisees might incite Herod against Jesus. They will later seek to get Christ into some sort of entanglement with Herod Antipas.[2] Jesus is suspicious of the Pharisees and concludes to make Galilee the scene of his ministry so as to get some distance from Jerusalem, the head-quarters of the Pharisees. Perhaps the disciples of Jesus had brought reports of remarks made by the Pharisees that Jesus was no better than John. They had carried their point with him and Jesus had better look out. The action of Jesus is not due to unmanly fear. His hour has not come. His work is not done. He cannot afford to be rash. The work of the kingdom needs him. The Pharisees are in reality now afraid that Jesus, in view of his success, which is surpassing that of John, may prove to be more formidable than John himself.[3] John apparently had more points of contact with the Pharisees than Jesus.[4] John had come to them "in the way of righteousness,"[5] but it was real, not ceremonial, righteousness with John. Besides, the Pharisees had resented John's baptizing.[6] At the time of the arrest of John he had on the whole been more popular than Jesus, and for a longer time. The rising tide of Christ's popularity had come to John's disciples and thus to John, but not to the Pharisees in Jerusalem.

[1] John 2 : 13–22.
[2] Luke 13 :31 ff.
[3] Godet, "John," p. 417.
[4] Westcott, "John," *in loco.*
[5] Matt. 21 : 32.
[6] Cf. John 1 : 25.

They were still more indignant at John, who had called them "a brood of vipers." That word had stuck and stung. Herod "had sent forth and had laid hold upon John." [1] It is entirely possible that the Pharisees had assisted in the arrest of John. They may have done more. It may have been the Pharisees who sent the first word to Herod about John's denunciation of his marriage, not that they approved it, but in order to get John into trouble. They are entirely capable of such tactics, as we know from their conduct in connection with Jesus and Herod Antipas.[2] The anger of the Pharisees toward John may have been greatly increased because of their growing dislike of Jesus and John's public endorsement of him as the Coming One. The Pharisees were responsible for the withdrawal of Jesus from the Jordan to Galilee. "We venture the suggestion that the imprisonment of the Baptist, although occasioned by his outspoken rebuke of Herod, was in great part due to the intrigues of the Pharisees." [3] The Pharisees took advantage of the personal resentment of Herod and Herodias to even up old scores of their own against John.

5. *The Political Excuse.*—Josephus[4] gives another version of the arrest of John which some writers have thought to be inconsistent with that found in the Synoptic Gospels. Josephus says: "Herod, who feared lest the great influence John had over the people might put it into his power and inclination to raise a

[1] Mark 6: 17. [2] Luke 13: 31 ff.
[3] Edersheim, "Life and Times," vol. I, p. 393.
[4] "Ant.," xviii, 5, 2.

rebellion (for they seemed ready to do anything he should advise) thought it best, by putting him to death, to prevent any mischief he might cause, and not bring himself into difficulties, by sparing a man who might make him repent of it when it should be too late." It may be that Josephus has here told what is true about Herod. Matthew[1] says that Herod "feared the multitude," and the narrative in Josephus may well be one aspect of that fear. His fear of John's power grew out of the fact that the people regarded him as a prophet. Josephus would naturally give the public aspect of the matter, while the Synoptic Gospels tell the inside facts. The Josephus narrative gives the excuse that Herod would offer for the arrest of John. He was a dangerous man, too dangerous to be allowed further liberty. The great crowds and the excitement up and down the Jordan bore witness to that fact. He had, besides, preached much about a kingdom that was at hand, and the popular mind was in an inflammable state and likely to burst into a conflagration at any moment. Herod could thus tell a plausible story to the public and to Cæsar for his treatment of John, if Cæsar cared to know. But Herod knew, if Josephus did not, that all this was mere excuse. The Pharisees may, indeed, have helped on this kind of talk. It was thus a threefold cord that was thrown around John (personal resentment, religious prejudice, political apprehension). John did have power enough with the people to stir them to rebellion against Herod for his licentious marriage.

[1] 14 : 5.

There was an element of truth in all three motives. The trouble came out of the personal resentment, but the religious aspect of it would easily lead to political excitement. The various motives are not at all inconsistent.[1] The heart of the matter is given in the Synoptic Gospels. John had hit Herod hard, had touched a sore place. There is nothing more terrible than the wrath of an evil woman, especially if she is a woman of ability. Herodias cared naught for Herod's political excuses and palaver. He could talk in that manner if he wished. She had a grudge against John that she could never forgive. It burned on steadily with unceasing energy. She was implacable. She watched the moods of Herod. She watched and counted the days. A convenient[2] day will come round some time. She can afford to wait. The life of John hangs on the failure of this woman with her vacillating husband. That is to say, it hangs by a slender thread. She knows no such word as "fail." In the end she will have her way or Herod will answer for the refusal. It is a strange providence that has brought the will of this imperious adulteress against the life of John the Baptist, the brave and pure spirit of the hills, who fears not priest nor rabbi nor soldier nor publican nor tetrarch nor woman. He is caught in the coils of Herodias.

[1] So Schuerer, "Jewish People," div. II, vol. II, p. 25. Sollertinsky (*Journal of Theol. Studies*, I, 507) shows that in regard to Herod Antipas we are bound to consider Josephus's statements with care. Cf. Tasker on John the Baptist, in "Hastings's One Volume Dictionary."

[2] Mark 6 : 21.

CHAPTER IX

GLOOM

"Art thou he that cometh, or look we for another?"
(Matt. 11 : 2).

1. *The Clouds of Doubt.*—John had been carried to Machærus a prisoner.[1] He was bound in prison.[2] We do not know what John thought of this sudden checking of his work as he went up the lonely bridle path that led up the only side of the heights of Machærus that was at all accessible. He doubtless knew that it was the bitter hatred of Herodias that was primarily responsible for his arrest. How long would he be kept in confinement here? It is one of the comforts of life that we do not always know what is ahead of us. As we go into the darkness we become accustomed to it. It is a mercy not always to know how near the darkness is nor how black it will be nor how hopeless we shall feel. Edersheim[3] imagines the Baptist on the summit of the mountain and looking westward. He is three thousand eight hundred feet above the Dead Sea. Beneath him lies the Jordan, hallowed with blessed memories of repentance, confession and baptismal vows. He has seen the light of a new life shine in many faces there. Memories of his

[1] Mark 6 : 17.
[2] *Ibid.*
[3] "Life and Times," vol. I, pp. 660 f.

preaching sweep up and down the Jordan and back into the wilderness of Judea. He would think of the years of waiting and of growth in the hills. Many of his old haunts could be seen along this crag or that wady. Yonder to the south-west is Hebron, and farther to the north lies Bethlehem. His own home in the Hill Country may have caught his eye; at least the general location is visible. The years have not been many since his glad childhood days in the hills. John is now only some thirty-two or thirty-three years old. Zacharias and Elizabeth have not lived to see their son a prisoner, but he is not ashamed. He is a prisoner for truth and righteousness, for loyalty to duty, for fidelity to man and to God. Perhaps he casts another glance upon the Jordan. There was the spot where he had baptized Jesus; where he had seen the vision of the descent of the Holy Spirit like a dove; where he had heard the voice of God proclaim Jesus as his Beloved Son. Farther up on this side of Jordan was Bethany, where he had twice seen and identified Jesus as the Lamb of God, the Son of God, the Messiah that was to come. It was a comfort to John to know that he had lived to see the actual coming of the Messiah. That was the goal of his life. He had not lived in vain. His words had come true. He was vindicated before men as the Herald of the Messiah. He had done his duty in denouncing Herod and Herodias. Prophets before him had won disfavor by their courage and loyalty to truth. There was Nathan, there was Elijah, there was Jeremiah, there was Daniel. John was determined to be a man, come what may.

God ruled and he was in God's work. Besides, the Messiah himself was now on earth, and he was the Messiah's Forerunner.

So John was led down into one of the dungeons of the castle. There was no trial, for Herod's will was law in such matters. There was no chance of escape, nor would escape have amounted to anything in the temper of Herod Antipas and his wife. John was not wholly cut off from the outside world. Herod and Herodias came and went and frequently sent for John to come up to the upper rooms of the castle where he "heard him gladly." [1] At such times John doubtless caught a brief glimpse of the outside world through openings in the castle walls. John came to exercise a curious power[2] over Herod, but not over Herodias. "It is a sign, such as has no parallel, of John's greatness, of the impressions he could produce in the soul of this not merely weak, but characterless man; of his power to awaken whatever nobility, whatever serious struggle of good against evil was possible in such a case, a power which the Man of God himself could bring to bear on the very stones of the wilderness. Thus, then, alarm and irresolution, conscious guilt and esteem worked together to secure the Baptist his life for a while longer, until the rancorous woman, whose removal John demanded, by stealth obtained the goal which her tempestuous wrath "had striven in vain to reach." [3] It was then a duel between John and Herodias, if one may so say. Geike[4] understands the words

[1] Mark 6 : 20. [2] Mark 6 : 19 f.
[3] Keim, "Jesus of Nazara," vol. II, p. 345.
[4] "Life and Words of Jesus," vol. I, p. 420.

of Jesus in Matt. 17 : 12 ("And they knew him not, but did unto him whatsoever they would") to mean that Herod and Herodias mistreated John in all sorts of ways. The words "point to torture, insult, and ill-treatment. The spirit that called for the blind Samson to be brought from his prison to make sport before the Philistine lords, was still in full vigor." The words of themselves[1] are capable of that meaning, and certainly Herodias is capable of anything mean. But the usual application among expositors is to the death of John, the final outcome rather than a long process of torture. Mark[2] expressly says that Herod kept John safe, but that after all means only safe from death, not from insult at the hands of Herodias. John doubtless knew every moment that Herodias watched or had watched his every movement.[3]

John had one crumb of comfort. His disciples were allowed to come and see him.[4] The disciples of John did not at once disband. They are doubtless dazed by the blow that has come to the Master; some of them may have felt that they were justified in the complaint that they had made to him about the greater success of Jesus; they may have imagined that somehow Jesus was partly responsible for the sad predicament of John. It had all turned out worse than they had feared. Jesus was the popular hero and was now in the full tide of success in his Galilean ministry. Many of the disciples of John had already gone to Jesus with the advice and approval of John.

[1] ἀλλὰ ἐποίησαν ἐν αὐτῷ ὅσα ἠθέλησαν.
[2] 6 : 20. [3] Mark 6 : 19. [4] Luke 7 : 18.

Now that John's voice is no longer heard along the Jordan, the crowds have all flocked to Galilee to hear the new prophet there; one with an even more wonderful message than John had; one who does marvellous cures; one whom many claim to be the very Messsiah himself. A feeling of bitterness would gradually come into the hearts of some of John's disciples. They could pray, for John had his disciples to pray.[1] John taught his disciples to fast as the Pharisees did. Perhaps at first unconsciously the disciples of John, forgetful or oblivious of the fact that the Pharisees were partly responsible for John's arrest, were drawn to take sides with the Pharisees against the disciples of Jesus. True, John had denounced the Pharisees, but here was Jesus with his disciples attending a great feast of publicans and sinners in the house of a prominent publican named Levi.[2] John would probably not[3] have attended a feast like that anywhere, most assuredly not in such a place and in such company. The Pharisees had made complaint to the disciples of Jesus[4] and the disciples of John probably sympathized with the criticism. At any rate it did look unseemly to them, all this levity on the part of Jesus (the Messiah, John's Messiah) and some of John's old disciples, while John himself languished in the dungeon at Machærus. Besides, it may have been on one of the weekly fast days that Levi's feast took place.[5] If so, that made it seem to them a real scandal. The

[1] Luke 11 : 1.
[2] Luke 5 : 29; Mark 2 : 15; Matt. 9 : 10.
[3] Matt. 11 : 18; Luke 7 : 33.
[4] Matt. 9 : 11; Mark 2 : 16; Luke 5 : 30.
[5] Edersheim, "Life and Times," vol. I, p. 663.

stricter Jews fasted twice a week.[1] The disciples of John naturally kept up his ascetic practices. It is very likely, therefore, that the feast of Matthew was on one of the nights after a fast had been begun by the disciples of John and of the Pharisees.[2] Hence the disciples of John feel emboldened and justified in coming to Jesus, even in company with the Pharisees,[3] to make complaint against him and his disciples for not fasting. The Pharisees are doubtless glad of a chance to drive the wedge in between the disciples of John and those of Jesus so as to make a wider separation. Swete[4] thinks that Mark shows that it was scribes, not disciples of John or of the Pharisees, who made complaint. But this is forcing the matter unduly in the face of Matt. 2 : 14, where it is expressly said that the disciples of John came to Jesus about the matter. The reply of Jesus seems like an echo of the last public testimony of the Baptist, when he had called Jesus the bridegroom and himself the friend of the bridegroom.[5] We have no means of knowing whether Jesus had heard of this testimony of the Baptist other than what occurs here. It is natural to think from this language of Jesus that he had been informed of the Baptist's noble words. There is no reflection in Christ's language on the Baptist, not the slightest. It is some of the disciples of John (not John himself) who have aligned themselves with Pharisaism in opposition to Jesus. John had evidently not made fasting an essential matter at all. We have no word

[1] Luke 18 : 12. [2] Swete on Mark, 2 : 18.
[3] Mark 2 : 18. Cf. Matt. 9 : 14; Luke 5 : 33.
[4] *In loco.* [5] John 3 : 29.

from him on the subject. He was still in the Jewish dispensation. It was not for John to furnish the new bottle, the new garment. That was for the Messiah. It is ceremonial Judaism that Jesus calls outworn, not John's message about repentance and real righteousness. So Jesus insisted in the presence of these disciples of John on the right of his disciples as "the sons of the bride-chamber" to feast instead of fasting. The time for fasting will come to them, real fasting and sorrow, when the bridegroom is no longer with them, for he will be taken away.[1] Was Jesus thinking of what Herod had already done to John, who had been spirited away to Machærus? Is he delicately saying to John's disciples that they have good reason to fast? He was also thinking of his own end, already foreseen. They will do unto Jesus as they have done unto John.

"John heard in the prison the work of the Christ." [2] Luke[3] says: "And the disciples of John told him all these things." We are thus under obligation to Matthew and Luke[4] for a glimpse of the intercommunication that was allowed to go on between John and his disciples. There was much to tell. Jesus was using John's text: "The time is fulfilled, and the kingdom of God is at hand: repent ye, and believe in the gospel." [5] At other times he used John's identical language: "Repent ye, for the kingdom of heaven is at hand." [6] Events had moved rapidly during the

[1] Matt. 9: 15; Mark 2: 20; Luke 5: 36.
[2] Matt. 11: 2.
[3] 7: 18.
[4] To quote (the Logia) the common non-Markan source so often used in Matthew and Luke. Cf. Allen on Matthew; Harnack, "Sayings of Jesus"; Hawkins, "Horæ Synopticæ."
[5] Mark 1: 14.
[6] Matt. 4: 17.

months that John lay in prison.[1] Jesus had wrought many wonderful miracles. He cast out demons, who went out crying: "Thou art the Son of God," but "he suffered them not to speak, because they knew that he was the Christ."[2] He had made a tour of Galilee and "there followed him great multitudes from Galilee and Decapolis and Jerusalem and Judea and from beyond Jordan."[3] It surpassed the exciting days of John's great ministry. Nobody ever saw anything like it. The crowds were so great at times that Jesus had to escape to the desert places to get away and pray. He could no more openly enter into a city.[4] The Pharisees were up in arms against Jesus for claiming to be the Son of man with power to forgive sins, but the people were amazed[5] at his miracles and glorified God: "We never saw it on this fashion." A sort of fear fell on many.[6] The more the Pharisees opposed Jesus, the closer he seemed to draw to the publicans and sinners, and actually feasted with them in the house of a publican.[7] This was more than many of John's own disciples could stand, and on his behalf they had joined with the Pharisees against the absence of fasting on the part of the disciples of Jesus.[8] They did not quite understand the comments of Jesus, but perhaps John would. The Pharisees had gone to the point of saying: "By the prince of the demons he casts out demons."[9] In Jerusalem there had been an open breach between Jesus and the Pharisees. They had accused him of equality with the Father, of being

[1] ἐν τῷ δεσμωτηρίῳ.
[2] Luke 4: 41.
[3] Matt. 4: 25.
[4] Mark 1: 45.
[5] Mark 2: 10–12.
[6] Luke 5: 26.
[7] Matt. 9: 10; Mark 2: 15.
[8] Mark 2: 18.
[9] Matt. 9: 34.

a Sabbath-breaker because he healed an impotent man on the Sabbath, and had actually tried to kill Jesus.[1] The address of Jesus on the occasion had left them speechless with rage because of the lofty claims[2] made by Jesus, but he had made a beautiful reference to John himself[3] in his rebuke of the Pharisees. He called John a witness to the truth and the lamp that burns and shines. But Jesus had stuck to his position on the Sabbath, and on two successive Sabbaths in Galilee had controversy with the Pharisees about his freedom from their rules for the observance of the day. Matters came to such a pitch that the Pharisees actually conspired with the Herodians[4] to put Jesus to death. If things went on this way no one could tell what the outcome would be. But so far Jesus was triumphant. He was master of the multitude. He had done remarkable and noteworthy things. He had chosen twelve men, half of them from among John's old disciples, to be a select band to be with him all the time, on his preaching tours and always. On that occasion Jesus had delivered the most remarkable sermon that people had ever heard.[5] He had outlined a policy about righteousness in the kingdom that was a stinging rebuke to the mere ceremonial righteousness[6] of the Scribes and Pharisees. It reminded John's disciples of his own denunciation[7] of the Pharisees and Sadducees down by the Jordan. On the whole, the teaching of Jesus was an expansion of that of John. From time to time various disciples

[1] John 5 : 10–18. [2] John 5 : 19–29. [3] John 5 : 33–35.
[4] Mark 3 : 6. [5] Matt. 7 : 28 f. [6] Matt. 5 : 20.
[7] Matt. 3 : 7.

of John came and told him what they knew and what he was anxious to hear. By and by the most startling news of all came to the dungeon in Machærus. Jesus had raised a girl who had apparently been dead.[1] But a widow was going with her only son to bury him near Nain, and Jesus stopped the procession and made the corpse sit up and speak and gave him to his mother.[2] This was the climax. "A great prophet is arisen among us: and, God hath visited his people." This news came to John in addition to all the rest that he had heard. We are not told the spirit in which the disciples of John reported these things to John.[3] John heard them as "the works of the Christ," and that is significant. They were apparently reported to him as the doings of the Messiah, for "the Christ" was not yet a proper name.

The news set John to musing, for he was by this time in "a prison mood."[4] He had listened with eager interest to every bit of news about Jesus as the Messiah. It was the one topic that most vitally concerned him. It is probably in the spring-time when John hears about the raising of the son of the widow of Nain. The plucking of the grains of wheat[5] in their hands as the disciples and Jesus walked through the wheat field shows that Luke is usually chronological. If so, the miracle and the report of it to John[6] followed the incident in the wheat fields. We have notice in John's Gospel[7] of another spring apparently a year sooner than this, when Jesus was in Jerusalem.

[1] Matt. 9 : 22–26; Mark 5 : 35–43.
[2] Luke 7 : 11–17.
[3] Bruce, "Matthew," *in loco.*
[4] *Ibid.*
[5] Luke 6 : 1.
[6] Luke 7 : 11–18.
[7] John 2 : 13.

Then John the Baptist was still at liberty, and preaching, though he was arrested not long afterward. We do not know at what point of the late spring or early summer[1] the disciples of John brought him this message which so stirred him. At any rate we may think of John as having been in prison about a year. What a change this year has wrought in the fortunes and feelings of John! Broadus[2] has ably pictured John's situation: "He had indeed been accustomed to comparative solitude for years 'in the deserts' (Luke 1:80); but at that time life was before him with its high hopes, and he doubtless felt himself to be preparing for a great mission, the nature of which was gradually growing clearer to his mind. Then came some eighteen months of public labors, during which he was attended by vast crowds, and his ardent nature must have revelled in the high excitement of his work. And now he is shut up, he, a 'son of the wilderness,' in one of the deep, dark, and frightfully hot dungeons of Machærus, deprived of fresh air and bodily exercise, of cheerful mental employment and opportunity to do good, and dependent for any future opportunities on the caprice of a weak king and a cruel woman. As Elijah sometimes got sadly out of heart, so John, who in many respects closely resembled him, would be likely to grow despondent in this season of enforced idleness and uncertain danger. Compare the occasional depression of Moses also." The very miracle at Nain would remind John "of Elijah and the widow of Sarepta; of Elisha and the

[1] Probably A. D. 28. [2] "Commentary on Matthew," p. 235.

lady of the not-far-distant Shunem. They, too, the greatest of the prophets, had restored to lonely women their dead only sons."[1] John has brooded long over his own fate and over the work of Jesus. What is his frame of mind? It would have been a miracle indeed if no doubts had come to him during the weary, dreary months of his imprisonment. The clouds had come and gone with John, and then they came again. It is a bitter thing for any man to feel that his work in life is over.[2] "We are in spirit by the mount of God, and about to witness the breaking of a terrible storm. It is one that uproots the great trees and rends the rocks; and we shall watch it solemnly, earnestly, as with bared head—or, like Elijah, with face wrapt in mantle."[3] Most of the time John was alone with his thoughts. On the whole this may have been best. The disciples of John did not fully understand him and were in danger of fossilization.[4] John himself had to face doubts about them, about himself, about Jesus that rose in that dungeon. "Like serpents that crept out of its walls, they would uncoil and raise their heads with horrible hissing."[5] Had some horrible mistake been made after all? Was it a nightmare? Was his life on the Jordan a dream? Was anything real or worth while? If Jesus was the Messiah, why did he leave him to languish in prison? If he could raise the dead, he could set him free. There was but one way to settle the matter. It was

[1] Farrar, "Life of Christ," vol. I, p. 286.
[2] Farrar, "Life of Christ," vol. I, p. 289.
[3] Edersheim, "Life and Times," vol. I, p. 666.
[4] *Ibid.* [5] *Ibid.*, p. 667.

to appeal to Jesus himself. John called two of his disciples and sent them to Jesus.

2. *The Cry from the Dungeon.*—John "sent by his disciples and said unto" Jesus: "Art thou he that cometh, or look we for another?"[1] The message of John was borne directly to Jesus. John thus spoke again to Jesus. Once the Pharisees had sent a committee of Sadducees from Jerusalem to John in Bethany to learn if he claimed to be the Coming One. They had put the sharp question to John: "Thou, who art thou?"[2] So now in John's turn he sends a committee to Jesus with the same sharp emphasis on "thou." The question was probably in Aramaic, but even so the Greek translation may be assumed to be accurate in tone and emphasis. The two messengers are abrupt, almost curt, in their approach to Jesus: "John the Baptist hath sent us unto thee, saying, Art thou he that cometh, or look we for another?"[3] The tone seems apologetic as much as to say, "We should not have come except that John, our master, has sent us. We do not wish to interrupt you or to interfere, but this is the message. We await your reply." We are probably justified in feeling that these two disciples of John were not particularly friendly to Jesus.

[1] Matt. 11 : 3; Luke 7 : 19. Σὺ εἶ ὁ ἐρχόμενος ἢ ἕτερον προσδοκῶμεν; The verb may be either the futuristic present indicative or the deliberative present subjunctive. More likely the latter. In Luke some MSS. (A. D.) read ἄλλον, but ἕτερον is the correct text. The idea is probably a different kind of a Messiah, not merely another (ἄλλον) of the same kind as Jesus. Note the emphasis on Σύ. Matthew and Luke preserve the logion in the same form.

[2] Σὺ τίς εἶ; John 1 : 19.

[3] WH read ἄλλον here following B, but ἕτερον is doubtless correct as it is supported by ℵ DL Ξ 33. Too much is not to be made of the point, since ἕτερον may mean only a "second," not "different."

They doubtless felt much that they would have enjoyed saying by way of reproach to Jesus for the apparent indifference which he had manifested toward John and his fate. Jesus, they mean to say, had sent no word of cheer to John. It is John who condescends to inquire of Jesus, the man whom John had baptized and introduced as the Coming One. Now Jesus is having all the glory and John all the woe. It is enough to make John lose faith in Jesus. As for themselves they had already done so. The disciples of John were right when they protested to John for his excess of kindness to Jesus, who had swept into the enjoyment of the fruit of John's toil, and was edging John off to one side and almost squeezing him out of the kingdom which John was the first to announce. The last words that John had spoken about Jesus were of the most laudatory nature, the very acme of eulogy for Jesus and of self-abnegation for John. It was all right for John to be humble and to feel that way, but they had their opinion of Jesus for taking it all to himself at the expense of John. If he could work so many miracles, why did he not do one for John? John had done everything for Jesus. What had he done for John? And now John had been driven in desperation to send them to Jesus for one word of comfort, for one ray of light in the darkness of his dungeon. They had come out of their love for John, not because they loved Jesus or expected any good to come out of the inquiry. As for themselves, they would have died in the dungeon in independence and self-respect rather than send this embassy. In their opinion John was just as good as Jesus, if not better. It was John who had had the courage to denounce the sins of Herod and Herodias. It was John who had inaugurated the new day in Israel. The disciples of Jesus had simply copied John's baptism and were not so pious as the disciples of John since they led a life of feasting and did not fast and did not know how to pray. But they had come because John wished it. And here they were. What did Jesus have to say in defence of himself under all the circumstances? They would like to know.

But surely John himself did not mean all this, though probably the two disciples did. Indeed, the disciples may have spoken with John and given their opinion to him before starting. The embassy is clearly sent on John's own impulse, "calling unto him two of his disciples." [1] But this was done after "the disciples of John told him all of these things." [2] Some of John's disciples had opened their hearts to him in the dungeon about "the works of the Christ." [3] What they said is conjecture, but we know the temper of the disciples of John who had come to him in the day of John's power with words about the rising star of Jesus.[4] It is hardly likely that all of John's disciples were kindly disposed to Jesus now that John's star had set. In fact, we know that some of them had actually lined up with the Pharisees against Jesus.[5] It is not straining the situation at all to suppose that some, if not all, of the disciples of John who brought news of the ever-widening power and fame of Jesus

[1] Luke 7 : 19. [2] Luke 2 : 18. [3] Matt. 11 : 2.
[4] John 3 : 26. [5] Mark 2 : 18.

betrayed a tone of disappointment, a tinge of resentment against Jesus because he had displaced John in favor and prestige. Not that John did not still have friends. He did have them, but a real breach had come, as they had foreseen while John was free, and now those who were most loyal to John held aloof from Jesus and let him go his way. It is natural for one's friends to color a situation to please the friend in sore distress. If a pastor has a division in his church, his party bear him reports favorable to him and derogatory to the other side. It was inevitable that talk of this nature came to John's ears in the dungeon. When it came before, John had nobly brushed it all aside.[1] Could he do it now after all that had happened in the past year? Perhaps these disciples of John had suggested to him that the only hope of his rescue lay in Jesus and they did not believe that he cared enough for John to do anything in his behalf.[2] The very narrowness and unprogressiveness of John's disciples may have been one of the elements in John's decision to appeal to Jesus.[3] John could not now handle the situation as he had done before. It was pitiful to think that John's disciples should drift away from Jesus, even become hostile to him. Chrysostom[4] long ago suggested that John made this inquiry for the benefit of his disciples. The trouble with the form in which this explanation of the message of John has been held is that it has

[1] John 3 : 27 ff.

[2] Edersheim, "Life and Times," vol. I, p. 661.

[3] *Ibid.*, p. 667.

[4] See "Oxford Library of the Fathers," X, p. 267. Practically all the fathers held this view except Tertullian. Cf. Plummer on Luke and Bruce on Luke. So Luther, Calvin, Beza, Grotius, Bengel, etc.

been offered as a substitute for the idea that John himself was in doubt. It was thought to be discreditable to John to admit that he was in real doubt. Hence he asked for the benefit of his disciples. But the two views are by no means exclusive. It was entirely possible for John to wish Jesus to help his disciples for the very reason that John himself was unable to do so. If Jesus would help John, then John could give his disciples the guidance which they needed, could heal the breach that had been made. We may admit, therefore, that desire to be of service to his disciples who had revealed to John their own anguish of heart was one of the motives that prompted John's inquiry. We do not see that it was the only one nor necessarily the main purpose of John. But any such notion as that of Theophylact that John merely "affects to inquire" or of Euthymius Zigabenus that John is "in pretence inquiring" may be dismissed as wholly unworthy of John or of the dignity and seriousness of the situation.[1] John may have had (probably did have) an interest in the attitude of his disciples, but it was a real interest, not a make-believe affair like that.

The view of Strauss may be unconditionally rejected. "Strauss cuts the knot by denying the historicity of the earlier narratives, especially the Fourth Gospel's, which represent John as recognizing and announcing the Messiahship of Jesus. He does not now begin to doubt whether after all Jesus is really the Messiah, but rather begins to wonder if he may not be the Messiah. 'We have here not a decaying,

[1] Broadus, "Commentary on Matthew," p. 236.

but a growing certainty.' "[1] This "budding faith hypothesis is based on too sceptical a view as to the historic value of even the synoptical accounts of John's early relations with Jesus."[2] Such a wilful setting aside of the sources of information makes historical study impossible and nugatory. This theory sets the pyramid on its apex. It may be safely thrown to the rubbish heap.

We may assume then that John himself was personally involved in the inquiry because he also needed help. Was John in doubt or was he merely impatient? Let us take the question of doubt first. "Many have thought it wholly inconsistent with John's position and previous testimony to suppose that he now felt personally the slightest doubt."[3] But that is the natural import of John's message, and it is best to take it so unless the difficulties are insuperable. "We need not suppose that he at any time wholly lost his persuasion that Jesus was the Messiah, but only that he became harassed by difficulties that he could not solve."[4] It was not psychologically impossible for John to have lapsed at times into doubt. He was in a real Doubting Castle if ever there was one. It is true what Herrick says:

"Stone walls do not a prison make,
Nor iron bars a cage;
Minds innocent and quiet take
That for a hermitage."

[1] Smith, "Days of His Flesh," p. 224.

[2] Bruce, "Matthew," *in loco*. Strauss is followed by Keim, Weizsäcker, Holtzmann in his "Hand-Commentar" ("beginnende Disposition zum Glauben an Jesu Messianität." For a complete answer to Strauss, see Hase, "Geschichte Jesu," sec. 39, ed. 1891.

[3] Broadus, "Matthew," p. 236. [4] *Ibid.*, p. 237.

But it is very difficult for one to be uninfluenced by his environment, to hold one's self to the highest all the time. We can point to the experience of Jesus himself in the Garden of Gethsemane[1] when under the stress of sore temptation Jesus with strong crying and tears[2] begged that he might escape the hour, the dreadful hour before him, when he should hang upon the Cross for the sin of the world. If it seems natural that Jesus had this instinctive shrinking from the terrible task before him, John may be pardoned if his mind became beclouded on the subject whether after all Jesus was proving to be the Lamb of God that taketh away the sin of the world as he had declared[3] him to be. Indeed, as it was now, things seemed to be turned round. John was the sufferer, while Jesus was "the idol of the populace, the hero of the hour."[4] This was John's highest conception of the Messiah, the sacrificial work. But he had also depicted him as a reformer. The axe was lying at the root of the trees ready for the Messiah to wield it.[5] The Messiah will take the fan in his hand "and he will thoroughly cleanse his threshing-floor; and he will gather his wheat into the garner, but the chaff he will burn up with unquenchable fire."[6] The mighty baptism of the Holy Spirit which John had foreseen and predicted[7] had not yet come in the full sense of John's idea. We need not say that John lapsed while in prison to the political conception of the Messiah held by the Jews in general, "that Jesus for a time at least raised John's

[1] Mark 14 : 35 f. [2] Heb. 5 : 7. [3] John 1 : 29.
[4] Smith, "Days of His Flesh," p. 225.
[5] Matt. 3 : 10. [6] Matt. 3 : 12. [7] Matt. 3 : 11.

mind to the height of his own insight; that when the influence of Jesus was withdrawn, John relapsed to his own familiar modes of thought."[1] He did have the heightened insight, but it is rather too easy a way out of the difficulty to suppose that this was due merely to the presence of Jesus. He had insight before he saw Jesus. It was raised by Jesus, but it remained high after he no longer saw Jesus. The doubt of John here does come as a surprise, but we are to remember that we have had no word from John for a year. The natural depression due to his surroundings had brought him to a pessimistic frame of mind. As a matter of fact, he could not see that Jesus was as yet either a reformer or a sufferer.[2] He could not see that the Cross was coming to Jesus, and that from the Cross Jesus would draw all men to him and so uplift and reform the race. The prophetic passion may have cooled in John at this time, but Elijah sat under the juniper-tree and wished to die. So fiercely had Jezebel beset him. Jeremiah, another great prophet, had poured out his soul in "Jeremiah" and "Lamentations." "Savonarola, and Jerome of Prague, and Luther were men whose courage, like that of the Baptist, had enabled them to stand unquailing before angry councils and threatening kings: who, in forming an estimate of their goodness and greatness, will add one shade of condemnation because of the wavering of the first and of the second in the prison-cells of Florence and Constance, or the phantasies of incipient

[1] Principal A. E. Garvie, *The Expositor*, VI, p. 375.
[2] Smith, "Days of His Flesh," p. 225.

madness which agitated, in the castle of Wartburg, the ardent spirit of the third?"[1] Just to be let alone for so long in this damp, dark, dismal dungeon was enough to bring one to despair. The fellowship that John had with his disciples now and then was a relief in one sense, this occasional glimpse of the great world outside; but from another point of view, it was like reopening an old wound. "To a child of freedom and of passion, to a rugged, passionate, untamed spirit like that of John, a prison was worse than death."[2]

It is possible also that the long confinement had had an effect on John's temper. "What ailed John was not so much a mistaken ideal as impatience."[3] The moral isolation of Jesus is brought out here by the apparent irritability of John.[4] Perhaps John felt that he could stir Jesus to more formal announcement of himself as Messiah, to a line of activity that would be more reassuring to John's disciples and in truth to John himself.[5] The Jews had an idea, many of them, that there would be a succession of forerunners. Without abandoning the conviction that he was himself a forerunner, John may have wished to raise with Jesus the question whether he was himself just another forerunner or in reality the Coming One.[6] Some thought Elijah himself would come to life, others Jeremiah; some thought "the prophet" spoken of by

[1] Farrar, "Life of Christ," vol. I, p. 292.
[2] *Ibid.*, p. 290. [3] Smith, "Days of His Flesh," p. 225.
[4] Bruce, "Matthew," *in loco.*
[5] Broadus, "Matthew," p. 237; Kohler, "Johannes der Täufer," S. 166 f.
[6] "The Coming One" is the Messiah. Cf. Ps. 118 : 26; Dan. 7 : 13; Mark 11 : 9; Luke 13 : 35; 19 : 38; Heb. 10 : 37. Cf. Plummer on Luke, *in loco.*

Moses would come. Most of those alternatives[1] had been presented to John himself by the Jerusalem committee. When so much was at stake and in the midst of so much perplexity it is not strange that John wished to have all uncertainty allayed. One on the bed of sickness in the hour of death loves to hear the reassuring words which he had himself spoken to others when in health. It was thus a combination of influences which led to the Baptist's obscuration of faith and hope.

> "Who listened to his voice? obeyed his cry?
> Only the echoes which he made relent
> Rang from their flinty caves, 'Repent! Repent!'"

"The Baptist's scepticism was real, but it was honest, and we may learn from him how to manage our own doubts."[2] Jesus was doing Messianic works, but he was not claiming in so many words to be the Messiah. Hence John may have argued that this silence indicated an uncertainty and even inconsistency in the mind of Jesus.[3]

To us it may seem a puzzle that at that crisis in the history of the kingdom of God the Baptist should have been thrown into prison.[4] God has often made "his best and greatest servants drink to the very dregs the cup of apparent failure."[5] It was to be true of Jesus himself as John had dimly foreseen in his phrase

[1] John 1 : 19 ff. [2] Stalker, "The Two St. Johns," p. 239.

[3] Plummer, "Matthew," p. 160. Edersheim ("Life and Times," vol. I, p. 668) scores a good point when he says that the mention in the gospels of the weakness of John after his strong testimony to Jesus is good evidence of the fidelity of the picture. It is drawn from life.

[4] Reynolds, "John the Baptist," p. 412.

[5] Farrar, "Life of Christ," vol. I, p. 291.

"the Lamb of God." It was true of Stephen, of Paul. But, when all is said, it may be seriously questioned whether a more noble and glorious end could have befallen John than the one which was his. The disciples of John had already become suspicious of Jesus. The prolonged activity of John would have accentuated that. The enforced retirement of John left the field clear for Jesus, as it should have been. John's light went out when it was at its brightest. He met a martyr's death and won a martyr's crown through no fault of his. Our hearts are with him in his struggles in the dungeon, but it is a short-sighted view of God and human life that can see only evil in the fate of John. God had not forgotten his servant when he let him remain in Machærus. Nor was Jesus unconcerned or heartless when he failed to interfere in John's behalf. But, with all the clouds of doubt that had gathered around John, let us never forget that he brought his doubts to Jesus. What can Jesus say that will dispel the clouds and send sunshine into the cell at Machærus?

3. *The Cheer for John.*—At first Jesus made no reply to the rather sharp inquiry of the messengers of John. It was apparently a moment of holy excitement[1] when great crowds pressed around the Master to hear his words and to be healed of their diseases. The disciples of John had not waited for a time of leisure to present their query. It had come in reality as an interruption. So Jesus worked on as if nothing had happened. "In that hour he cured many of dis-

[1] Stalker, "The Two St. Johns," p. 240.

eases and plagues and evil spirits; and on many that were blind he bestowed[1] sight."[2] Probably the disciples grew impatient and may even have manifested signs of it. This was surely a fine way to treat a message of the Baptist after all that John had done for Jesus, and considering the present plight of the Baptist. But Jesus meant no discourtesy nor was he careless about John. Is it any reflection on Jesus to say that he was meditating while he worked? The disciples of John watched Jesus. Finally he spoke: "Go your way, and tell John what things ye have seen and heard."[3] There was nothing new in that. John knew of "the works of the Christ" already.[4] Yes, he knew, but he did not understand. "It seems a stern, almost unfeeling reply. He spoke no word of sympathy. He sent no message of cheer to that brave soul languishing in prison and questioning whether the crowning act of his heroic ministry had not been a fatal blunder. It seems almost a cruel reply, but in truth Jesus spoke both kindly and wisely."[5] Jesus went on: "The blind receive their sight, the lame walk, the lepers are cleansed and the deaf hear, the dead are raised up, the poor have good tidings preached to them."[6] The most of these things had just passed under their eyes. The disciples had the benefit of experience to take to John. The case of the raising of the son of the Widow of

[1] *ἐχαρίσατο*. Graciously bestowed as a free gift. Cf. a modern oculist who saves sight for many.

[2] Luke 7 : 21.

[3] Luke 7 : 22.

[4] Matt. 11 : 2.

[5] Smith, "Days of His Flesh," p. 226.

[6] Luke 7 : 22. Cf. Matt. 11 : 4 f.

Nain was very recent.[1] There was only one new point in the message. That was the preaching to the poor. This was a Messianic sign as John would probably recognize.[2] They are all works of mercy, none mere works of power or display such as the Pharisees expected the Messiah to perform.[3] The works of Jesus that John had heard of in the prison might prove only that Jesus was a great prophet. Elijah and Elisha had raised the dead. Jesus had himself claimed the preaching to the poor to be a Messianic sign.[4] It was a new thing in Jewish life for a rabbi to honor the poor. The message of Jesus to John therefore is symbolical, like that of Tarquinius Superbus to his son Sextus at Gabii.[5] They are to tell John what they have seen Jesus doing. Actions speak louder than mere words. It would be easy for Jesus to say the word Messiah, but a mere claim would not make it true. Jesus does not seem concerned whether the messengers will understand his symbolism or not.[6] But surely John will comprehend.

Jesus does not mention the word Messiah[7] nor the phrase of John "the Coming One." If he had done so on this occasion, he would have violated his custom at this period of his ministry. After the first few months we find Jesus carefully abstaining from applying the term Messiah to himself. The jealousy of the Pharisees had already been aroused against him and they would understand the use of "Messiah" by

[1] The tenses are all present (iterative present).
[2] Bruce, "Matthew," *in loco*. Cf. Isa. 35 : 5; 61 : 1.
[3] Plummer, "Matthew," p. 160.
[4] Luke 4 : 18–21.
[5] Plummer, "Matthew," p. 160.
[6] Plummer, "Matthew," p. 160.
[7] Sanday, "The Life of Christ in Recent Research," p. 57.

Jesus in the political sense which was untrue in itself and which would lead to insurrection against Rome or at least violent popular disturbance.[1] These very disciples of John might have been misled by the use of the term by Jesus. Jesus could not afford to imperil the course of his ministry by giving a categorical reply to the question of John. He therefore sends John an affirmative answer, but in symbolism; a cryptogram, but not a very hard one to read. "It was not indeed the sort of evidence that John was looking for; but it was his expectation that was at fault, and Jesus had faith in his sincerity, his candor, his open-mindedness, his willingness to reconsider his opinions and abandon them if he found them untenable."[2]

4. *The Gentle Reproof*.—"And blessed is he, whosoever shall find none occasion of stumbling in me."[3] This is a beatitude that Jesus sends John. It is expressed in general terms, but John will certainly understand what Jesus means. Jesus does not place a premium on doubt, not even on honest doubt such as that in the case of John. With all the natural causes that led to John's doubt, it was weakness, not strength. There was pathos in the use of the word "happy" by Jesus. John was certainly not happy, and doubt had made him more unhappy than ever. Many will find

[1] Broadus, "Harmony of the Gospels," p. 24.

[2] Smith, "Days of His Flesh," p. 226.

[3] Luke 7 : 23; Matt. 11 : 6. *καὶ μακάριος ἐστὶν ὃς ἐὰν μὴ σκανδαλισθῇ ἐν ἐμοί*. The use of *μακάριος* is like that in Matt. 5 : 3 ff. The use of *σκανδαλίζω* (common in the New Testament) may be compared with Isa. 8 : 14. "John was in a dangerous state of mind. If he had given way to his pessimistic mood he might have stumbled over the stone which he had been sent to lay in Zion as the chief corner-stone" (Stalker, "The Two St. Johns," p. 245).

Jesus a stumbling-block, but that ought not to be true of John. He had been enlightened beyond the men of his time. He ought to understand Jesus. This message of tender rebuke would confirm the implicit claim of Jesus to be the Messiah. The import of all that Jesus has said in his message to John is that he is what John had proclaimed him to be. He sends renewed proof of his power. John should not doubt. There was nothing in Jesus to justify doubt. He was going on with the work of the kingdom in the way that he had begun. It would all come out right in the end. Jesus was doubtless deeply touched by this sad wail from John, for Jesus could only love the Herald of the Messiah. He sent him the best possible message out of a heart that lovėd him and sympathized with him. John had somehow misunderstood Jesus, and Jesus was deeply grieved to find it so. It was almost a tragedy that there should come the least misunderstanding between John and Jesus. But John is right at heart as Jesus knows. Jesus was in no way responsible for the present predicament of John. The disciples of John left with this message of Jesus and bore it to John, perhaps dubious what comfort John would get out of it. But Jesus was concerned about John's insight, not about theirs. Let us hope that John did see all that Jesus wished him to understand, that his heart was permanently refreshed by the words of Christ. One can almost feel sorry that these two disciples of John had not heard the generous praise that Jesus gave to John when once they were out of hearing.[1] It seems as if Christ made

[1] Matt. 11 : 7; Luke 7 : 24.

a point of waiting till they were out of ear-shot before "he began to say unto the multitudes concerning John." [1] From one stand-point this noble eulogy would have been meat and drink to John in his loneliness and grief. Bits of it probably were carried to John afterward by other disciples of his. Farrar[2] even supposes that Jesus spoke privately to John's messengers other words of affection and encouragement "for the grand prisoner whose end was now so rapidly approaching—words which would be to him sweeter than the honey which had sustained his hunger in the wilderness, dearer than water-springs in the dry ground." But there is no real basis for that supposition. Perhaps Jesus felt that his praise would seem more sincere and genuine if not meant as a direct message to John. It was more delicate, as it was, and shows how much Jesus really loved John, how he had done all to cheer him that lay in his power. The purpose of Jesus may have been partly to vindicate John in the minds of some in the multitude who thought "John irresolute or cowardly." [3] Plummer[4] suggests also that if the disciples of John had heard this glowing eulogy it would have counteracted the effect of the rebuke which Jesus had given. "This panegyric is almost the funeral oration of the Baptist; for soon after this he was put to death." [5]

[1] Luke 7 : 24. [2] "Life of Christ," vol. I, p. 293.
[3] Smith, "Days of His Flesh," p. 226.
[4] "Luke," p. 204. [5] Plummer, *ibid.*

CHAPTER X

APPRECIATION

"Among them that are born of women there hath not arisen a greater than John the Baptist" (Matt. 11 : 11).

1. *The Courage of John.*—John had often borne testimony to Jesus, and Jesus now bears glad witness to his great worth and work.[1] "In society men are commonly praised to their face, or the faces of their friends, and blamed behind their backs. Jesus does the opposite in the case of John." [2] "Gossip only waits till the door is shut behind a visitor before canvassing every defect in his appearance and ripping up the seams of his character." [3] Jesus probably knew that the by-standers "were charging the Baptist with vacillation and cowardice. His faith, once so assured, was shaken; adversity had broken his spirit." [4] In the minds of the people, now that the messengers of John are gone, Jesus will not seem to be using words of fulsome flattery. It is clear that Jesus was not willing for the inquiry of John and his reply to have the effect on the crowd of depreciating John. Jesus was not willing for the people to draw injurious inferences[5] from what had just occurred, so that he

[1] Broadus, "Matthew," p. 238. [2] Plummer, "Matthew," p. 161.
[3] Stalker, "The Two St. Johns," p. 247.
[4] Smith, "Days of His Flesh," p. 226.
[5] Bruce, "Matthew," p. 170.

began at once, as the messengers departed, his defence of John. He spoke with poetic intensity[1] in discharge of a debt[2] of love to John. It is Jesus who thus interprets for men the real significance of John. It was John who first apprehended Jesus and interpreted him to some of his disciples. Now in turn Jesus "in language of rhythmic and perfect loveliness"[3] shows the perfect solidarity between himself and John, finds John's niche in the temple of history and places him securely in it. No one can dislodge John from the high pinnacle on which Jesus put him. No one had so perfect an understanding of the human heart as Jesus. His judgments of men are final.[4] Jesus spoke such glorious praise of no other man. It is all true, but was probably occasioned by the very pathos of John's situation. It was a fine opportunity to do John justice, and Jesus quickly seized it. "What went ye out into the wilderness to behold? a reed shaken with the wind? But what went ye out to see? A man clothed in soft raiment? Behold, they which are gorgeously apparalled, and live delicately, are in kings'."[5] These questions of Jesus brought the crowd back to a sane stand-point concerning John. The catechetical method is lively and impressive[6] always, but it was the quickest way to change the current of thought in the crowd. The present attitude of many of them was nothing less than a caricature of the real John[7] as Jesus knew him to be. At

[1] Stalker, "The Two St. Johns," p. 248.
[2] Godet, "Luke," *in loco.*
[3] Farrar, "Life of Christ," vol. I, p. 293.
[4] John 2 : 25.
[5] Luke 7 : 24 f.
[6] Bruce, "Matthew," *in loco.*
[7] Stalker, "The Two St. Johns," p. 248.

bottom John was highly esteemed still by the masses and Jesus was not willing to see that good reputation destroyed. The bulk of those before Jesus had probably gone to the wilderness to behold [1] John. He was the greatest spectacle of his time and many had gone from mere curiosity. It is always so in times of religious excitement. Some go to mock and remain to pray. The "reed [2] shaken in the wind" is still to be seen by the Jordan. "Yet the stream flows in the old bed. Still gently blows the wind among the sighing reeds." [3] The words can be taken literally, to mean that people flocked to the Jordan to see the reeds shaken in the wind. But that is rather jejune in spite of great names which support it.[4] The people went to see John the Baptist. It is a rhetorical question and the idea is that, if John had been fickle and vacillating like a reed in the wind, the people would not have continued to go to see and hear him. Even the rulers paid John the tribute of a visit and rejoiced in this bright and shining light "for a season." [5] The picture of one reed shaking in the breeze is the image of a weak inconstant man. That is precisely what John was not, and those who had just heard his cry for light must not think so. Jesus calls them from John's moment of temporary doubt due to his prolonged imprisonment to the real character of the man as they themselves had known him in the days of his

[1] *θεάσασθαι* in Matt. 11:7 (but Luke has *ἰδεῖν*) as a spectacle. Cf. theatre.

[2] *κάλαμον ὑπὸ ἀνέμου σαλευόμενον.*

[3] Furrer, "Wanderungen," S. 185. Translated by Bruce on Matthew, *in loco.*

[4] De Wette, Fritzsche, Grotius, etc.

[5] John 5:35.

power in the wilderness. It is not fair to a man to judge his whole career by those moments of depression which come to all. The question answers itself and Jesus asks another:[1] "But what went ye out to see? A man clothed in soft raiment?"[2] The question is again rhetorical and keenly ironical. The image of John in his garment of rough hair-cloth with his leathern girdle is brought vividly to their minds by the "soft raiment" of silk or fine linen such as one finds in the gorgeous apparel of those in kings' courts who live in delicacy and luxury in contrast to John's locusts and wild honey. If John were a coward, he would have been a courtier and would have fawned upon Herod and Herodias with flattery. This bold, rudely clad, uncompromising witness to the truth was not won from the straight path by the smile of a king nor intimidated by the hate of a queen. He stood "like an iron pillar and a brazen wall"[3] against error and wickedness. John was no worldling like Herod Antipas, no hypocrite like the Pharisees. He was courage incarnate, no demagogue, no courtier.

2. *The Last of the Prophets.*—Jesus went on. He had brushed out of the way the possible misconceptions of John by the two previous pointed questions. Now he is ready to give the positive side of John's character. "But what went ye out to see? a prophet?"[4] "Yea" Jesus adds, that they may not think this a mere rhetorical question like the rest.

[1] The ἀλλά waves aside the former question.
[2] *ἐν μαλακοῖς ἱματίοις ἠμφιεσμένον.*
[3] Stalker, "The Two St. Johns," p. 249.
[4] Luke 7 : 26. Cf. Matt. 11 : 9.

"Right at last; a prophet, indeed, with all that one expects in a prophet—vigorous moral conviction, integrity, strength of will, fearless zeal for truth and righteousness; utterly free from the feebleness and time-serving of those who bend like reeds to every breath of wind, or bow obsequiously before greatness."[1] Jesus had struck the popular chord about John, for the people held him to be a prophet[2] if ever there was one. The long weary years when no prophet had appeared in Israel gave heightened interest to John.[3] He had the prophetic gift in all its reality and power, and that is the explanation of his tremendous power with the people. He was a true fore-speaker[4] as well as a for-speaker. Stalker[5] notes "that every man of prophetic endowment has to pass through the stages of criticism against which John was defended by Jesus" (a mere demagogue who bent to the popular breeze; then a man who pandered to the rich and powerful and moved in the king's court as a courtier in soft raiment). It is true also of many a modern preacher that he has to live down suspicion, misunderstanding, envy. "Only after running the gauntlet of such criticism does he at last wring from the minds of his contemporaries the acknowledgment that he is a prophet."[6] John was the last and the greatest of the prophets. Like Samuel, the last and greatest of the judges who inaugurated a new era (the monarchy succeeding the theocracy), so John was the last pro-

[1] Bruce, "Matthew," *in loco.*

[2] Matt. 21 : 26.

[3] Broadus, "Matthew," p. 239.

[4] προ-φήτης.

[5] "The Two St. Johns," pp. 249 f.

[6] Stalker, "The Two St. Johns," p. 250.

phetic voice under the old dispensation and introduced the new age, the Messianic era. "For all the prophets and the law prophesied until John."[1] The point is in "until John."[2] John was not a mere continuator of the prophetic line who kept repeating the prophecy that the Messiah will come.[3] John went further. He said: "The kingdom of heaven is at hand." Yes, and he finally said that the Messiah had come. John is the last predictor of the kingdom, the first preacher of it.[4] That ended the old order. John, then, is the great mile-post between the old order and the new. He marked the close of one epoch, the beginning of another. He stands as a great mountain peak in solitary grandeur, the last and highest in the long range of mountains.

3. *Much More than a Prophet.*—He is a prophet, the greatest of the prophets, but he is what no prophet ever was. The phrase[5] was one to catch the ear. But, at first, one is puzzled to see how John could be greater than a prophet, even his own prophetic office. The explanation is found in the quotation from Malachi[6] given by Jesus:

> "Behold, I send my messenger before thy face,
> Who shall prepare thy way before thee."[7]

Here in the fullest and frankest manner Jesus recognizes John as his Forerunner just as John had claimed.

[1] Matt. 11:13.

[2] ἕως Ἰωάνου. Luke (16:16) has Jesus saying another time: "The laws and the proph ts were until John."

[3] Bruce, "Matthew," *in loco*.

[4] Broadus, "Matthew," p. 242.

[5] περισσότερον προφήτου.

[6] 3:1.

[7] Matt. 11:10; Luke 7:27. Cf. Mark 1:2.

He sets the seal of his approval upon John's ministry as John had baptized and introduced Jesus. The real relation between John and Jesus thus comes out clearly in a way to remove all ambiguity. Jesus is addressing those supposed to be in sympathy with him and this public and precise endorsement of the work of John removes all ground for misunderstanding. John is just what he always claimed to be. "This is he," says Jesus, of whom the prophet Malachi wrote. Once John had said of Jesus: "This is he."[1] John is himself the subject of prophecy. That is more than being a prophet. Jesus is here exalting his own position in exalting John.[2] He is virtually claiming to be the Messiah of whom John is the Forerunner, but he avoids using the term as he did in the message to John. It is in a sense an accident that the high honor of being the Forerunner falls to John,[3] since some prophet had to fulfil that office. It is thus more a matter of good fortune than of merit that John happens to be the "Elijah which is to come."[4] This remark of Jesus would catch the popular ear because John had denied to the Jerusalem committee that he was Elijah.[5] Jesus, in fact, calls special attention to it, as if to emphasize it: "He that hath ears to hear, let him hear."[6] Jesus is very fond of this way of winning attention if interest flags or he wishes to drive the point home, or if ignorance or prejudice has to be overcome.[7] "We can scarcely conceive how difficult

[1] John 1 : 30.
[2] Broadus, "Matthew," p. 239.
[3] Bruce, "Matthew," *in loco.*
[4] Matt. 11 : 14.
[5] John 1 : 21.
[6] Matt. 11 : 15.
[7] Cf. Matt. 13 : 9, 43; 24 : 15. Cf. Broadus, "Matthew," p. 242.

it was for the Jews to accept the assertion that the prophecy of Elijah's coming was fulfilled in John the Baptist. And we have abundant need to fear lest we ourselves lack ears to hear, lack the spiritual perception and sympathy, the candor and willingness to follow truth, the readiness to let the Bible mean what it wishes to mean, which are necessary to a thorough understanding of Scripture."[1] "If ye are willing to receive it," says Jesus. It was opposed to the popular ideas on the subject, and to John's express denial because of that popular misconception. Much as the people thought of John, they were hardly willing to go that far. They liked him best when he was attacking the sins of others. "His stern demand for repentance, and for conduct worthy of a penitent, was not liked by many; and his declaration that descent from Abraham gave no claim to admission into the kingdom was disliked by all."[2] But Jesus probably also meant that they must take the identification of John with Elijah *cum grano salis*, not in a baldly literal way as the Jews had expected and as John had properly denied. "Christ idealizes, seizes the essential truth. John was all the Elijah that would ever come, worthy to represent him in spirit, and performing the function assigned to Elijah *redivivus* in prophecy."[3] This was all that was ever promised of John by the angel Gabriel.[4] So, then, John is the Forerunner of the Messiah and stands above all the prophets. "In that

[1] Broadus, "Matthew," p. 242 f.
[2] Plummer, "Matthew," p. 163.
[3] Bruce, "Matthew," *in loco*.
[4] Luke 1 : 17. Cf. what Jesus said later in Matt. 17 : 11; Mark 9 : 13.

long procession the King comes last, and the highest is he who walks in front of the Sovereign."[1]

4. *The Greatest of Men.*—Jesus is rising in his expressions of praise. It is a mighty *crescendo.* To change the figure, he is piling Pelion on Ossa. "Among them that are born of women there hath not arisen a greater than John the Baptist."[2] It is easy to say off-hand that a man is the greatest man who ever lived, and not mean it. Jesus did make use of hyperbole at times as all speakers do. But we are accustomed to measure his words, to weigh them, and we do not find them wanting. We cannot think that here Jesus passed an exaggerated compliment on John that he knew would be properly discounted. His language is very solemn and formal: "Verily I say unto you."[3] It is his personal conviction and must be accepted at its face value. Jesus has just been speaking of John's historic position as the Forerunner, but he now turns to discuss the character of John, his own intrinsic worth as a man.[4] Some manuscripts[5] in Luke 7:28 do have "prophet," but it is rightly left out of the Revised Version. It was evidently inserted by some scribe to relieve the manifest difficulty of the saying. If John was merely the greatest prophet, the matter would be much simpler. Indeed, many, probably most, scholars to-day take the remark of Jesus to refer solely to the position of

[1] Alexander Maclaren.
[2] Matt. 11:11. Cf. Luke 7:28. μείζων Ἰωάνου τοῦ βαπτιστοῦ.
[3] Matt. 11:11.
[4] Bruce, "Matthew," *in loco.*
[5] But not ℵBL, most versions.

John as the Forerunner.[1] He was so great because he occupied that lofty position. That is true, but I cannot myself feel that this is all that Jesus meant to say in such a solemn way. It is not necessary to say that Jesus has all men who will ever live in mind. His own case is a peculiar one and stands apart from the rest. It may even be that the comparison of Jesus moves in the circle of Jewish life and history.[2] That is probably true, though the expression "among them that are born of women" seems like a "solemn periphrasis for the whole race of mankind."[3] There are difficulties from any point of view, and this word of Jesus was not probably accepted by the people who usually rank the dead above the living.[4] Instantly the minds of the audience would challenge that statement with the names of Abraham, Moses, David, Elijah, Isaiah, Jeremiah. Surely Jesus could not mean to place John above these men! They would not likely think of Homer, Plato, Buddha, or Confucius.[5] But they would easily call to mind Judas Maccabeus, Hillel, Shammai among recent men. The solution lies in one's conception of greatness. Who is really great? What is greatness? Men have varying standards. Some care more for power, others for money, others for brilliance of intellect, others for achievement in statecraft, in battle, in industrial pursuits. Herod was called "Great"; so was Alexander;

[1] Broadus, Godet, Plummer, etc. Zahn ("Evangelium des Matthäus," S. 428) suggests that Jesus does not have in mind the writing prophets like Isaiah, Jeremiah, since John wrote nothing, but only prophets like Samuel, Elijah, Elisha.

[2] Bruce, "Matthew," *in loco.*

[3] Plummer, "Matthew," p. 162.

[4] Bruce, "Matthew," *in loco.*

[5] Stalker, "The Two St. Johns," p. 251.

so were Sophocles, Socrates, Thucydides, Praxiteles, Demosthenes. "We measure greatness by the size of the brain—by what men call brilliance, talent, genius."[1] We may be quite sure that Jesus has in mind no such superficial measure of greatness as that. "God's way of estimating greatness is different: greatness is to be sought in faithfulness to duty, in the humility with which the gifts of God are received and utilized; above all, in nearness to God."[2] This is the point that men overlook in their estimate of John, but it was just the matter that Jesus cared most about. The angel Gabriel had said that John would be "great in the sight of the Lord."[3] The career of John the Baptist in a striking way illustrates the Parable of the Householder and the Laborers in the Vineyard.[4] John's ministry was short and came at the end of the long day, but he did a full man's work in the eleventh hour. "So the last shall be first and the first last." John was both last and first; last in time, first in the quality of his service. John had taken his pound and made it come to ten pounds,[5] to use another parable of Jesus. Faithfulness is the true measure of greatness. In God's eye greatness and goodness are very nearly equivalent terms. I would not say that Jesus excludes the superior position of John in his estimate of his greatness, but that he does not confine his measure of greatness to that. John was a real prophet; he was the last and greatest of the prophets;[6] he was much more than a prophet because he was the Fore-

[1] Stalker, "The Two St. Johns," p. 251.
[2] *Ibid.* [3] Luke 1 : 15. [4] Matt. 20 : 1–16. [5] Luke 19 : 16.
[6] Zahn, "Evangelium zu Matt.," S. 423.

runner of the Messiah, Elijah that was to come; he was equal to the greatest of men. Thus the argument runs. The last point is the necessary climax. The solemn "verily I say unto you" and the extension of the comparison to all those "born of women" lifts the comparison to the summit. It is a supreme position that John occupied. He stood next to the Son of God himself. That was honor beyond that received by Abraham, Moses, David, Isaiah, Socrates, Plato, Demosthenes, Alexander, Judas Maccabeus, Hillel, Shammai. It was largely reflected glory and greatness that came to John, as the moon reflects the beauty of the sun. But not wholly so, in my opinion. In the supreme place where John stood right beside the Sun of Righteousness he was "the lamp that burneth and shineth."[1] That is great praise. The brightest electric light makes a poor figure in the face of the noon-day sun. I once saw natural-gas lamps ablaze in broad daylight all over Calgary, Canada, because it was cheaper to let them burn than to put them out and relight them each day. But the lights were miserable tapers in the Canadian summer sun. John burned with the bright and steady light of loyalty to truth and righteousness when he came into the presence of the Son of God himself. He was, like all mortals born of woman, still a man of weakness and frailty, sorrow and sin.[2] Jesus does not mean to crown John with the garland of perfection. But, under the very shadow of the recent exhibition of John's weakness and doubt Jesus calls him equal to the greatest

[1] John 5:35.

[2] Zahn, "Evangelium zu Matt.," S. 424.

of men, a negative way of saying that he is the greatest. I would not press the point too far to the disparagement of other men, but by the highest standard of true greatness known to us, that of loyalty to duty in a supreme place, John meets the test squarely and fairly. We use the term "inherent greatness," but we probably mean only genius. The moral quality of supreme loyalty overtops mere genius. The point of view of Jesus here is "capacity to render effective service to the kingdom of God." [1] There John stands supreme.

5. *The Least in the Kingdom.*—John was the last link [2] with the past. He stood upon the shoulders of the past, the bravest and truest of them all, "Yet he that is but little in the kingdom of heaven is greater than he." [3] It is a most astonishing turn to the sentence and to the thought. The first has suddenly become last. Jesus is fond of paradox and startling turns of expression. It was part of his power as a speaker and teacher of audiences of varied intelligence. It is part of the power of his words to-day to grip and hold the attention and interest of men. But Jesus does not deal in paradoxes just to be striking. If there is not a real, even great, thought in the paradox, it becomes wearisome. The translation "he that is but little" [4] is unfortunate and conceals the real idea.

[1] Bruce, "Matthew," *in loco.*

[2] Edersheim, "Life and Times," vol. I, p. 670.

[3] Matt. 11 : 11. Cf. Luke 7 : 28.

[4] ὁ μικρότερος. The comparative with the article should be taken either as a true comparative or as the equivalent of the superlative. In the modern Greek the usual way of expressing the superlative is by the article and the comparative. The idiom is common in the New Testament both with and without the article. Cf. μείζων in Matt. 18 : 1;

The Authorized Version has it more in accord with the Greek idiom, "he that is least in the kingdom." The Revised rendering is really quite out of place[1] and ignores the current Greek idiom. We may pass by as quite beside the mark the notion of Chrysostom, though followed by so many of the fathers and later writers, [2] that "the least in the kingdom" is Jesus himself. This interpretation is that Jesus, though less in age and fame than John, is in reality greater. This is a truth, but it is more than doubtful if Jesus would choose this occasion to speak thus of himself. The inquiry from John had without doubt raised the problem of the relation between John and Jesus, and Jesus had spoken on that point in calling John the prophetic Forerunner or Elijah. But the interpretation in question would place Jesus in the position of appealing to the multitude to think more of himself than of John, a difficult thing to think of at this juncture. That was not involved.[3] Jesus means, therefore, to say that the least in the kingdom of heaven is greater than John, any one of the crowd before Jesus who was really in the kingdom. What did he mean? Was it due to defects in John's spirit and temper? "He utterly misconceived the Messianic kingdom—John conceived the Messiah as a stern Reformer, and he was eager for the inauguration of the new and

I Cor. 13 : 13; ὁ μείζων 18 : 4; 23 : 11. See Robertson, "Short Grammar of the Greek New Testament," p. 66. The superlative form μικρότατος is absent from the New Testament.

[1] Broadus, "Matthew," p. 240.

[2] Hilary, Ambrose, Theophylact, Enthymius Zigabenus, Erasmus, Luther.

[3] Bruce ("Matthew") calls this notion of Chrysostom an exegetical curiosity."

better era. He had broken with the old order; he had forsaken Temple and Synagogue, and assailed the rulers with fierce denunciation. He had inflamed the zealot-temper and set the land afire. Men were thinking to establish the Kingdom of Heaven by violent and revolutionary methods. This spirit and these methods Jesus viewed with profound disapprobation, recognizing as He did the value of the ancient faith, as a preparation for His perfect revelation, and the spirituality of the Kingdom of Heaven. He had the Baptist in His eye when He said at the outset of His ministry: 'Whosoever looseth one of these least commandments and teacheth men so, least shall he be called in the Kingdom of Heaven.' And now He reiterates the declaration with still greater emphasis: 'One that is but little in the Kingdom of Heaven is greater than he.'"[1] It seems to me that Dr. Smith has here put John in the strait-jacket of the Pharisees whose perfunctory traditionalism John had denounced. The disciples of John, some of them, had come to affiliate with the Pharisees in opposition to Jesus, but there is no proof that they really represented John in this attitude. There were evidences in John's own preaching (the baptism of the Holy Spirit in the Synoptic Gospels,[2] the Lamb of God in John's Gospel[3]) that the Baptist had grasped the spiritual conception of the kingdom and of the Messiah. Besides, the eschatological apocalyptic language of John can be paralleled with similar words from Jesus himself.

[1] Smith, "Days of His Flesh," pp. 227 f.
[2] Matt. 3 : 11; Mark 1 : 7; Luke 3 : 16.
[3] John 1 : 29, 35.

John certainly did not have the fulness of knowledge that was possible to those under the immediate tutelage of Jesus, but it is going further than the words of Jesus justify to put John in the category of the Pharisees. It is certainly true that, in calling the least in the kingdom of heaven greater than John, Jesus has in mind position and privilege, not character or performance.[1] In the description of John as the greatest born of women it was urged that Christ had reference to John's fidelity as well as to his high station. There would thus be a change in the point of view somewhat like that in the double use of "life" in the saying: "Whosoever would save his life shall lose it."[2] John is only the friend of the Bridegroom, as he had said, while the followers of Jesus are his spouse.[3] He is the greatest servant of the King, while they are the sons of the bride-chamber.[4] John did have moral sternness,[5] but it may be seriously questioned if Bruce[5] is right in holding that quality responsible for John's doubt of Jesus and inferiority in rank to the disciples of Jesus. He says: "It made him doubt Jesus, kept him aloof from the kingdom, and placed him below anyone who in the least degree understood Christ's gracious spirit, e. g., one of the Twelve called in x. 42 'these little ones.'" I think that John's graciousness of spirit is quite on a par with that of the disciples who "disputed one with another in the way, who was the greatest,"[6] who wanted to call down fire to burn up a Samaritan village,[7] who forbade men to cast out

[1] Stalker, "The Two St. Johns," p. 251.
[2] Matt. 16 : 25.
[3] Plummer, "Matthew," p. 162.
[4] Matt. 9 : 15.
[5] "Matthew," *in loco.*
[6] Mark 9 : 34.
[7] Luke 9 : 54.

demons in the name of Jesus unless they followed the disciples,[1] who wanted the chief places in the kingdom,[2] who could have a contention for personal promotion at the last passover meal of Jesus,[3] to go no further. These matters are not mentioned for the purpose of disparaging the disciples in the least, but to show that Bruce is in error in depreciating the spirit of John in comparison with that of the twelve apostles.

The truth about John is that Jesus here looks upon him as the last in the old dispensation. The kingdom of heaven is here used in the sense of the new dispensation or New Testament era.[4] "The law and the prophets were until John."[5] John marked the close of the old era, the beginning of the new. It must be repeated that the sense of "kingdom of heaven" is not that of inward experience of grace or the reign of God in the heart, the usual idea in the New Testament. In this sentence Jesus uses the phrase for the new spiritual order. In this technical sense of the term John was not in the kingdom of heaven. He belonged to the old order. Meyer[6] quotes a legal maxim: "The least of that which is greatest is greater than the greatest of that which is least." In privilege and opportunity the lowest in rank in the new order are ahead of John who was the highest of the old order. It is not true that the lowest in character in the new order is superior in character or performance to John. John's standing in that respect has already

[1] Mark 9 : 38 f. [2] Luke 18 : 37. [3] Luke 22 : 24.

[4] Stalker, "The Two St. Johns," p. 252. [5] Luke 16 : 16.

[6] "Matthew," *in loco*, from Maldonatus: *Minimum maximi est majus maxime minimi*. Cf. Farrar, "Life of Christ," vol. I, p. 294.

been made secure by the word of Jesus. He now turns to another matter, that of opportunity. Jesus was pouring forth a wealth of spiritual knowledge that the world had not possessed before. His teaching is still to-day the wonder and joy of the whole earth. John had come right up to Jesus, but, so far as we know, did not hear a single discourse from the Master Teacher and Preacher[1] of the ages. He came so near and missed so much. Jesus has therefore used his high encomium of John as a hammer to drive home to his audience in a powerful way their own tremendous responsibility. John had lived up to his light with loyalty and fidelity. They need not be worried about him. What were they going to do with their own transcendent privilege? Capernaum, Bethsaida, Chorazin will put to blush Sodom and Gomorrah, Tyre and Sidon. Broadus[2] compares the position of John to that of a landing-place in a stairway which turns at that point. It is the highest part of the stairway up to that point. It is the lowest of the next flight of steps. Chrysostom has likened him to the hour between dawn and sunrise. It is the close of night, the beginning of day. Stalker[3] has illustrated John's position by the three kingdoms (mineral, vegetable, animal). The lowest of the vegetable is higher than the highest of the mineral. The lowest of the animal is higher than the highest of the vegetable. This illustration is all the more pertinent in view of scientific discoveries like radium which obscure the

[1] Cf. Bond, The Master Preacher.
[2] "Commentary," p. 241.
[3] "The Two St. Johns," p. 252.

distinctions drawn. That is to say, it is hard to put your finger down and say which is wholly mineral and not vegetable, which is wholly vegetable and not animal. The border-line disappears. In a true sense, therefore, John is both in and out of the kingdom. Jesus treats him here as out of the kingdom to illustrate this point. The beginning of John's ministry was dawn, while Pentecost was the full blaze of the Messianic era.[1] Stalker[2] aptly reminds us that Paul makes precisely the comparison that Jesus here draws between the two dispensations. "For verily that which hath been made glorious hath not been made glorious in this respect, by reason of the glory that surpasseth. For if that which passeth away was with glory, much more that which remaineth is in glory."[3] It is the shame of Christians that they do not rise to the height of their opportunity and responsibility. "It is from the sense of being ideally lifted up into a region of holiness and blessedness through our connection with Christ that we are supplied with the motive and the power for a real conflict with evil."[4]

So far John. But has his work been a success? That is one test of a man's work, though not the only one. Paul appealed to the success of his work as an apostle against the Judaizers.[5] Could there be success to a man's work when he lay in prison? "And from the days of John the Baptist until now the kingdom of heaven suffereth violence, and men of violence

[1] Broadus, "Matthew," p. 241.
[2] "The Two St. Johns," p. 252.
[3] II Cor. 3 : 10 f.
[4] Stalker, "The Two St. Johns," p. 253.
[5] Bruce, "Matthew," *in loco*. Cf. II Cor. 11.

take it by force."[1] Luke[2] gives this saying in another context and in a slightly different form. It is so excessively difficult that we need all the light possible: "The law and the prophets were until John: from that time the gospel of the kingdom of God is preached and every man entereth violently into it."[3] If the translation in Luke is correct, the saying in Matthew[4] probably corresponds with it. Zahn[5] takes it to mean: "the kingdom forces its way" like a mighty rushing wind.[6] That is true, for at that very moment the kingdom of God under the leadership of Jesus was forging ahead. But it is more than doubtful if it is the correct interpretation. The use of "take it by force"[7] is against it. But it is not a hostile attack, but the moral energy shown by those who seek to enter the kingdom of God. It is thus a powerful picture of the moral enthusiasm generated by John the Baptist. He began the movement which, under Jesus, was gathering momentum every day. "His preaching had led to a violent and impetuous thronging to gather around Jesus and His disciples, a thronging in which our Lord apparently saw as much unhealthy excitement as true conviction."[8] It is probable that by "men of violence" Jesus meant to describe "the publicans and sinners" who welcomed him[9] as they had John.[10] "For John came unto you in the way of

[1] Matt. 11 : 12. [2] 16 : 16.

[3] *καὶ πἀς εἰς αὐτὴν βιάζεται.* The intransitive use of *βιάζομαι* is illustrated in the inscriptions. Cf. Deissmann, "Bible Studies," p. 258.

[4] *ἡ βασιλεια τῶν οὐρανῶν βιάζεται, καὶ βιασται ἁρπάζουσιν αὐτήν.*

[5] "Evangelium zu Matt.," *in loco.*

[6] Plummer, "Matthew," p. 162. [7] *ἁρπάζουσιν αὐτήν* equals attack.

[8] Hort, "Judaistic Christianity," p. 26.

[9] Matt. 9 : 10. [10] Luke 7 : 29.

righteousness, and ye believed him not: but the publicans and the harlots believed him."[1] Those who responded to the message of John were not all of the so-called respectable class. Many of them came from the down-trodden class. In times of excitement such work is sharply criticised by many. But certainly Jesus is not here criticising John nor his converts. These converts had many imperfections and shortcomings, but they had at least this to their credit. They had pushed on with eagerness into the kingdom of heaven while the scribes and Pharisees held aloof and criticised those who did enter in. "And ye, when ye saw it, did not even repent yourselves afterward, that ye might believe him."[2] But the movement inaugurated by John, whatever the shortcomings of those swept on by it, was a proof of his power and abiding influence. These very men of violence prove John's great moral force and high prophetic endowment.[3] "Christianity was born in a great revival,"[4] and it has grown by means of revivals.

6. *Rejection of Both John and Jesus.*—It is not certain how we are to take verses 29 and 30 in Luke 7: "And all the people when they heard, and the publicans, justified God, being baptized with the baptism of John. But the Pharisees and the lawyers rejected for themselves the counsel of God, being not baptized of him." Bruce,[5] for instance, is absolutely certain that the words are a historical reflection of the evangelist: "Its prosaic character, as compared with what

[1] Matt. 21 : 32.
[2] *Ibid.*
[3] Bruce, "Matthew," *in loco.*
[4] Broadus, "Matthew," p. 241.
[5] "Luke," *in loco.*

goes before and comes after, compels this conclusion, as even Hahn admits. Then its absence from Matthew's account points in the same direction." The Authorized Version had inserted "And the Lord said"[1] in verse 31, to indicate that the two verses preceding were remarks by Luke. But these words are not genuine and do not appear in the Revised Version. It is possible that Luke did this to explain how far John's work was really successful with the people. But it is certainly strange to have such an extended comment in the midst of a discourse of Jesus. Plummer[2] considers it "without a parallel and improbable." On the whole, therefore, it is best to take the words as part of the address of Jesus. They really come in very well after the paragraph in Matthew (not given by Luke) about the violent energy displayed by men in entering the kingdom of God. That enthusiasm was true of some, but not of all. The people as a whole justified God in sending John and accepted baptism at his hands in proof of their attitude toward him. It is to be feared that the great mass of these did not possess the spiritual qualification demanded by John for his baptism. But the fact that they submitted to baptism by him showed that they believed in his worth and the truth of his claims. And John did "turn" many of the children of Israel to the Lord their God as the angel had said to Zacharias.[3] Some of the disobedient were walking in the wisdom of the just. A people was made ready for the Lord Messiah

[1] εἶπε δὲ ὁ κύριος.
[2] Plummer, "Luke," p. 205 f.
[3] Luke 1 : 17.

when he came. Even the publicans[1] accepted his baptism.[2] "Wherever the publican penetrates, there is no justice for any one."[3] It was just because the mob, the *am-ha-aretz*, believed in John that the Pharisees and the lawyers drew back. It was so as to Jesus. "The Pharisees therefore answered them, Are ye also led astray? Hath any of the rulers believed on him, or of the Pharisees? But this multitude which knoweth not the law are accursed."[4] The coming of the publicans to the side of John drove the Pharisees still further away.[5] But it was God's counsel[6] that even the Pharisees and lawyers[7] should repent. In truth, none needed repentance more.[8] But the Pharisees and lawyers (scribes) had come out against Jesus also, so that Jesus does not consider their hostility to John to his discredit.

So then in spite of all the enthusiasm excited by John in some classes, the people had not really turned from their sins. Least of all had the religious leaders met the appeal of John, as was to have been expected. As a matter of fact, John was now in prison partly because the Pharisees had conspired with Herod against him. This generation is not the one to be casting stones at John. It lives in a glass house. He has in mind, as is plain from Luke's report, chiefly these religious leaders who are already jealous of Jesus himself. "Whereunto shall I liken the men of this

[1] *καὶ οἱ τελῶναι.* Here *καὶ* equals even. [2] Matt. 21 : 32.
[3] Livy, quoted by Davis, "The Influence of Wealth in Imperial Rome," p. 27. 1910.
[4] John 7 : 47 f. [5] Matt. 21 : 32. [6] *τὴν βουλὴν τοῦ θεοῦ.*
[7] *οἱ νομικοί* equals *γραμματεῖς.* These lawyers were ecclesiastical and civil lawyers, but particularly ecclesiastical students.
[8] Bruce, "Luke," *in loco.*

generation, and to what are they like? They are like unto children that sit in the market-place, and call one to another; which say, We piped unto you and ye did not dance; we wailed, and ye did not weep." [1] Bruce[2] is not certain that this vivid parable was spoken by Jesus at the same time as the rest of the discourse. But surely this is hypercriticism, since both Matthew and Luke report it so. It is perfectly natural that, after Jesus has pronounced his wonderful panegyric on John and his relation to himself with some sketch of the success of his work, he should turn to a characterization of the people among whom John and Jesus have labored, especially those who have rejected them. It is a sharp transition, but not too sharp. The "but" here is not by way of disparagement of John, as is so often true of conversation.[3] Jesus includes himself in this picture, which is in every way like the style of Christ. Jesus had watched the children at play in the market square. He dearly loved children and their ways. One child played chief mourner in the game of funeral, while the rest wailed behind.[4] Then one child played the pipe at the game of wedding, while the rest danced at the wedding. Then all grew tired and wanted a change. Curiously enough this is the only place in the Bible where a children's game is described.[5] The parable points its own application, but Jesus does not leave the matter to chance. He expounds it himself. "For John the Baptist is come, eating no bread nor drink-

[1] Luke 7 : 32. Cf. Matt. 11 : 16 f.
[2] "Matthew," *in loco.*
[3] Stalker, "The Two St. Johns," p. 255.
[4] *Ibid.*, p. 256.
[5] Broadus, "Matthew," p. 244.

ing wine; and ye say, He hath a devil. The Son of Man is come eating and drinking; and ye say, Behold a gluttonous man, and a winebibber, a friend of publicans and sinners!"[1] These children were petulant and peevish. They revealed not the good, but the bad, qualities of children. They were childish in the extreme. Exactly so the Pharisees and lawyers had acted toward both John and Jesus. They were playing at religion[2] like fretful children, who refused to play if they could not have their way. They demanded of John that he play like a Pharisee. They demand the same of Jesus. But they are fickle and inconstant in their criticisms. Both of the groups of children found fault, if they were not the same group in reality. That point is not made perfectly clear. In Matthew[3] the correct text seems to draw a distinction between the two groups of children, though that is not necessary. They played funeral and the most of them disliked it. They played wedding and most of them disliked that. In truth these fault-finding children do not want to play at all unless they can have their way about everything. John with his sternness and ascetic habits was like playing funeral. He did not eat or drink as most people did. The language is not to be pressed too literally. It is less open to misunderstanding in Luke, who mentions bread and wine. John did eat locusts and wild honey, and most assuredly drank water, but he was unusually abstemious

[1] Luke 7 : 33 f. Cf. Matt. 7 : 19.

[2] Bruce, "Matthew," *in loco*.

[3] 11 : 16. τοῖς ἑτέροις (Luke has ἀλλήλοις), not τοῖς ἑταίροις. BCDL read in Matthew ἑτέροις, but the word does not always mean "different." It may still be equivalent to Luke's ἀλλήλοις.

in his diet. The reward that he received from the Pharisees and lawyers, who acted with peevish childishness, was that they said: "He has a demon." He was so peculiar, so different from other people. By the use of "ye say" in Luke[1] Jesus seems to imply that some of these critics are present as he speaks. If so, this fact partly explains his comment about the Pharisees and lawyers.[2] They had not only rejected John's message and mission, but are now ridiculing him.[3] John had called the Pharisees and Sadducees a brood of vipers for their hypocrisy. So now they find a satisfactory retort in calling him crazy and possessed with a demon. A lunatic was usually considered demoniacal. The reality of demons is a perplexing problem for many people at the present day. The subject does not come before us in an acute form at all in the ministry of John, since he did not cast out demons or work other miracles. However, it may be said in passing, that the modern researches in physiological psychology concerning the intimate relation between mind and matter make it less difficult to understand how spirits of evil, if they exist, can influence human nature. Certainly, the intense profanity, blasphemy and love of evil in some deranged persons make plausible the idea of possession, whether cause or effect. It is possible that, when one has lost his mental balance, he is less able to resist the spirits of evil who, in some cases, take possession of him and greatly intensify the physical and mental malady. The existence of the devil is the chief diffi-

[1] 7 : 33 f. [2] Luke 7 : 29 f. [3] Broadus, "Matthew," p. 244.

culty concerning the question of demons. The origin of evil is a dark and dreadful problem from any point of view. But it is not rendered easier by denying the existence of the devil or of demons. One can easily call to mind men and women who seem bent on evil.[1] In the case of John it is, of course, slander pure and simple. The Pharisees had already said[2] that Jesus did his miracles by the prince of demons. He was able to drive out demons because he was in league with their prince, the devil himself. They will very soon repeat this very accusation against Jesus, who will expose their hypocrisy in making it by showing that, if it were true, Satan would be casting out Satan, an absolute absurdity.[3] The charge against John was due to jealousy on the part of the Pharisees, as it plainly was in respect to Jesus.[4]

They would not play funeral with John, nor will they play wedding with Jesus. Jesus had attended a wedding[5] early in his ministry. He had, unlike John, mingled in the social life of the people. The Pharisees were quick to find fault with him for that. He was so different from John. He played wedding, not funeral.[6] The two criticisms cancel one another. But fault-finders are not bothered by inconsistency. The excuses advanced merely betray an attitude of mind and heart, not the real motive. They feared John's "glittering axe" and "the winnowing fan of Jesus."[7] That was the real motive. They feared

[1] Cf. Broadus, "Matthew," p. 189 f.
[2] Matt. 9 : 34.
[3] Matt. 12 : 24–26; Mark 3 : 22 ff.
[4] Matt. 12 : 23 ff.
[5] John 2 : 1–11.
[6] Stalker, "The Two St. Johns," p. 257.
[7] *Ibid.*

and hated both John and Jesus. The Pharisees slandered John by saying: "He is a little off. He has a demon. You will have to excuse him for what he says. That is why he called us a brood of vipers. That is why he lives on locusts and wild honey and dresses so queerly. That is why he talks in such an excited manner about the Messiah and the kingdom. That is why he has gotten into all this trouble with Herod. It is best just to pay no attention to his talk." They slandered Jesus by saying: "He is a regular glutton.[1] He eats everything in sight. He is a wine-bibber,[2] and, worst of all, he is a friend of publicans and sinners. He is a regular man of the world and no ecclesiastic and certainly not religious. He is an unsafe man in religion and morals." Jesus was not over-sensitive to criticism, and he does not mention the pitiful narrowness of the Pharisees because he was unduly irritated. He is not ashamed of being the friend of publicans and sinners. It is one of the chief glories of Jesus that he could reach the lost, and he knew it and claimed it.[3] The term "friend" is here "used in a sinister sense, and implies that Jesus was the comrade of the worst of characters, and like them in conduct. A malicious nick-name at first, it is now a name of honour: the sinner's lover. The Son of Man takes these calumnies as a thing of course and goes on His gracious way."[4]

[1] φάγος equals eater, but they mean "eater" with emphasis, a voracious gormandizer.

[2] οἰνοπότης equals drinker of wine. The light wine used at that time was generally mixed with water and was about as strong as our tea or coffee. Cf. Broadus, "Matthew," p. 244.

[3] Luke 5 : 31 f.; 15 : 1–32.

[4] Bruce, "Matthew," p. 175 f.

7. *The Consolation.*—What is one to do about such a situation? John had gone boldly about and done his duty. He has not escaped trouble, but he did right and his vindication will come. The course of Jesus spoke for itself. He was certainly not pandering to popular favor nor to ecclesiastical power. He was not seeking to curry favor with the rulers nor to excite the prejudices of the masses. In the case of both John and Jesus "wisdom is justified by her works."[1] So the true text in Matthew reads.[2] Luke[3] has it: "Wisdom is justified of all her children." In Luke the children who are wise are the ones who justify wisdom. The foolish children will carp and criticise as the Pharisees and lawyers have done toward John and Jesus. But the faithful minority welcome John and Jesus. The report in Matthew puts the emphasis on the works done by the children of wisdom. It is the appeal to fruit which was insisted on by both John[4] and Jesus.[5] In the long run wisdom is justified by the life and deeds of those who practise the truth.[6] Wisdom is here personified as in the Wisdom Books of the Old Testament.[7] But, even if "children" be the right meaning in Matthew, it does not mean that wisdom is justified from the attacks of her children. The true idea is that the method of John and that of Jesus are both justified by results.[8] It is not likely that Jesus is here quoting

[1] Matt. 11 : 19. ἐδικαιώθη ἡ σοφία ἀπὸ τῶν ἔργων αὐτῆς.
[2] Many manuscripts read τέκνων as in Luke, but ℵB have ἔργων.
[3] 7 : 36. [4] Matt. 3 : 8. [5] Matt. 7 : 20.
[6] Bruce, "Matthew," *in loco*.
[7] Cf. Prov. 8, 9. So Sirach 24; Wisdom of Solomon 6–8.
[8] Plummer, "Matthew," p. 163.

from his critics who sneered at his followers with the remark that time would tell how they would hold out.[1] That is, alas, too often the case. Jesus speaks of the matter as already a fact.[2] It is always true, and certain to be so in the case of those who have taken the side of John and Jesus against the Pharisees. The word "justify" here is the one so freely used by Paul with the notion of declaring one righteous. Wisdom will be pronounced right in the end. Folly may usurp the leadership for a time, but in the very nature of things that situation of things cannot last. John had friends in spite of the ill-fortune that had come upon him. These men are the wise ones. Time has rolled on. Where to-day is the man who will stand up for the Pharisees and lawyers against John and Jesus? The verdict of history is with John and Jesus. The men who do a wrong to gain a temporary triumph have a short-lived glory. The courage of John and of Jesus in the midst of opposition and misrepresentation is an inspiration to every exponent of truth and righteousness. "Every sort of preacher will be found fault with by the ungodly world; but every truly devout and wise preacher will be justified by the effects of his ministry."[3] The true preacher to-day must have the vision of Moses who "looked away[4] unto the recompense of reward," "accounting the reproach of Christ greater riches than the treasures of Egypt," who "endured, as seeing him who is invisible."[5] He

[1] Bruce, "Luke," *in loco*, opposes this notion of Bornemann.
[2] ἐδικαιώθη. Timeless aorist.
[3] Broadus, "Matthew," p. 245.
[4] ἀπέβλεπεν equals kept looking away (imperfect).
[5] Heb. 11 : 26 f.

may get a living from the children of wisdom or he may not, for even they are fickle and not always responsive, but he must sustain himself by the consciousness of duty done and the approval of Jesus. The spiritual conception of life, the constant vision of the unseen God, is the chief incentive to work in the ministry, the chief reward for the privations inevitably experienced. The people grow dull and listless. "One day it is too hot, another too cold; one church is too empty, another too full; one preacher is too learned, another not learned enough, one congregation is too genteel, another too common."[1] The people may be fickle, but the preacher must be faithful. Jesus knows all about that problem.

[1] Stalker, "The Two St. Johns," p. 257.

CHAPTER XI

MARTYRDOM

"Give me here in a charger the head of John the Baptist" (Matt. 14 : 8).

1. *Herodias Biding Her Time.*—Luke[1] mentions the bare fact of the death of John in connection with its influence on Herod Antipas. The details of this terrible tragedy are told with more fulness by Mark,[2] who is followed in briefer form by Matthew.[3] But for superstitious fears of Herod about Jesus as John *redivivus* we might have no report of the details of John's death in the gospels.[4] It is a horrible story, but it is necessary to know the worst that befell John. There was no change in the attitude of Herodias toward him. With the persistence and stealth of a tigress she watched for her opportunity. She was sure that it would come. Herod at times had "the murderous mood,"[5] but it vanished with him under nobler impulses. With Herodias it did not vanish. It was her settled purpose,[6] "and she desired[7] to kill him." In the nature of the case there could be but one issue in this matter when a furious woman like

[1] 9 : 7–9. [2] 6 : 14–29. [3] 14 : 1–12.
[4] Bruce, "Mark," *in loco*. [5] *Ibid.*
[6] Mark 6 : 19. Whether we supply χόλον with ἐνεῖχεν (equals had a grudge) or not (equals fixed hate).
[7] ἤθελεν. Imperfect.

Herodias was bent on John's blood. Her only obstacle was Herod himself, who was enamoured of her. He was too weak to stand out against the will of his wife. It may be placed, however, to the credit of Herod that he resisted her direct attacks in spite of impulses to yield.[1] The convenient day[2] came on the birthday[3] of Herod. Herod may have felt that he had to make public announcement of his marriage with Herodias on this occasion.[4] Herodias may have feared that on this occasion Herod might fall again under the spell of John's power and yield to his advice and dismiss her from court in disgrace. The feast was to be celebrated at the palace at Machærus. Herod may have chosen this palace for the celebration partly because it had recently belonged to Aretas, the father of his former wife. That may have been the plan of Herodias to give a little added sting to the daughter of Aretas, whom she had displaced. Here then are assembled at Herod's invitation "his lords and the high captains and the chief men of Galilee."[5] They were the magnates, the military officers and the men of importance.[6] It was a splendid gathering of the grandees of Galilee. It was in itself a defiance of John, for the feast in the palace was not far from John's prison. Did John suspect the crisis in his

[1] Geike, "Life and Words of Jesus," vol. I, p. 429.

[2] *ἡμέρας εὐκαίρου.* Mark 6 : 21.

[3] *τοῖς γενεσίοις.* Cf. Gen. 40 : 20 ff. In Attic Greek *τὰ γενέθλια* was the word used for offerings on birthdays and then for birthdays, *τὰ γενέσια* being used for offerings for the dead. But in the later Greek *γενέσια* is used for birthdays also.

[4] Reynolds, "John the Baptist," p. 439.

[5] Mark 6 : 21. *τοῖς μεγιστᾶσιν αὐτοῦ καὶ τοῖς χιλιάρχοις καὶ τοῖς πρώτοις τῆς Γαλιλαίας.*

[6] Cf. Acts 26 : 1 ff.

affairs? At any rate Herodias was more than ever on the alert and was determined that John should be gotten out of the way. His very presence at Machærus was intolerable.

2. *The Dance of Herodias.*—The main function in the celebration of the birthday festivities was the dinner.[1] The guests had eaten much and drunk the various wines. Herod himself, as host and as the one in whose honor the feast was given, had to lead in the potations. Herodias had laid her plans well. "The vulture was swooping on her prey."[2] "As the procession wound up the mountain pass, with the bravery of nuptial banners and music, and while Roman officers with flashing armour and plumed helmets rode as body-guard of the princesses, and all the grandees and wealthy lords of Galilee and Perea were gathering from various approaches to this eagle's eyrie, and when the garrison stood forth and presented arms as the great nobles entered the gates, and the city crowd of many tribes—among them Greeks and Bedouins, white-robed Essenes and Oriental traffickers, priests and Levites from Jerusalem, and disciples of the prophet eager for his release—sent up their shout of welcome; accustomed as men in that age were to deeds of vengeance and blood, it could hardly have occurred to any that the veiled ladies of the court were revolving a murderous plot, as godless and foul as any that had already stained the

[1] δεῖπνον. It was in the evening, but the formal dinner. Cf. the dinner by Herod Agrippa I to the Emperor Caius in order to win a favor (Josephus, "Ant.," xviii, 8, 7).

[2] Reynolds, "John the Baptist," p. 440.

annals of the house of Herod."[1] And now the hour has come. Herodias had to stoop to the very depths of degradation in order to carry her point. But she had become desperate and her very nearness to John probably irritated her beyond endurance. It is possible that John may have heard the sound of revelry. One is reminded of the feast of Belteschazzar[2] and the handwriting on the wall. Herodias was willing to use the physical charms of her own daughter by her former husband,[3] Herod Philip, to gain her purpose. When maudlin with drink she knew that Herod would prove an easy mark to the lascivious dance which she had trained Salome to execute. It was and is a common Oriental custom[4] to have dancing-girls come in at the close of the feast and dance for the delectation of the guests. Jewish maidens had danced of old at times of public rejoicing with no thought of disgrace, but this was a religious act.[5] The Greeks had their *hetairæ*[6] who performed at such functions, and finally the Romans fell in with the ways of the voluptuous East. But a Latin inscription reads: "It was disgraceful both to dance and for a virgin to come into the banqueting-hall to men who had drank freely."[7] It would have been demoniacal enough for Herodias to have hired a professional dancing-girl, whose char-

1 Reynolds, "John the Baptist," p. 440 f.

2 Dan. 5.

3 The reading τῆς θυγατρὸς αὐτοῦ Ἡρῳδιάδος (equals his daughter Herodias) is accepted by Westcott and Hort. If true, it can mean only his daughter by marriage (step-daughter) and that she was named Herodias as well as Salome.

4 Cf. the Hindoo nautch-girls.

5 Broadus, "Matthew," p. 318. Cf. Ex. 15 : 20; I Sam. 18 : 6; II Sam. 6 : 21.

6 ἑταῖραι. Public characters like the Japanese geisha girls.

7 Quoted by Broadus, "Matthew," p. 318.

acter and reputation were already lost, to come and make the licentious dance for the purpose of overcoming Herod with her charms. But the very bottom of iniquity is reached when Herodias prostitutes her own daughter to that foul purpose. It is an unspeakable commentary on the corruption of the times, and more than justifies all that John the Baptist had ever said about her if it needs any justification in any one's mind. The daughter had been thoroughly drilled in her part, perhaps only too willing a victim, for she was the daughter of her mother. At the proper moment Salome was to come to Herodias for further instructions, when once she has Herod in her power. That is not all, however, bad as it is now. By the marriage of Herodias with Herod the daughter is a member of the court. She was already a princess of royal blood, a great-granddaughter of Herod the Great. The maliciousness of Herodias would not brook defeat. She was willing to stoop to any humiliation in order to conquer. "The music and the wine and the laughter are all at their height, and the sounds of the revelry reverberate through the marble corridors. Purple shadows of the mountain peaks are beginning to fall across the deep ravines, and to shroud the towers of the fortress in their gloom." [1] Then at the auspicious moment, long planned by Herodias, "the daughter of Herodias herself came in and danced." [2] Matthew[3] remarks that she "danced in the midst," right in the presence of the whole company. The dance was a bewildering success from the point of Herodias, and

[1] Reynolds, "John the Baptist," p. 441. [2] Mark 6:22. [3] 14:6.

Salome "pleased Herod and them that sat at meat with him."[1] Herod became oblivious of the fact that it was his wife's daughter who had shown such bewildering grace and "daredevil sauciness."[2] The guests greeted her performance with tumultuous applause. Herod is now excited beyond all bounds. The girl dances on and the half-drunken crowd become tempestuous with excitement. Herod is wholly in the girl's power. "Ask of me whatsoever thou wilt, and I will give it thee." Apparently Salome ignores his remark and dances away. Herod probably leaps up. At any rate he now swears to her: "Whatsoever thou shalt ask of me, I will give it thee, unto the half of my kingdom."[3] Perhaps Herod in his drunken excitement is reminded of Esther and Ahasuerus. He feels his own importance and is grandiloquent in his generosity. It was the custom for the dancing-girls on such occasions to receive presents. Herod will be equal to the occasion and will reward such magnificent dancing. As a matter of fact, he could not give away a bit of his kingdom without the consent of Cæsar. Mark[4] here calls Herod "king," and Herod speaks of his "kingdom." That was common usage, a matter of courtesy, not meant to be taken literally. But Herod had made his promise, a public promise, and with an oath. This was the victory.

3. *The Demand of Herodias.*—Salome knew well how to play her part. At this juncture "she went out,

[1] Mark 6:22. Reclined, συνανακειμένοις, according to Oriental custom.
[2] Stalker, "The Two St. Johns," p. 267.
[3] Mark 6:23. One thinks of Esther 5:3 f.
[4] 6:22 f. Cf. Matt. 14:9. Cf. Smith, "Days of His Flesh," pp. 229 f.

and said to her mother, What shall I ask?"[1] Herodias had herself remained outside of the hall, not to betray her hand too clearly. The ladies were not expected in the banqueting-hall. Matthew[2] says that Salome, "being put forward by her mother," made her request at once. There is no contradiction here. Matthew merely passes by the detail of the visit outside to her mother. It was all done in a moment. The spell must not be broken. Herodias did not need time for reflection. She had only to say, "The head of John the Baptist." Her hour had come at last. She had waited long for triumph and now it was at hand. She would soon see the silent lips that would never more malign her. Salome "came in straightway with haste."[3] There was no time to lose. The fires of drink and passion must not be allowed to cool. The conscience of Herod must not be given a chance to get control of him. The daughter of Herodias was not apparently abashed by the horrible request of her mother. She evidently knew her mother well. Indeed, Salome acted with so much glee that she probably shared her mother's resentment against John, and was glad of the chance to put him out of the way. Whether she was in her mother's secret before this moment is not made clear. But, when she hears her mother's word, she does not hesitate. She said with unblushing effrontery to Herod Antipas: "I will that thou give me forthwith in a charger the head of John the Baptist."[4] She wishes

[1] Mark 6 : 24. [2] 14 : 8. προβιβασθεῖσα. [3] Mark 6 : 25.
[4] Mark 6 : 25. Cf. Luke 11 : 39 for "charger," ἐπὶ πίνακι here.

the head "forthwith." She has taken Herod at his word. "In hotter haste than Herodias herself she seeks to clutch the ghastly trophy of her rage and spite."[1] She was apparently glad also to show her power over her step-father,[2] this "wretched offspring of the once noble Maccabees," "out of whom all maidenhood and all princeliness have been brazed by a degenerate mother."[3] Did a shiver run through the crowd of men that so beautiful a girl could be so blood-thirsty? It was enough to bring them all to their senses.

4. *The Maudlin Acquiescence of Herod.*—He was squarely caught in the trap set by Herodias. He was tipsy, but he knew that he would be the butt of ridicule. He was not willing to face the laugh of his companions. He cared more for what people would say of him than for what was right or wrong. He belongs to that class "to whom a breach of the decalogue is less dreadful than a breach of etiquette."[4] Herod's sorrow[5] was probably sincere. John had made a marvellous impression upon the mind and conscience of this unprincipled ruler.[6] His perplexity now reached a culmination. He feared the multitude. He knew that it was wrong, and, what was worse, that it would be unpopular, for the people counted John as a prophet.[7] So Herod did not join in the laughter of the revellers at "the pretty wickedness"[8] of the merry

[1] Reynolds, "John the Baptist," p. 442.
[2] Swete, "Mark," *in loco.*
[3] Edersheim, "Life and Times," vol. I, p. 672.
[4] Plummer, "Matthew," p. 202.
[5] περίλυπος γενόμενος.
[6] Mark 6 : 20.
[7] Matt. 14 : 5. Cf. Broadus, "Matthew," p. 320.
[8] Stalker, "The Two St. Johns," p. 268.

dancer. He is probably superstitious and hesitates at such a cold-blooded murder, but he has "a nest of scorpions in his bosom."[1] But what he dreaded most of all was Herodias, "the blood-thirsty Fury,"[2] whom he must meet. She would tell him that he had violated a gentleman's "code of honor"[3] and was beneath contempt. He had not kept his word, his promise, his oath. So, while the girl waits for her reward,[4] he trembles for a moment in sore distress between the disgrace that was inevitable, if he refused to stand by his word, and the dread of John and his own conscience, if he yielded to the demand of Herodias through Salome. Fear conquered, and he caught at his oath as his excuse. "For the sake of his oath, and of them that sat at meat, he would not reject her."[5] He was afraid to give Salome a public slight[6] and add her fury to that of Herodias. A rash promise better broken than kept. So he gave the order for a soldier[7] of his guard to bring in John's head. This soldier was a sort of spy or scout kept to be on the lookout like a picket or to carry messages. It is sometimes objected that Herod could not have given such a command at such a time, but Broadus[8] reminds us that "Herodias' ancestor, Alexander Jannæus, while holding a feast with his concubines, commanded eight hun-

[1] Reynolds, "John the Baptist," p. 442.

[2] Stalker, "The Two St. Johns," p. 268.

[3] Smith, "Days of His Flesh," p. 230. Cf. "Herod.," ix, 109; Ovid. "Met.," ii, 44–52; "Jud.," xi, 30–35.

[4] Broadus, "Matthew," p. 320.

[5] Mark 6 : 26. Cf. Matt. 14 : 9.

[6] ἀθετῆσαι equals set aside.

[7] σπεκουλάτορα equals Latin "speculator." Cf. Greek σκέπτομαι. Nowhere else in New Testament.

[8] "Matthew," p. 320. Cf. Josephus, "Ant.," xiii, 14, 2.

dred rebels to be crucified in full view, and their wives and children to be slain before their eyes."

5. *The Death of John.*—The gospels have drawn the veil of silence over this dreadful scene.[1] Mark merely states the melancholy fact: "And beheaded him in the prison." But our thoughts inevitably turn from the revelry and horror of the banqueting-hall to the cell of John the Baptist. He doubtless knew of the presence of his enemies in the palace by the glitter and glare of the festival. Sounds of laughter and of applause may have reached his ears. Was John asleep when the scout came to the door of his dungeon? It was now doubtless far into the night. Was he beheaded in his sleep? Did he go to sleep never to wake again on earth, but to awaken in heaven? That is possible. He may have been hurriedly awakened and then beheaded.[2] If so, "when the apparition of death confronted John so suddenly, how did he receive it?"[3] Did he still have his great doubt[4] about Jesus? Did he feel the love of life that is natural in one so young? Is it not possible, yea, probable, that the message of Jesus in reply to John's pathetic appeal had removed[5] the last lingering doubt? He had been in prison more than a year, but his death was sudden after all. In the case of Paul it was different. Paul was an old man, and he felt sure that his work was accomplished. He faced death with calmness and content. He knew his fate. We have

[1] Swete, "Mark," *in loco*.
[2] Broadus, "Matthew," p. 320.
[3] Stalker, "The Two St. Johns," p. 269.
[4] *Ibid.*, p. 269.
[5] Broadus, "Matthew," p. 320.

no word from John as to his own emotions and outlook. Had Herod given him a word of hope? John must have looked death in the face many a time during the long year of his confinement. Perhaps at times he may have longed for it to come. It is not dreadful to die suddenly "if one has lived the life of faith." [1] Did John know that Herodias was responsible for his death? Let us hope that he did not know that a lewd dancing-girl, though of royal blood, had literally danced his head off. The head of the greatest of the prophets fell as the price of the rude oath of a Herod in a tipsy mood to his voluptuous charmer. The scene is inconceivably horrible. We turn away from it in revolt. And yet "this murder of the greatest of the prophets was in itself hardly so shocking a sight as the scene yonder in the banqueting-hall." [2]

6. *The Gift to Herodias.*—The disgusting demand was carried out to the letter. The scout of Herod brought the head of John on a charger. "There stood the maiden, her cheek still flushed with her recent exertion, while the guests sought to drown their painful emotions in wine." [3] The executioner comes in with his ghastly trophy[4] to present to the fair damsel. She acts her part out probably with the same gay and flippant manner that marked her dancing and her demoniacal request.[5] The soldier passed it on to Salome "and she brought it to her mother." [6] She bore it as a treasure. Mark[7] adds simply: "And the

[1] Broadus, "Matthew," p. 320. [2] *Ibid.* [3] *Ibid.*
[4] Smith, "Days of His Flesh," p. 230.
[5] Stalker, "The Two St. Johns," p. 268.
[6] Matt. 14:11. [7] 6:28.

damsel gave it to her mother." What a gift, this noble head dripping with blood! Salome no doubt "took it daintily in her hands lest a drop of blood should stain her gala dress, and tripped away to her mother, as if bearing her some choice dish of food from the king's table."[1] The victor often had the head of his fallen foe brought before him. The ancient civilizations had not gotten beyond that species of barbarism which is still practised by modern savages. Fulvia, the wife of Antony, spat upon Cicero's head, drew out the once eloquent tongue and pierced it repeatedly with her hair-pin. That tongue would never denounce her nor her husband again.[2] We do not know how Herodias behaved. It is not difficult to imagine her look of triumph as her eyes flashed satisfaction upon the mouth that had denounced her sins, the eyes that had made her cower with dread and hate. Jerome,[3] indeed, tells a story of the way in which Herodias took her bodkin and pricked the tongue of John, the tongue that now could rebuke her no more. It is probably a mere tradition, but Herodias was none too good to do such a thing in the first moments of her passion. It would be so Roman, besides, and she had lived in Rome. She has triumphed over the mighty preacher before whose voice a nation once quailed. "She remained Herod's evil genius to the end. The death of the Baptist filled the tetrarch's subjects with horror."[4]

[1] Broadus, "Matthew," p. 320. Salome afterward married her uncle, Philip the Tetrarch, and, according to legend, died from a fall on the ice. Cf. "Niceph." I, 20.

[2] Cf. Broadus, "Matthew," p. 320; Stalker, "The Two St. Johns," p. 268.

[3] *Contra Rufin.*, c. 11, quoted by Witsius. Cf. Reynolds, "John the Baptist," p. 443.

[4] Stalker, "The Two St. Johns," p. 269.

Aretas made war on Herod for his treatment of his daughter and Herod was defeated. Some of the Jews "thought that the destruction of Herod's army came from God, and that very justly, as a punishment of what he did against John."[1] Herodias's turn will come. Some ten years afterward, when her scapegrace brother Agrippa is appointed by the Emperor Caligula to be king of the tetrarchy of Philip, she is so envious that she gives Herod Antipas no rest till they go to Rome to demand the title of king for Herod. But Agrippa makes counter-charges so that they are sent in banishment and disgrace to Gaul or Spain.[2] Herodias is now in her glory. She cares naught for the shame of her daughter nor for the embarrassment of Herod. She has carried her point and has a Satanic delight in that. "They did unto him whatsoever they would."[3] John has met his turn. That of Jesus will come next. "Even so shall the Son of Man also suffer of them."[4]

7. *The Burial.*—"And his disciples came and took up the corpse, and buried him."[5] These disciples were probably on the hill at the time, though it is not certain. One may at least hope so, for otherwise the headless body of the Baptist lay all night and most of the next day in neglect in the dungeon. But John's disciples did hear[6] of the tragedy. The news would spread quickly all over the palace. It was a melancholy duty, but these disciples were loyal to John as

[1] Josephus, "Ant.," xviii, 5, 2.
[2] Josephus, "Ant.," xviii, 7, 2; "War," ii, 9, 6. Smith ("Days of His Flesh," p. 230) calls Herodias "that she-devil."
[3] Mark 9 : 13.
[4] Matthew, 17 : 12.
[5] Matt. 14 : 12.
[6] Mark 6 : 29.

he was loyal to Jesus. They laid his body in a tomb,[1] probably in one of the rock-hewn tombs around Machærus. There is a late story that John's body was found at Sebaste (Samaria), in the time of the Emperor Julian, when his bones were burnt and most of the dust scattered by the pagan party, the rest being kept by the Christians as relics.[2] But little credence is to be placed in that report. It is not inconceivable that disciples of John may have removed the body of their Master from Machærus. If the burial was at Machærus, it was probably hurried. John's disciples would be too dazed for utterance. He has been cut down in his prison, but his life was not in vain. Courage and humility were combined in John in a remarkable way. He practised self-denial, not merely preached it for others. "Had his honors been ten thousand times brighter than they were, he would have laid them all at Christ's feet. John in his ministry was not like the evening star—sinking into the darkness of the night, but like the morning star—lost to our view in the brightness of day."[3] They have killed him, but at the cost of eternal infamy to themselves, the execration of mankind, misery untold to their own hearts and lives. The blood of the martyrs is the seed of the church. In one sense John was the first of the Christian martyrs, though Stephen is usually so designated.[4] He has met death in the path of duty. He lived like a saint, he preached like a prophet, he died like a hero.

[1] ἐν μνημείῳ.

[2] Swete, "Mark," *in loco.*

[3] Belfrage in Kitto.

[4] Broadus, "Matthew," p. 320.

8. *Telling Jesus.*—"And they went and told Jesus."[1] They knew not where to go but to Jesus. Not long ago John himself had sent two of them to Jesus with a message of doubt. Now they bear to Jesus the word of despair. How could a man like Herod and a woman like Herodias be allowed to slay John the Baptist? The mystery of evil remains unsolved.[2] What has the world now in store for the disciples of John? What will Jesus say? What did he say? We are not told. But Jesus loved John. He wept by the grave of Lazarus. He had already pronounced the noblest eulogy on John. Did he not drop a tear for John, whose mission was so closely allied to his own? Did his own heart not grieve at the dastardly deed that had taken John away in such lawless, barbarous fashion? Did he not speak words of comfort to the sorrowing disciples of John? Did he not draw them closer to himself? They had no possible grounds for jealousy now. John's momentary doubt had vanished. They go to Jesus with "a true instinct."[3] It was what John would have advised. Indeed, he may have told them what to do in case the inevitable end came suddenly upon him. "They went to Jesus" with many thoughts on all the wondrous events of the last few years. "Ah, blessed road, whereon thousands upon thousands have followed them since! It is the right road, whatever be the trouble."[4] We leave Jesus with memories of John, with prophecies of his own fate. He was walking in the footsteps of his great

[1] Matt. 14 : 12. καὶ ἐλθόντες ἀπήγγειλαν τῷ Ἰησοῦ.
[2] Stalker, "The Two St. Johns," p. 270.
[3] *Ibid.*
[4] *Ibid.*

Forerunner. His own hour was hastening. The clock was running round and would strike. How little the people understand the tragedy of soul which is going on in the heart of Jesus as he steps forward to meet his cross. Matthew[1] represents Jesus as leaving the dominion of Herod Antipas as soon as he heard the news of John's death: "Now when Jesus heard it he withdrew from thence in a boat to a desert place apart." Jesus went into the tetrarchy of Herod Philip and is in Galilee very little thereafter. According to Mark[2] Jesus withdrew after hearing the report of the disciples when they returned from their preaching tour over Galilee. The two events probably came close together.[3] Herod did become much concerned about the work of Jesus so that his departure was wise.[4]

[1] 14:13. [2] 6:30 f.
[3] Broadus, "Matthew," p. 322; Bruce, "Matthew," *in loco.*
[4] Matt. 14:1 f.; Mark 6:14; Luke 9:7.

CHAPTER XII

LINGERING ECHOES

"John baptized with the baptism of repentance, saying unto the people that they should believe on him that should come after him, that is, on Jesus" (Acts 19 : 4).

1. *A Terror to Herod.*—The court of Herod Antipas left Machærus after the birthday festival was over. It had been a magnificent occasion with lavish extravagance and splendor of entertainment. The dance of Salome had given a peculiar zest to the celebration and was for long the talk of the guests. The daring of Herodias and her daughter in demanding the head of John the Baptist was something of a shock, but, the grandees argued, one must get used to such things if he moved in court circles. He must not be too particular nor squeamish about small matters. As a matter of fact, John was a mere adventurer, a religious demagogue, who gained his importance purely from his favor with the masses. It was for this reason that Herod had wished his endorsement of the marriage with Herodias. If he had shut his eyes to that weakness of Herod and treated it as *un fait accompli*, he would be still alive and the people would have followed him in his endorsement of Herod's marriage. Princes, the courtiers would argue, cannot be held to

the ordinary rules of morality to which other people are expected to conform. One in court circles must have a blind eye to many things. After all John had brought his fate on himself by his bluntness, ill manners, and lack of common-sense. He had no policy, no suavity, no spirit of accommodation. It was a pity, but he had only himself to blame in his resistance to the will of Herodias. Thus the flatterers of Herod's court probably argued and satisfied themselves with little regret about John. The actual outcome was rather bad in its details, as there was no formal trial, but the thing had happened, and now

> "On with the dance,
> Let joy be unconfined."

The court is again at Tiberias with all its wonted brilliance.

Herod Antipas, with all his faults and sins, was not wholly degenerate as was Herodias. Herod's conscience still worked occasionally. He was superstitious also. John had troubled him while in prison. He had been "much perplexed" [1] what to do about him. He is "much perplexed" [2] now that John is dead. Herod had John on the brain.[3] "It is said that when Theodoric had ordered the murder of Symmachus, he was haunted and finally maddened by the phantom of the old man's distorted features glaring at him from a dish on the table; nor can it have been otherwise with Herod Antipas." [4] In spite of his

[1] Mark 6 : 20. πολλὰ ἠπόρει.
[2] Luke 9 : 7. διηπόρει. Note imperfect tense and δια.
[3] Bruce, "Matthew," *in loco*.
[4] Farrar, "Life of Christ," vol. I, p. 394.

maudlin condition at the feast, Herod had seen the head of John the Baptist on the charger. He saw the sightless eyes many a night as they glared at him out of the darkness from the foot of his bed and charged him with the murder of John. He could still hear that wonderful voice as it accused him of his sins of which he knew his guilt. "If we mistake not, that dissevered head was rarely henceforth absent from Herod's haunted imagination from that day forward till he lay upon his dying bed." [1] He was tasting hell beforehand. The lashing of a guilty conscience is hell.

News came to the golden palace of Herod in Tiberias about a new prophet in Galilee. Jesus himself had studiously avoided Tiberias, Herod's capital. It may seem strange that Herod had not heard of Jesus before this time. In reply it may be stated that Herod was often away from Tiberias and sometimes outside of his own dominions. A prince often knows less about what is going on than his subjects.[2] He may, in truth, have heard of Jesus in an incidental way that made no impression on him. The religious movements among his people probably concerned him very little. Jesus had been actively at work in Galilee for over a year.[3] He had labored all over Galilee, and particularly at Bethsaida, Capernaum, Chorazin, which places were not far[1] from Tiberias. It was not, however, the mere fact of the preaching of Jesus or even of his works that excited at this time. It was

[1] Farrar, "Life of Christ," vol. I, p. 394.
[2] Plummer, "Matthew," p. 200. [3] Broadus, "Matthew," p. 315.

the explanation of the power of Jesus that agitated him. The tour of the twelve apostles was just completed, and much talk about Jesus was the result. People were trying to explain Jesus. The Pharisees had already said that he was in league with the devil.[1] But the masses rightly attributed that explanation to jealousy. Some of the people said that Jesus was one of the old prophets risen again to life.[2] The people had an expectation that Jeremiah would return to life.[3] Others thought Jesus a prophet equal to any of the Old Testament prophets, "as one of the prophets." Some, who had not seen that John the Baptist was Elijah in spirit and power, and who expected Elijah back in person, wondered if Jesus might not be Elijah himself. "It is Elijah," they said. He has appeared at last.[4] These knew that John had refused to be identified with Elijah. But there was a group, who apparently knew nothing of the early ministry of Jesus that was parallel with that of John, who said: "This is John the Baptist; he is risen from the dead." [5] There is a late story to the effect that Jesus and John resembled each other in personal appearance, or rather Origen[6] suggests the idea. John wrought no miracles, but the advocates of this view used the miracles of Jesus as one element in the proof that he is John *redivivus*. John can now work so many and such wonderful miracles because he has come back from the grave. "Therefore do these

[1] Matt. 12 : 24 f.
[2] Mark 6 : 15; Luke 9 : 8.
[3] Matt. 16 : 14. Cf. Sirach 19 : 10 f.
[4] Mark 6 : 15; Luke 9 : 8.
[5] Matt. 14 : 2; Mark 6 : 14; Luke 9 : 7.
[6] On John 6 : 30. Cf. his notes on Matt. 10 : 20.

powers work in him."[1] "The powers of the invisible, vast and vague in the king's imagination,"[2] are now at work in John who has come to life. This interpretation of Jesus is what stirred Herod. "John I beheaded; but who is this about whom I hear such things?"[3] The "I" is emphatic in the Greek: "As for John *I* beheaded him."[4] Herod is here arguing against accepting the new theory of Jesus that he is John come to life. He had killed John. There was no doubt of that. He had too many nightmares on the subject not to know it. Now he is to have all this trouble over again! Will John not let him alone? "He sought to see him,"[5] in order to determine if he were the Baptist or not. He could tell, for he could never forget that face. It glared at him now. He kept trying to see Jesus (in perfect tense), but did not succeed till the trial of Jesus, when Pilate sent the prisoner to him.[6] Herod doubtless felt himself an injured man about John. His wife was responsible for his death. As for himself, he had tried, but with poor success, to forget the murder, but the memory of it kept coming back to him, "and now the murdered man himself seemed to have risen again to rebuke him."[7] To his courtiers[8] he finally said: "This is John the Baptist; he is risen[9] from the dead; and

[1] Matt. 14:2; Mark 6:14. *διὰ τοῦτο αἱ δυνάμεις ἐνεργοῦσιν ἐν αὐτῷ.* Note that *αἱ* is almost demonstrative.

[2] Bruce, "Matthew," *in loco.*

[3] Luke 9:9.

[4] Plummer, "Luke," *in loco.* Ἰωάνην ἐγὼ ἀπεκεφάλισα.

[5] Luke 9:9. *ἐζήτει ἰδεῖν αὐτόν.*

[6] Luke 23:8. By this time he wants to see Jesus work a miracle and no longer dreads him as John the Baptist come to life.

[7] Plummer, "Matthew," p. 201.

[8] *τοῖς παισὶν αὐτοῦ.* Matt. 14:2. Cf. Mark 6:14.

[9] *ἐγήγερται.* Present perfect, a living reality to Herod's fears.

therefore do these powers work in him." The idea became an obsession with him. Herod in this mood could find no peace at Machærus where he could see the ghost of John walk. His terror is greatly increased by the news about Jesus. John, though dead, was goading Herod to fury.

2. *The Puzzle of the Disciples of Jesus.*—The months go by. Jesus has kept out of the territory of Herod Antipas as much as possible. It is late summer or early autumn. Christ has his disciples with him in the region of Cæsarea Philippi.[1] The greatest tragedy of the ages is before Jesus. The shadow of the Cross lies across his path, just a little over six months ahead. It may be about the time of the feast of tabernacles as has been suggested by Colonel Mackinlay in his book, "The Magi" (p. 222). As the group of Christ's disciples get away from the gloom of the death of the Baptist, they enter the cloud and are afraid.[2] They are afraid of the cloud on the Mount of Transfiguration, with its mystery and its messengers of comfort to Jesus about his decease. They fear as they hear the voice[3] out of the cloud, the same voice which John the Baptist had heard at the Jordan: "This is my beloved Son, in whom I am well pleased; hear ye him."[4] All the synoptics have "hear ye him." Matthew[5] says: "They fell on their face, and were sore afraid." When Jesus touched them, they suddenly saw Jesus alone. Moses and Elijah had gone with the cloud. They go down the

[1] Matt. 16:13; Mark 8:27. [2] Luke 9:34. [3] *Ibid.*
[4] Matt. 17:5; Mark 9:7; Luke 9:35. [5] 17:6.

mountain in awe under the strict command of Jesus not to tell what they had seen till the Son of Man should rise from the dead. They talked about the rising from the dead, and then about Elijah. He had come back, as Malachi had said. They had just seen and heard him. He did not stay, it is true.[1] Besides, Jesus as the Messiah had come before Elijah. How can that be? They have evidently forgotten what Jesus had said about John the Baptist as Elijah.[2] It made little impression on their minds at the time, if indeed they heard it. They may have been otherwise occupied at the moment. The puzzle is too great for these three disciples (Peter, James and John). They bring it to Jesus: "Why then say the scribes that Elijah must first come?"[3] It is the old perplexity now revived in a new form. "How was Elijah's appearance at the Transfiguration to be reconciled with the official doctrine of his return?"[4] The scribes held from Mal. 3:23; 4:4 f. that Elijah himself would return to earth. The question is certainly suggested by the appearance of Elijah at the Mount, whether the disciples took that to be the predicted coming and too late for the prophecy in Malachi[5] or whether they were troubled by the fact that the Messiah had come while Elijah had not come.[6] In either case John the Baptist is not in the thoughts of the disciples. It is hard to understand a great contem-

[1] Plummer ("Matthew," p. 240) takes the question to mean that Elijah had not yet come.

[2] Matt. 11:15.

[3] Matt. 17:10. Cf. Mark 9:11.

[4] Swete, "Mark," *in loco*.

[5] So Meyer, Weiss, etc.

[6] Broadus, Bruce, etc. The "then" (οὖν) points back to the Transfiguration experience. They are puzzled over "first" (πρῶτον).

porary. They were not quite far enough away from John to take the measure of his stature, though Jesus had interpreted him for them. The answer of Jesus is very significant. He is patient with his dull pupils in spiritual things and repeats his identification of John with Elijah. The scribes were right in their interpretation of Malachi (except as to Elijah *in person*, though he does not put in this *caveat* in words). "Elijah indeed cometh first, and restoreth all things." [1] This is the prophecy and God's plan about the Forerunner and the Messiah. Jesus here quotes the Septuagint "restoreth all things," a more general phrase for the Hebrew[2] text: "He shall turn the heart of the fathers to the children" as in the prediction of Gabriel.[3] He was to make ready the people for the Messiah, to bring to pass a moral renovation. Jesus sadly adds: "But I say unto you, that Elijah is come already, and they knew him not, but did unto him whatsoever they listed." [4] So then Jesus expected no literal coming of Elijah. John the Baptist was all the Elijah who would ever come. He passes by the brief visit of the real Elijah on the Mount. They did not recognize[5] John as Elijah nor understand his true mission as men did not know Jesus in his true light.[6] Jesus refers to John's death in euphemistic language.[7] Mark[8] quotes Jesus as saying: "Even as it is written of him." The fate of Elijah was a type of the death of John.[9]

[1] Mark 9:12. [2] Mal. 4:6. [3] Luke 1:17.
[4] Matt. 17:12. [5] οὐκ ἐπέγνωσαν. Note ἐπί.
[6] John 1:10.
[7] ἐποίησαν ἐν αὐτῷ. Literally "did in his case." Cf. Gen. 40:14.
[8] 9:13.
[9] I Kings 19:2, 10. Cf. Swete, "Mark," *in loco*.

The identification of John with Elijah in spirit and power is made so plain by Jesus this time that the disciples saw his meaning clearly. "Then understood the disciples that he spake unto them of John the Baptist."[1] "Then" is "at that time," then at last they understood, but "what a disenchantment: not the glorified visitant of the night vision, but the beheaded preacher of the wilderness, the true Elijah."[2] At one blow Jesus has disposed of the notion of the scribes that Elijah himself was to come and "lead Israel to the *Great Repentance*,"[3] and the idea of the disciples that the appearance of Elijah on the mountain was the fulfilment of Malachi's prophecy. But the heart of Jesus is concerned about a more important matter than the interesting parallel between Elijah and John the Baptist. Elijah and Moses had been talking with him on the Mount about "his decease which he was to accomplish at Jerusalem."[4] He had spoken of his resurrection from the dead just a little[5] before their inquiry about Elijah. The fate of Elijah will be repeated in that of Jesus. Jesus asks the disciples how his own death can follow the restoration by John?[6] "That he should suffer many things and be set at naught."[7] There is to be a suffering Messiah as there has been a suffering Forerunner.[8] The glory of the Transfiguration is followed by the prophecy of the cross. In truth, the Cross was the chief theme of converse in the Transfiguration.

[1] Matt. 17 : 13.
[2] Bruce, "Matthew," *in loco.*
[3] *Ibid.* Cf. Weber, "Die Lehren des Talm.," S. 337.
[4] Luke 9 : 31.
[5] Mark 9 : 9; Matt. 17 : 9.
[6] Mark 9 : 12.
[7] Cf. Matt. 17 : 12.
[8] Plummer, "Matthew," p. 240.

Jesus has no illusions about his own future. He knows what is ahead of him, and he will meet it bravely as John did. If Elijah's fate was a prophecy of John's death, that of John foretells the doom of Jesus. The disciples had been puzzled about the resurrection from the dead and then about the coming of Elijah. The problem of Elijah is cleared for them, but they are still unable to understand the words of Jesus about his own death.

The Rev. F. B. Meyer[1] has drawn a very helpful parallel between the life of Elijah and that of John the Baptist which may be useful to modern disciples who are puzzled over the matter. I give it here in condensed form. They were similar in their dress. Each of them lived awhile in Gilead (Perea). Each was abstemious in his diet (Elijah was fed by ravens, John lived on locusts and wild honey). They were both persecuted by a wicked king and queen (Ahab and Jezebel, Herod and Herodias). Each had a distinct sense of the presence of God. Elijah said to Ahab: "As the Lord, the God of Israel, liveth, before whom I stand." John said: "The kingdom of heaven is at hand." They both had a "God-consciousness." Each had moments of depression (Elijah under the juniper-tree, John in prison). They both hold a relation to fire (Elijah called down fire from heaven to consume the wood drenched with water in the test on Carmel; John prophesied the baptism of fire by the Messiah). Each turned the people back to God (Elijah made the people cry, "Jehovah, he is God";

[1] "John the Baptist," 1910, pp. 239–245.

John turned the hearts of the fathers to the children and to God). Each had also a gentler ministry (Elijah anointed Elisha, John baptized Jesus). Each had a sudden end (Elijah caught up in the chariot of fire, John suddenly beheaded). Some of these points are more striking than others, but they illustrate well the prophecy of Malachi about the return of Elijah and the fulfilment in the career of John as interpreted by Jesus himself.

3. *The Power of the Silent Voice.*—John dead was, for a time at least, more powerful than when alive. He was now a martyr and a hero with the masses who had heard his wondrous message and had received baptism from him. Jesus had said to the three disciples that, as John had suffered martyrdom, so would he. On the great Tuesday in Passion Week, the Tuesday of the Debate, Jesus taught for the last time in the Temple. The power of Christ over the masses was never so great. The Triumphal Entry had filled the Galilean multitudes at the Passover with wild enthusiasm. The Jewish rulers sought to kill Jesus, "for they feared him." [1] Jesus had done what John had never attempted. He had come right into the Temple itself and won the favor of the masses away from the accredited teachers of the law. This was a triumph that was unendurable to Pharisees and Sadducees, but "they could not find what they might do. for all the people hung upon him listening." [2] The rulers finally decided upon a formal challenge of the authority of Jesus. Mark and Luke[3] mention that

[1] Mark 11 : 18. [2] Luke 19 : 48. [3] Mark 11 : 27; Luke 20 : 1.

"the chief priests, and the scribes, and the elders" (the Sanhedrin, in a word, which was composed of these three classes) came to Jesus and said: "Tell us: By what authority doest thou these things? or who is he that gave thee this authority?"[1] The object was to entrap Jesus and to break his hold upon the people. The crowds in the Temple were even now hanging on his teaching and preaching.[2] A dilemma was presented to Jesus by this challenge. If he claimed to be the Messiah and to have direct authority from God, they would interpret this to be treason against Cæsar by giving a political turn to his claim to be king and to have a kingdom. They finally used this very argument with Pilate[3] to force his acquiescence in the death of Jesus. The other horn of the dilemma was the favor of the people. If Jesus denied that he was the Messiah or asserted only human authority like other teachers, the spell of the Triumphal Entry would be broken. The rulers felt sure that they would ruin Jesus with the masses or get him into trouble with Rome. It is the mission of John the Baptist that gives Jesus the way out of the dilemma. He meets the dilemma of the rulers with another and one pertinent to their query. It was not a dodge on the part of Christ to evade a categorical answer. They had asked Jesus "who" gave him his authority. This "who" has two aspects, the divine origin or source and the human agent who conveyed it. The claim of Jesus to divine authority will be scouted by them without human endorsement, prophetic ap-

[1] Luke 20: 2. [2] Luke 20: 1. [3] John 19: 12.

proval by an accredited spokesman of God. So Jesus properly takes up first the divine endorsement through a prophetic agent. That had come through John the Baptist as all men knew. John had made no secret of his identification of Jesus as the Messiah. But who was John? The rulers had once[1] investigated John and had refused to deny his claim to be the Forerunner of the Messiah. They did not endorse John formally, though "ye were willing to rejoice for a season in his light."[2] They were afraid to condemn John. It was the business of the Sanhedrin to pass on John's claims[3] to be a prophet, not to say Forerunner of the Messiah. They had not done so, and were therefore not in a position to challenge Jesus who was formally and publicly endorsed by John. Was John a prophet of God? "I also will ask you a question; and tell me: The baptism of John, was it from heaven, or from men?"[4] Just "one" question Matthew and Mark have it. The rulers said "Tell us" to Jesus; he says "Tell me" to them. The "baptism" of John is not singled out by Jesus for any ecclesiastical or sacramental reasons, but simply because the baptism of repentance stood for the whole work of John.[5] It was the objective symbol. If the rulers will take up a position on the ministry of John, that will clear the way for Jesus to make an intelligible reply to their query. If John was a prophet, then Jesus had prophetic endorsement such as the Messiah

[1] John 1:19 ff. [2] John 5:35.
[3] Plummer, "Matthew," p. 293.
[4] Luke 20:3 f. Cf. Matt. 21:24 f.; Mark 11:29 f.
[5] Cf. Swete on Mark, Bruce on Matthew, Plummer on Matthew, Broadus on Matthew.

should have. He had just the kind of authority that ought to have weight with the religious leaders of God's people. The rulers ought to have taken a public stand on John's career long before this.[1] They were squarely and fairly caught. No wonder "they reasoned with themselves."[2] There was no time for prolonged conference. The pause was embarrassing. The people noticed their difficulty and were on the alert to see if the rulers would say an unkind word about the martyred prophet. The rulers knew that they were caught, hopelessly caught in the meshes of their own net. The reasoning seems to have been aloud; perhaps they were excited and spoke louder than they knew in their conference. As a matter of fact, John's work was both from heaven and from men.[3] He was not divine as Jesus, but his authority came from God, not from the ecclesiastics. But the rulers would not dare deny that John's baptism was both divine and human. They confess their defeat to themselves in the most naïve manner as reported by Matthew:[4] "If we shall say, From heaven; he will say unto us, Why then did ye not believe him?" They knew the power of Jesus in debate too well to risk that retort. "But if we shall say, From men; we fear the multitude; for all hold John as a prophet." In Mark [5] there is an anacoluthon "—they feared the people." Luke[6] adds: "All the people will stone us." They are in a *cul-de-sac*, and meekly come back and

[1] Plummer, "Matthew," p. 293.

[2] διελογίζοντο παρ' ἑαυτοῖς. Matt. 21 : 25. Note imperfect tense. παρά suggests a conference a little aside. Mark (11 : 31) has πρός.

[3] Bruce, "Matthew," *in loco*.

[4] 21 : 25 f. [5] 11 : 32. [6] 20 : 6.

say: "We know not."[1] Their rout is complete. "They had publicly declared that they were unable to settle such questions, thus abdicating their authority in religious questions of the highest moment, and they do not venture to press him further."[2] John was dead, but he wielded a sceptre over the hearts of the Jewish masses. The Pharisees and Sadducees had quailed before John as he denounced them to their faces. They shrink now before the power of that silent voice. They know that a storm[3] of hate will burst upon them. They actually fear stoning in such case. No words can add anything to this grip which John has on the hearts of the people as the rulers come into collision with Jesus. Herod feared John's ghost. The Pharisees and Sadducees fear John's upright character and hold upon the love of all the people. Jesus had probed to the root of the unbelief of the rulers, and they winced at his home thrust.[4] But Jesus is not done with the problem of John the Baptist. He drove home the lesson of their admission about John by the parable of the two sons. One said he would and did not, like them. Another said he would not and did, like the publicans and harlots who repented at John's preaching and at that of Jesus. These "go into the kingdom of God before you. For John came unto you in the way of righteousness, and ye believed him not: but the publicans and the harlots believed him: and ye, when ye saw it, did not even repent yourselves afterward, that ye might believe

[1] Matt. 21 : 27; Mark 11 : 33; Luke 20 : 7.
[2] Plummer, "Matthew," p. 293.
[3] Swete, "Mark," *in loco*.
[4] Smith, "Days of His Flesh," p. 308.

him."[1] It was a terrible turn in the argument. They had not escaped Christ's dilemma. He boldly charged them with not believing John when they saw that he was a prophet. This was one horn that they had tried to escape,[2] but Jesus now pillories them on it. They had escaped stoning from the crowd, but not the exposure from Jesus. The ministry of John thus plays an important part in the closing day of Christ's own public work. We sigh

> "But oh, for the touch of a vanish'd hand,
> And the sound of a voice that is still."

But John's hand wields a sceptre and John's voice still rings in the ears of men, calling them to righteousness, pointing out Jesus as the Lamb of God.

4. *The New Epoch in History.*—We pass on beyond the great event whose shortening shadow was coming upon Christ. The fate of John did meet Jesus. The manner of his death was different, but he was killed as the great martyr to truth and righteousness. Like John, Jesus was cut down in his prime. The forms of a trial were gone through with in the case of Jesus, but only the forms were observed, and by no means all of them were kept. As with John, so with Jesus, hate, jealousy, intrigue on the part of the ecclesiastics compassed his death. There was not toward Jesus the personal resentment of a tigress like Herodias. But the political rulers were used against him, and Jesus himself appeared before Herod Antipas,[3] who now assumed an air of careless curiosity about Jesus.

[1] Matt. 21 : 32. [2] Matt. 21 : 25. [3] Luke 26 : 6–12.

He had gotten over his fright about John's having returned to life. He actually "mocked"[1] Jesus now that he is a prisoner. He is very brave before the defenceless. But in Acts[2] we are beyond the tragedy. Jesus has risen from the grave and has returned to his place at the right hand of the Father. It is Peter who interprets the present situation to the disciples of Jesus. They have passed through the most wonderful experience that had ever fallen to the lot of men. They must now apprehend the significance of it all. They must face the world with courage. They possess the great facts of the spiritual revolution that has begun. Peter says: "Beginning from the baptism of John, unto the day that he was received up from us, of these must one become a witness with us of his resurrection." Our purpose is not here to discuss the address of Peter about the selection of a successor to Judas. Our concern is with the single point of the reference to the baptism of John as the new epoch in human history. The baptism is again mentioned as the thing which signalized the ministry of John. They can now look back over the ministry of both Jesus and John. They go together in the large view. John's was first and introduced the new age. The disciples are now no longer puzzled over Elijah that was to come. The manner of Peter's reference to John shows clearly that they now accept the interpretation of Jesus as a matter of course. It is not from the close of John's ministry that Peter dates the new dispensation, but the beginning. When John lifted

[1] ἐμπαίξας.

[2] 1 : 22.

up his voice in the wilderness, that was the opening of the new dispensation. It is interesting to note that Mark begins his gospel with the baptism of John. It is commonly supposed that Mark was the interpreter, if not amanuensis, of Peter. There is another allusion to John's baptism by Peter in the same epochal way, "beginning from Galilee, after the baptism which John preached." [1] This mention again reminds us of the Gospel of Mark which, after the baptism of John, takes us at once to the Galilean ministry of Jesus. "The law and the prophets were until John." [2] It is a great thing to mark a new time. That John did. Human history will never again be what it was before John was able to say: "Behold, the Lamb of God that taketh away the sin of the world." [3] Peter's speeches show that the disciples soon began to take the right measure of John and of his proper relation to Jesus. He has never lost that place in the estimation of the world and never will. Whether Jesus referred to him as the porter[4] or not, he did open the door and usher in the Good Shepherd of the sheep. That was honor enough for John, to be the Doorkeeper for Jesus.

5. *Impression on Paul.*—It is Luke in Acts who reports the addresses of Paul. But we are not justified in saying that Luke made up Paul's speeches after the fashion of Thucydides. The speeches of Peter, Stephen, Paul differ in style, and each of Paul's addresses has a special appropriateness to time and

[1] Acts 10 : 37. [2] Luke 16 : 16. [3] John 1 : 29.
[4] John 10 : 4.

place.[1] Paul had spent much time in Jerusalem while a Pharisaic student and leader, and could very well have heard the current reports of John the Baptist and his sayings. His words had left a deep mark on his age. Among the Christians they would in particular be cherished because of John's testimony to Jesus as the Messiah. In the first extended report of one of Paul's discourses he makes express mention[2] of the Baptist. "Of this man's seed hath God according to promise brought unto Israel a Saviour, Jesus; when John had first preached before his coming the baptism of repentance to all the people of Israel. And as John was fulfilling his course, he said, What suppose ye I am? I am not he. But behold, there cometh one after me the shoes of whose feet I am not worthy to unloose." Paul is speaking in the Jewish synagogue at Antioch in Iconium to both Jews and Gentiles. His reference to John is brief, but clear and full enough for his point. He is proving that the promise made to David was fulfilled in Jesus, John the Baptist being witness. John did not consider himself to be the Messiah, but he knew who was the Messiah. The words of John are not quoted exactly in the form in which they occur in the Synoptic Gospels,[3] but more nearly resemble the form in Luke. The essential point is the same in all four reports. John himself repeated it in a still different way.[4] But with Paul, as with Peter, John is the man who introduced the new age. He first preached the

[1] Cf. M. Jones, "St. Paul the Orator," 1910.
[2] Acts 13 : 23 ff.
[3] Matt. 3 : 11; Mark 1 : 7; Luke 3 : 16.
[4] John 1 : 26 f.

baptism of repentance and it was just before the coming of Jesus. John was filling out his course[1] when he spoke the words quoted. It was not long before his imprisonment. Paul thus reveals considerable knowledge of the life and teaching of the Baptist. He understands his priority to Jesus, his preaching about repentance, his baptism, his disclaimer about being the Messiah, his knowledge that the Messiah was near, the cutting off of the Baptist's career. He probably knew much more, but these facts suited his purpose on this occasion. That Paul did know about John's message is shown by another brief exposition of his teaching made by Paul on a later occasion. Paul is in Ephesus, and has to explain John's real views to some ill-taught disciples of John. Paul said: "John baptized with the baptism of repentance, saying unto the people, that they should believe on him who should come after him, that is, on Jesus." [2] John often spoke of "the Coming One," and Paul is sure that he meant Jesus.[2] The baptism of John marked by repentance continues the chief characteristic of his ministry. That was the point that appealed most to the imagination of men and that gave him his name of the Baptizer, but the heart of John's ministry was his testimony to Jesus as the Messiah. This he came to feel himself.[3] Paul sees it also in this passage. Here, then, we have the great apostle after Christ joining hands with the great prophet before Christ in full accord. They both accept Jesus as the Messiah—the

[1] ἐπλήρου τὸν δρόμον. Cf. Paul's language in Acts 20 : 24; II Tim. 4 : 7.
[2] Acts 19 : 4.
[3] John 1 : 34.

hope of Israel. John was the clasp between the old dispensation and the new. Jesus is the common bond between John the man of the wilderness and Paul the man of the schools. There is fellowship in Christ between men of every age, race and condition. Paul is glad to honor John as the Forerunner of Jesus.

6. *A Great Disciple of John.*—What became of the disciples of John after his death? He organized no apostolate as did Jesus, though he had disciples who accompanied him and were loyal to him, some even to the point of jealousy of Jesus, as we have seen. There was a circle of disciples who clung close to John during his imprisonment and buried his corpse.[1] The great bulk of John's disciples naturally blended with the followers of Jesus. After the death of John his disciples went and told Jesus. In Palestine especially this union took place more easily. But the influence of John extended far beyond Palestine. Over twenty years after John's death there are proofs of his abiding power in Alexandria and in Ephesus. The attitude of these belated disciples of John toward Jesus will depend on the amount of information which they possess of the teaching of John. If they have the later as well as the earlier words of John, his identification of Jesus as the Messiah as well as his prophecy of the Messiah, they will either be already disciples of Jesus or predisposed to that step. There would naturally be varieties among the lingering disciples of John. Some would be ignorant of Jesus, some would be ignorant of John's real position. Some would know

[1] Matt. 4:12; 9:14; 11:2 f.; Mark 6:29.

well John's teaching and that of Jesus and not be familiar with the later developments since Pentecost. We have seen that John the Baptist made his impress on Peter and Paul. But he made a deeper mark on Apollos, of Alexandria, one of the most learned or eloquent[1] men of the first century. He was a Jew who was "mighty in the Scriptures,"[2] evidently, like Paul, a man of the schools. He was a man of prowess as an interpreter and speaker before he comes to Ephesus. In Alexandria he was in touch with the Jewish teaching and the Greek philosophy, and probably knew the combination of the two in Philo the Jew. There is no real evidence for attributing to him the authorship of the "Wisdom of Solomon." He is held by some to be the writer of the Epistle to the Hebrews. When he went later to Corinth, he so "powerfully confuted the Jews, *and that* publicly, showing by the scriptures that Jesus was the Christ,"[3] that he at once divided honors in that church, and was the occasion, though through no fault of his, of a schism in the church there.[4] It is significant that this man of learning, native gifts and force of character is a representative of the "baptism of John," "knowing only" that when he appears before us.[5] But we are not at liberty to interpret this language to mean that Apollos knew nothing of Jesus and was not a disciple of Jesus. The correct[6] text here expressly states that Apollos "spake and taught accurately the

[1] ἀνὴρ λόγιος. The word is ambiguous. Acts 18 : 24.

[2] δυνατὸς ὢν ἐν ταῖς γραφαῖς,

[3] Acts 18 : 28.

[4] I Cor. 3 : 4; 16 : 12.

[5] Acts 18 : 25.

[6] ℵABDEL. ἐλάλει καὶ ἐδίδασκεν ἀκριβῶς τὰ περὶ τοῦ 'Ιησοῦ. Note imperfect tense.

things concerning Jesus." He was an experienced teacher of the story of Jesus, and he did it accurately. He made no mistakes as far as he went. He was fervent in spirit and "instructed in the way of the Lord." How much did he know? Rendall [1] groups these facts clearly. "He had (a) received the baptism of John, (b) been instructed in the way of the Lord, and he (c) knew the things concerning Jesus. This represents the stage reached either by those who themselves had been disciples of Jesus, or brought very near to him, but had returned to a distant home before Pentecost or for some other reason had not maintained communications with the apostolic church; or by those who had been instructed by such disciples." In other words, Apollos seems to occupy the standpoint of those disciples of John who accepted Jesus as the Messiah, but who knew nothing of Pentecost and the developments since. What did Apollos lack? "But when Priscilla and Aquila heard him, they took him unto them, and expounded unto him the way of God more accurately." [2] They took him to themselves[3] and set forth more fully[4] the way of God which he already knew. There was no correction of what he did know, but rather addition to his stock of knowledge. We are left partly to conjecture as to what the new teaching was. There is no evidence that Apollos was baptized anew. The case of the twelve disciples in Acts 19 is not necessarily similar.[5] These disciples

[1] "The Acts of the Apostles," p. 341. [2] Acts 18 : 26.
[3] προσελάβοντο. Middle voice. [4] ἐξεθεντο. Middle voice also.
[5] Knowling (*Acts* in "Expositor's Greek Testament") argues from Acts 19 : 5 that Apollos was also baptized. But Meyer (*in loco*) does not think so, nor does Hackett (*in loco*) consider it probable.

were poorly taught in John's own message, while Apollos was accurately instructed. It cannot be maintained that the disciples of John were all rebaptized, that the baptism of John was not "valid" with the early disciples of Jesus. That is all the baptism possessed by Jesus and the first half-dozen of his apostles, so far as we have any record. The trouble with Apollos was not in his baptism. The mention of John's baptism was for the purpose of dating him, so to speak. He occupied the pre-Pentecost stand-point. There is no hint that Priscilla and Aquila taught Apollos the insufficiency of John's baptism. Blass[1] suggests that Apollos may have had the Gospel of Mark or one of the early accounts of the life of Jesus which stopped short of Pentecost. Mark's Gospel begins with John's baptism and ends with the resurrection and appearance of Christ. If Apollos knew all that was in Mark's Gospel, he would still have much to learn by way of understanding the things of Christ. Mark's Gospel gives the primitive narrative of the ministry and death of Jesus, and probably covers the extent of the knowledge of Apollos when he appears in Ephesus. The word "instructed"[2] usually refers to oral teaching, but not always. He is a well-equipped expounder of the scriptures and of the work of Jesus, but he apparently is ignorant of the baptism of the Holy Spirit as a fact.[3] John had described the Messianic work under that figure, suggested by his own baptism. Perhaps Luke notes here that Apollos knew only the baptism

[1] "Acta Apostolorum," *in loco*. [2] κατηχημένος. Cf. Luke 1:4.
[3] Rendall, "Acts of the Apostles," p. 442.

of John because he did not know the baptism of the Holy Spirit, which John had said the Messiah would bestow.[1] Priscilla and Aquila could explain how that prophecy of John was fulfilled so wondrously on the Day of Pentecost.[2] Jesus had, indeed, himself breathed the Holy Spirit upon the disciples after his death and resurrection.[3] But that was only an earnest of the fuller blessing which he had promised and for which he bade the disciples to wait.[4] There is, in truth, some hint that Apollos received this baptism of the Holy Spirit after (or during) his visit with Priscilla and Aquila (two saints of rare sympathy and wisdom, who knew how to perform a delicate task). The hint lies in the tremendous power[5] of his work in Corinth, whither he went. But, all in all, Apollos stands only to the credit of John's work. He had grasped the vital elements in the work of both John and Jesus, and was ready to learn more of the significance of the life of Jesus under the tutelage of the Holy Spirit. The baptism of John stood for nothing unless there was first the new heart. It was the pledge of the new life in Christ which could only be entered into with fulness under the leading of the Holy Spirit. Apollos was going straight ahead in line with John's own teaching when he was taught more accurately the way of God.

7. *Misguided Disciples.*—Apollos is gone to Corinth and Paul comes to Ephesus on the third great mis-

[1] Matt. 3 : 11; Mark 1 : 8; Luke 3 : 16; Acts 18 : 25.
[2] Acts 2 and 3.
[3] John 20 : 22.
[4] John 15 : 26–16 : 16; Luke 24 : 49; Acts 1 : 3–8.
[5] Acts 18 : 28.

sionary tour.[1] Paul "found certain disciples"[2] in Ephesus. The expression is very vague and raises a number of problems. How did these "disciples" escape[3] the notice of Apollos? As a matter of fact, there is no evidence that they had come to Ephesus before Apollos left. The words of Luke in Acts quite well admit of this interpretation.[4] If this is true, there is no problem concerning their connection with Apollos. But, even if Apollos did not leave till after the arrival of these "twelve,"[5] there is still no proof that Apollos saw them or had any dealings with them.[6] In favor of the idea that Apollos was quite independent of these twelve men is the fact that Priscilla and Aquila apparently take no interest in them.[7] Apollos would surely have sought to impart to these men the fuller light which he had learned from Priscilla and Aquila, if they were disciples of his. Even if Apollos had been suddenly called to Corinth, which does not seem to be the case in view of the careful preparation for going by way of a letter of introduction,[8] he would almost certainly have urged[9] Priscilla and Aquila to lead them into the fuller light. It is Paul who discovers this group of "disciples" and seeks to indoctrinate them. His method is quite different from that of Priscilla and Aquila with Apollos. The difference hardly lies wholly in Paul's temperament. The cases

[1] Acts 19 : 1.
[2] εὑρών τινας μαθητάς.
[3] Ramsay, "St. Paul the Traveller," p. 270; Felten, "Apostelgeschichte," S. 351.
[4] Knowling, "Acts," *in loco*.
[5] Acts 19 : 7. οἱ πάντες ἄνδρες ὡσεὶ δώδεκα. The number was, of course, accidental. It was not another circle of twelve like the twelve apostles.
[6] Rendall, "Acts," *in loco*.
[7] *Ibid.*
[8] Acts 18 : 27.
[9] Rendall, "Acts," *in loco*.

called for different treatment. The whole tone of the narrative in Acts 19 : 1–7 is that of a separate incident with no actual connection with the work of Apollos in ch. 18. The one note of similarity is the fact that they, like Apollos, have only the baptism of John.[1] But we must not be misled by a phrase. The context is entirely different in the two incidents. The facts about Apollos have already been set forth. What are the facts about these twelve "disciples"? Can we get a clear idea of them? They were undoubtedly disciples of John.[2] Were they also disciples of Jesus? McGiffert[3] says that they were not. This has been the common notion from the time of Chrysostom,[4] and some writers even hold that these men were baptized by John the Baptist himself.[5] But Blass[6] contends that the use of the term "disciples" and "believed" proves that they were also disciples of Jesus. That is, of course, possible, though the word "believed"[7] occurs in Paul's question and cannot be pressed into a positive assertion about them. There is more force in the word "disciples," but it must not be overlooked that the term was applied in the gospels freely to the followers of the Baptist.[8] The story in the Acts is naturally from the stand-point of disciples of Jesus, however, and the most obvious meaning of the word here is that these men were in some sort disciples of Jesus. But even so, it does not follow that they

[1] Acts 19 : 3. [2] *Ibid.* [3] "Apostolic Age," p. 286.
[4] "Acts," *in loco.*
[5] Knowling, "Acts," *in loco.*
[6] "Acta Apostolorum," *in loco.*
[7] Acts 19 : 2. πιστεύσαντες.
[8] Mark 2 : 18; 6 : 29; Matt. 9 : 14; 11 : 2; Luke 5 : 33; 7 : 18 f.; 11 : 1; John 1 : 35, 37; 3 : 25; 4 : 1.

were on the same plane with Apollos, who taught accurately or carefully the things concerning Jesus, though he knew only the baptism of John.[1] It is not certain that these men knew accurately the things of John or of Jesus. We do not have to assume that they took John to be the Messiah. That error arose in John's own time and, in spite of his resolute disclaimer, did not disappear at once.[2] Neander[3] supposes that the Zabians (Mendæans or Nazoreans), discovered in the East in the seventeenth century, are a remnant of this sect who clung to John as the Messiah instead of Jesus. A sect of Hemerobaptists claim John the Baptist as one of their number. They appear in the second century in proconsular Asia.[4] These Hemerobaptists have perverted John's teaching and misrepresented his office.[5] They baptize daily for atonement of sin and for sanctification.[6] Baptism is no longer a single symbolic ordinance. John is himself the Messiah with these people. It needs no argument to prove that they owe nothing in reality to John. They have seized on his name and misused it.[7] There is little likelihood (none, I think) that the twelve disciples at Ephesus were tainted with this heresy. If they are Christians, they are certainly very imperfectly informed [8] disciples of Jesus, far below the level

[1] Acts 18 : 25.
[2] Hackett, "Acts," *in loco*.
[3] "Church History," vol. I, p. 376.
[4] Justin Martyr, "Dialogue with Trypho," Clem. Hom. ii, 23; Hegesippus in Eus. H. E. IV, 22. Cf. Lambert in "Hastings's D. C. G."
[5] Lightfoot, "Colossians," p. 401.
[6] "Apost Const.," vi, 6.
[7] Justin Martyr even ("Dialogue with Trypho," 10) alludes to them as "Baptists," but they have no real connection with Christianity, certainly not with the great body of Christians now called Baptists.
[8] Lightfoot, "Colossians," p. 400.

of Apollos. But they betray a lamentable ignorance of important elements in the teaching of John, to such an extent that one hesitates to call them Christians at all. It could have been true only in a nominal sense, or at most "they possessed the elements of a true faith, and acknowledged the name of Christ as soon as the apostle made it known to them."[1] They did not know that the Holy Spirit had been bestowed, if, indeed, they knew of the existence of the Holy Spirit. Paul's question[2] was whether they had received the gift of the Holy Spirit when they believed. The inquiry seems abrupt because we probably do not have all the conversation.[3] Paul assumes that they are familiar with the promise of the Holy Spirit to all who call upon the name of the Lord.[4] This fact may argue that he had not had much discussion with them and did not know the depth of their ignorance. They answered: "Nay, we did not so much as hear whether the Holy Spirit was."[5] The Revised Version adds "given" to the word "was." But it is by no means clear that that is the idea here as in John 7:39. Knowling[6] urges that these disciples knew of the existence of the Holy Spirit because of John's teaching and the Old Testament also. But the trouble is that these "disciples" may have been ignorant of John's portrayal of the Messiah. Still, it is charitable to them to interpret the language as referring to the bestowal of the Holy Spirit. Paul expresses astonish-

[1] Hackett, "Acts," *in loco*.

[2] Acts 19:2. The two aorists refer to the one event. εἰ πνεῦμα ἅγιον ἐλάβετε πιστεύσαντες;

[3] Hackett, "Acts," *in loco*.

[4] Acts 2:39.

[5] 'Αλλ' οὐδὲ εἰ πνεῦμα ἅγιόν ἐστιν ἠ κούσαμεν.

[6] "Acts," *in loco*.

ment at their ignorance and inquires for the significance of their baptism. "Unto what then were ye baptized?"[1] To Paul's mind a baptism in water that had no symbolic relation to the Holy Spirit's work was an absurdity whether they had received the baptism of the Holy Spirit or not. These disciples reply simply: "Unto John's baptism."[2] They had received John's baptism, that and no more. How did Paul understand this reply? Paul said: "John baptized with the baptism of repentance, saying unto the people that they should believe on him that should come after him, that is, on Jesus."[3] Did Paul mean to say that John's baptism was inadequate and therefore they must receive a new water baptism? So Knowling[4]: "John's own words showed that his baptism was insufficient." Insufficient for what? John said that the baptism of the Holy Spirit at the hands of the Messiah was more important than his water baptism.[5] But that was a very different thing from saying that those who had received water baptism from John should receive another water baptism from Jesus or his disciples. As a matter of fact, till now, we have no instance of such a repetition of water baptism in the New Testament. Rendall[6] gets rid of the difficulty by saying that John's baptism "was only a preparation for, as also a profession of faith in, the coming Messiah, whose baptism was to be with water

[1] Acts 19:3. *εἰς τί οὖν ἐβαπτίσθητε*; the use of *εἰς* does not demand "into" in English. Cf. Matt. 10:41; 12:41. Paul means to ask for the higher meaning of the ordinance to them.

[2] *εἰς τὸ Ἰωάνου βάπτισμα.*

[3] Acts 19:4. *Ἰωάνης ἐβάπτισε βάπτισμα μετανοίας, τῷ λαῷ λέγων, εἰς τὸν ἐρχόμενον μετ αὐτὸν ἵνα πιστεύσωσι, τουτέστιν εἰς τὸν Ἰησοῦν.*

[4] "Acts," *in loco.* [5] Matt. 3:11. [6] "Acts," p. 246.

and the Spirit." But he here adds "water" to the words of the Baptist. That argument required the rebaptism of all the Johannine disciples, the six apostles of Jesus included. Hackett[1] comes much nearer to the heart of the matter when he says: "John indeed preached repentance and a Saviour to come (as you know); but the Messiah whom he announced has appeared in Jesus, and you are now to believe on him as John directed." This interpretation assumes that they had not exercised faith in Jesus. Paul probably meant even more than this. John's water baptism was preceded by repentance, which was a spiritual act under the influence of the Holy Spirit. Thus Paul means to say, that, if they really understood the significance of John's baptism, they should have known of the baptism of the Spirit of which he had first asked them, since John preached about that great characteristic of the new dispensation. Paul is, then, not discrediting John's baptism, but interpreting the real significance of John's baptism, and exposing their defective comprehension of John's baptism, which they claimed to have received. The rest of Paul's explanation is in harmony with this idea. John urged belief in the Coming One at the same time that he spoke of the baptism of the Holy Spirit.[2] These "disciples" were evidently very backward in their knowledge of John's earlier preaching. In his later ministry John even identified the Coming One with Jesus: "This is he of whom I said."[3] So then Paul is justified in adding "that is, on Jesus." In effect,

[1] "Acts," p. 219. [2] Matt. 3:11. [3] John 1:30.

therefore, Paul has administered to them a rebuke for their ignorance of John's teaching. They had, in fact, received the form of John's baptism without any conception of its spiritual import. It would appear from Luke's narrative that Paul's exposition of John's teaching came as a fresh ray of light to them. They illustrate how John's work, which accented with tremendous power the reality of spiritual experience, had become hazy at this distance in the minds of a group of well-meaning men. John's new ordinance was called a repentance-baptism to distinguish it from the mere ceremonial ablutions of the Pharisees. But here at last "John's baptism of repentance" has dwindled into just "John's baptism" and the addition of "repentance" by Paul comes as a brand-new idea to these followers of the Baptist. "When they heard this, they were baptized in the name of the Lord Jesus."[1] Paul's brief exposition set the whole matter in such a new light that they felt that they had not been baptized at all. They are baptized afresh, not because they had only John's baptism, but because they did not really have that. The original question of Paul about the baptism of the Holy Spirit has for the moment receded into the background. These men did not even have a real water baptism, let alone the spirit baptism. So they are baptized in the name of the Lord Jesus, probably as representing that of the Trinity.[2] It is surely gratuitous to insist on the addition in "Codex Bezæ" "for the forgiveness of sins"[3] and to explain it as showing "that

[1] Acts 19:5. [2] Cf. Matt. 28:19. [3] εἰς ἄφεσιν ἁμαρτιῶν D.

John's baptism did not convey forgiveness; hence the repetition of the baptism of water."[1] It is obviously just a repetition of the language of Mark 1 : 4 about the baptism of John. In point of fact neither the water baptism of John nor that in the name of Jesus "conveyed" forgiveness of sins. In each instance the baptism in water presumed that the forgiveness had already been received. Now it is that "when Paul had laid his hands upon them, the Holy Spirit came on them; and they spake with tongues and prophesied."[2] The water baptism was not a prerequisite to the baptism of the Spirit. In the case of Cornelius and his household the baptism of the Spirit preceded the water baptism.[3] The same order was true of Paul's Spirit baptism and water baptism.[4] But the discussion between Paul and these twelve disciples led back from the baptism of the Spirit to the water baptism of John. They had not really received the water baptism. This defect was remedied on their confession and request apparently. Then came the baptism of the Holy Spirit of which Paul had first inquired. The proof was at hand, for they spake with tongues and prophesied as at Pentecost and at Cæsarea. The bestowal of the Holy Spirit preceded the speaking with tongues and was independent of it, nor was this proof always on hand. It was a great experience for these twelve men. They had come a long way during their interview with Paul. They had farther to come than Apollos. Paul had laid hold of their loyalty to John

[1] Rendall, "Acts," p. 346.
[2] Acts 19 : 6. [3] Acts 10 : 44–48. [4] Acts 9 : 17 f.

to bring them out into the full truth as set forth by John and Jesus.

8. *The Last Look at John.*—Many years go by. Paul and Peter have joined the roll of martyrs headed by John and Jesus, Stephen and James. John the Apostle lingers on till the end of the century. It is possible that the principles of the Hemerobaptists spread in Asia Minor. At Ephesus John the Apostle probably lived to see the name of John the Baptist bandied about as a party shibboleth. These heretics tried to appropriate John the Baptist. "His name is no longer the sign of imperfect appreciation [as in the case of the twelve at Ephesus], but the watchword of direct antagonism; John has been set up as a rival to Jesus."[1] So then in this Fourth Gospel, written at the end of the first century, we see John the Apostle interpreting John the Baptist and Forerunner in the light of the misuse of his name by the Hemerobaptists. He calls him simply "John." To the aged Apostle he was *the* John. He had himself been John's disciple, and it was at John's instance that he went that day to follow Jesus.[2] He cannot bear to see that glorious name become a by-word among these narrow opposers of Jesus. To us John's great disciple is *the* John.[3] John the Apostle loved both John and Jesus. He knew that these heretics were wrong. He knew that John was not jealous of Jesus, but placed the crown on his head as the Lamb of God and the Bridegroom whose friend he was.[4] John was great, but Jesus was

[1] Lightfoot, "Colossians," p. 401.
[2] John 1 : 35–42.
[3] Dods, "John," *in loco.*
[4] John 1 : 29 ; 3 : 28 f.

greater, as John himself knew and gladly acknowledged. John was the lamp (a bright and shining one), but Jesus was the sun.[1] "He was not the light, but came that he might bear witness of the light."[2] Nothing could give John greater offence, if he only knew, than for people to set him up as the rival of Jesus. "He must increase, but I must decrease." As the Apostle looks back across two generations since he first heard the wonderful words of John by the Jordan, he can see in a clear light the relation between John and Jesus. Jesus is the eternal Logos, the Son with the Father, the Life and the Light of men, the Light that shines on in the darkness and that the darkness did not overcome or put out.[3] "There came a man sent from God, whose name was John."[4] The introduction of John the Forerunner into this context appears abrupt, but it is not so. The conflict between Light and Darkness took a new turn when this man of God appeared on the scene.[5] John entered the lists on the side of the Light. He came as the Morning Star to prophesy the coming of the Sun of Righteousness. He was the Herald of the King, the Harbinger of the Day. "The same came for witness, that he might bear witness of the light, that all might believe through him."[6] The mission of this God-moved man was to testify about the Messiah before he was manifested and afterward, "that all might believe through him." That was his real aim, not that men should take him to be the Messiah. He had

[1] John 5 : 35; 1 : 4, 9 f.
[2] John 1 : 8. [3] John 1 : 1–5. [4] John 1 : 6.
[5] Westcott, "John," *in loco*. [6] John 1 : 7.

denied that repeatedly.[1] His purpose was to help men, whose eyes were blinded, to see the Light. This mission he fulfilled grandly, gloriously. He was able to brush aside the misconceptions of current rabbinism and help men to see how Jesus as the Messiah fitted into the Old Testament picture. He found the point of contact between Jesus and Malachi. He was himself the link between the two. As the last of the prophets he set his seal of approval upon the Messiah, and then stepped aside or was pushed aside by Pharisee and Herod, not by Jesus. John's mission had not failed. He lived to be able to say: "This was he of whom I said, He that cometh after me is become before me: for he was before me."[2] When he was able to say that, he had fulfilled his mission.

Rev. F. B. Meyer, in his helpful book, "John the Baptist,"[3] has drawn a striking parallel between John and Jesus. The lives of both were strenuous and short. Each met boundless enthusiasm of the masses, followed by the bitter hatred of the religious leaders. In each case a little handful of disciples laid the dead body in the tomb without hope. But here, Mr. Meyer urges, the parallel ends. John's death was a martyrdom; that of Jesus was a sacrifice. John's body has not risen from the dead, while Jesus came out of the grave. The disciples of John were scattered and absorbed or perverted. Those of Jesus after the sight of the Risen Christ united to wait for the power of the Holy Spirit to go forth on a world conquest. The influence of John has decreased, as he said it

[1] John 1: 19 f.; 3: 28. [2] John 1: 15. [3] Pp. 11 f.

would, while to-day the name of Jesus is mightier than ever before, King of kings and Lord of lords.

This is all as it should be, as John foresaw and wished. It is not honoring John the Baptist to suggest possible jealousy in his heart toward Christ. I have called him "John the Loyal" because it is true, and because I wished thus to set in clear light his devotion to Jesus. That is his real glory. I have sought to expound his greatness and his power as we see these qualities in the gospels. But I cannot write the last lines in this book about John without the humble tribute of my own heart's love. Few personalities in history hold my admiration and enthusiasm with a firmer grip than does the rugged and picturesque figure who still stands silhouetted on the horizon at Bethany beyond Jordan in Gilead, the land of Elijah of old. I see him standing "and he looked upon Jesus as he walked." His heart has gone with that look; he keeps on looking till he says: "Behold, the Lamb of God." He can say no more. There is no need to say more, not for John. And he never saw him more on earth.

BIBLIOGRAPHY

The Bible dictionaries, lives of Christ, commentaries on the gospels, all have valuable discussions of the ministry of the Baptist. The most important separate treatises on John the Baptist are given below.

Barde, "Jean Baptiste" (1892).
Boissonas, "De l'Attitude de Jean Baptiste."
Bornemann, "Die Taufe Christi durch Johannes."
Breest, "Johannes der Täufer" (1881).
Breuil, "Du Culte de S. Jean Baptiste."
Chenot, "Jean le Baptiste."
Coleridge, "Ministry of St. John the Baptist." (Vol. I of his "Public Life of Our Lord.")
Douglas, "More Than a Prophet" (1905).
Duncan, "Life, Character, and Acts of John the Baptist" (1853).
Feather, "John the Baptist."
Gale, "The Prophet of the Highest."
Gams, "Johannes der Täufer" (1853).
Geux, "Jean Baptiste."
Haupt, "Johannes der Täufer" (1874).
Holmes, "On the Prophecies and Testimony of John the Baptist" (1783).
Houghton, "John the Baptist—His Life and Work" (1889).
Huxtable, "Ministry of St. John the Baptist."
Innitzer, "Johannes der Täufer" (1908).
Köhler, "Johannes der Täufer" (1884).
Lofton, "John the Baptist" (1905).
Mandel, "Die Vorgeschichte Jesu."
McCullough, "The Peerless Prophet; or, the Life and Times of John the Baptist" (1888).
Meyer, "John the Baptist" (1901).
Penick, "More Than a Prophet" (1881).
Reynolds, "John the Baptist" (1874).

Rymington, "Vox Clamantis: Life and Ministry of John the Baptist" (1882).
Simpson, "The Last of the Prophets."
Smith, "Johannes de Dooper" (1908).
Stalker, "The Two St. Johns" (1895).
Van Rohden, "John the Baptist" (1853).
Wilkinson, "A Johannine Document in the Early Chapters of St. Luke's Gospel."

GENERAL INDEX

SCRIPTURE INDEX